MR ROGER BROCKBANK MR D BROCKWELL MS L BRODERICK MS M BRODERICK MISS M BRODERICK MR D BRODIE MRS J BRODIE MS C BRODIN DR PETER BRODRICK MRS P BROGAN MR DAVID BROMFIELD MAJOR J BROMHEAD MR D BROMLEY MS A BROMLEY-DERRY MRS A BROMWICH MRS
BROOK MR NIGEL BROOK MS TRACEY BROOK MR A BROOKE MR D BROOKE MRS J BROOKE MR OLIVER BROOKE MR P BROOKE MS PENELOPE BROOKE MR PETER BROOKE MISS S BROOKE MRS V BROOKES MR A BROOKS MRS DOROTHY BROOKS MRS E BROOKS MS E BROOKS MR JOHN BROOKS M
KATHERINE BROOKS MR L BROOKS MRS M BROOKS M BROOKS DR P BROOKS MR R BROOKS MR P BROOK-SMITH MRS E BROOKWICK MISS E BROOM MR D BROOME MR DEEN BROSNAN MRS DELLA BROTHERSTON C BROTHERTON MRS R BROTHERTON MS A BROUGH MISS B BROUGHTON MR
BROUGHTON MR R BROUGHTON MR SIMON BROUGHTON MR R BROUTT MR A BROWN MS A BROWN MRS A BROWN MR ADRIAN BROWN MISS AMANDA BROWN MR AND MRS R BROWN MS B BROWN MISS B BROWN MR B BROWN MRS B BROWN DR C BROWN MR C BROWN MRS C BROWN LADY C J E BROW
CAROLINE BROWN MR CLIFFORD BROWN MR D BROWN MR DAVID BROWN MR DOMINIC BROWN MR E BROWN PROFESSOR EDWINA BROWN MS ELIZABETH BROWN MR ERIC BROWN MR F BROWN MS F BROWN MISS G BROWN G BROWN MR G BROWN MRS G BROWN MS GABRIELLE BROWN MS GA
BROWN MR GEOFFREY BROWN MRS GRACE BROWN MR HENRY BROWN MRS I BROWN MISS J BROWN MR J BROWN MRS J BROWN MRS JANET BROWN MS JANET BROWN MR JEREMY BROWN MISS JILL BROWN REVEREND JOHN BROWN MR K BROWN MRS K BROWN MS LOUISA BROWN MR M BROW
MRS M BROWN MRS MANDY BROWN SIR MERVYN BROWN MISS N BROWN MR P BROWN MS P BROWN MRS PATRICIA BROWN MR R BROWN MRS R BROWN MR & MRS R BROWN MR AND MRS ROBERT BROWN MS ROZ BROWN MR RUSSELL BROWN MR S BROWN DR S BROWN MISS SANDRA BROWN MIS
SUE BROWN MS SUSAN BROWN MRS V BROWN MRS VALERIE BROWN MR J BROWNE MS J BROWNE MR K BROWNE MR O BROWNE MR R BROWNE MRS A BROWNING DR J BROWNING MS RACHEL BROWNING MRS I BROWN-LANA MR TIMOTHY BROYD DR A BRUCE MRS B BRUCE MS C BRUCE H BRU
MRS J BRUCE MRS JACQUELINE BRUCE THE HON JAMES BRUCE FCA MS PATRICIA BRUCE MISS S BRUCE MR TREVOR BRUCE MS M BRUCE-KONUAH MR N BRUCKHEIMER MRS R BRUCKNER MISS C BRUELL MRS NATASHA BRUELL MR M BRUMBY MS ANN BRUMFIT MR R BRUN MR HERVE BRUN
MR W BRUNN MRS H BRUNNER MS S BRUNNER MRS J E BRUNNING MRS J BRUNSKILL MRS K BRUNT MR P BRUPBACHER MS J BRUSTIK MR M BRUTON MR TORBEN BRUUN MR URBAIN BRUYERE MRS J BRYAN MRS MARY BRYAN MS P BRYAN MRS R BRYAN MR AND MRS BRYANT MRS C BRYAN
MISS ELAINE BRYANT MR M BRYANT MR N BRYANT MR NICHOLAS BRYANT MR S BRYANT MR Q BRYAR MRS N BRYCE MR J BRYDEN MRS D BRZESKA MRS E BUCHAN MISS J BUCHAN MRS J BUCHAN MS CAROL BUCHANAN MRS E BUCHANAN MRS ENA BUCHANAN MRS JANE BUCHANAN MRS ODET
BUCHANAN MRS M BUCHMAN MRS A BUCK MR C BUCK MR G BUCK DR P BUCK MR P BUCK MR ALLAN BUCKINGHAM MISS EILEEN BUCKINGHAM MRS J BUCKINGHAM MR R BUCKINGHAM MR R BUCKLAND MRS S BUCKLAND MS C BUCKLE MR H BUCKLE MR B BUCKLEY MR G BUCKLEY MRS
BUCKLEY MS M BUCKLEY SIR M BUCKLEY MALCOLM BUCKLEY MS N BUCKLEY MS P BUCKLEY MRS D BUCKTON MR DAVID BUDD MR F BUDD MR R BUDDEN MS P BUDDERY MR R BUDDLE MR R BUDGETT MR D BUDWORTH MS M BUEKETT MR G H BUFFARD MRS J A BUGG MRS JEAN BUHR ANTHO
BULL MR B BULL MRS ELIZABETH BULL MRS KAREN BULL MRS M BULL MR R BULL MRS T BULL DR P BULLET MR D BULLMAN MR & MRS BULLOCK MRS K BULLOCK MRS RUTH BULLOCK MS P BULLOCK-CHASE MR D BULLOUGH MR PAUL BULLOUGH MRS S BULMER MRS I BUNCE REVEREND
BUNCE MS Z BUNCE MR JOHN BUNGEY MRS R BUNKER MRS S A BUNKER B BUNN MISS SUSAN BUNN MR J BUNNEY MRS S BUNTEN MISS V BUNTIN MS REBECCA BUNTING MISS W BUNTING MR K BUNYAN MR A BUNYARD MRS J BURBEA MRS C BURBEDGE MR JEFF BURBIDGE MR H BURBRID
MR R BURBURY MISS A BURCH MR I BURCH MR NIGEL BURCH MS L BURCHELL MRS S BURCHELL MR A BURCHER MS MARY-JANE BURCHER MISS J BURDEN MR L BURDEN MS L BURDETT MR ROGER BURGE MRS A BURGER MR DAVID BURGES WILL BURGES MR ALAN BURGESS MS BRIGIT
BURGESS MR C BURGESS COLIN S BURGESS MRS E BURGESS MS L M BURGESS MR M BURGESS MRS M BURGESS MR N BURGESS MR R BURGESS-ALLEN MS C BURKE MRS DIANA BURKE MRS DIANE BURKE MISS E BURKE MRS J BURKE KOFI BURKE MR PATRICK BURKE MS SHELLEY BURK
MR G BURKILL MR JOHN BURKILL MRS M BURKINYOUNG MR DAVID BURKLE MRS M BURLAND MS K BURLEIGH MR R BURLTON MRS D BURMAN DR N BURMAN MR I BURMETT MRS D BURN MRS J BURN MRS R H BURN MS S BURN MR AND MRS R BURNESS MR A BURNET MR G BURNETT MS H
BURNETT MRS H BURNETT MS HELEN BURNETT MR JOHN BURNETT MR R BURNETT MR DAVID BURNS MRS HELEN BURNS MR ROBERT BURNS MR CHRISTOPHER BURR MR I BURR MS S BURR MS J BURRAGE MRS C BURRASTON MR A BURREE MR & MRS RICHARD BURRELL MRS L BURRIDGE MRS
BURRILL MS CAROLIN BURROW MRS A BURROWS MR A BURROWS CLIFF BURROWS MISS EMMA BURROWS MRS SUSAN BURSLEM MS CHRISTINA BURSTIN MRS M BURSTON MRS D BURT MR E BURT MS J BURT MR NICK BURT E BURTON MISS J BURTON MRS J BURTON MR M BURTON MS M BURTO
MISS M BURTON MR N BURTON MR M BURY MS H BUSH MR J G BUSH MRS JULIE BUSH MR R BUSH MRS S BUSH MS V BUSH MR C BUSHELL MS J BUSHELL MRS M BUSHELL MR PAUL BUSHELL MRS A BUSHNELL MRS MYRNA BUSTANI MR FRANZ BUSUTTIL MS J BUTCHER MR L BUTCHER MR
BUTCHER MICHAEL BUTCHER MRS P BUTCHER MS R BUTCHER MRS ROSEMARY BUTCHER MRS C BUTKUS MRS A BUTLER MR C BUTLER MR CLIVE BUTLER MS CORTINA BUTLER MR D BUTLER MS D BUTLER MR GEOFF BUTLER MS H BUTLER MRS HELEN BUTLER MS J BUTLER MRS LINDA BUTL
MISS M BUTLER MRS M BUTLER MR PETER BUTLER MR R BUTLER MR STEPHEN BUTLER MR T BUTLER MR T F BUTLER MS V BUTLER MRS W BUTLER MR A BUTNICK MS CAROLINE BUTT MRS CHRISTINE BUTT MR R BUTT MR A BUTTERFIELD MR D BUTTERFIELD MRS DOROTHY BUTTERS MRS A
BUTTERWICK MRS M BUTTERWICK MS N BUTTERWICK MRS D BUTTERWORTH MISS P BUTTERWORTH DR S BUTTERWORTH MR T BUTTERWORTH MR C BUTTERY MS L BUTTIGIEG MR I BUTTON MR D BUXTON MR J BUXTON MR M BUXTON MR NICK BUXTON MS S BUZZA MS S BYARD MR PETER BYCRO
MRS A BYE MR B BYER MRS L BYERS MR HUGH BYFORD MRS R BYFORD MR A BYRNE MS DANIELLE BYRNE MS G BYRNE MS M BYRNE MRS P BYRNE MR R BYRNE MR STEPHEN BYRNE MR T BYRNE MS V BYRNE MR R BYRNES MR M BYRON-EDMUND MR A BYRT MR COLIN BYTHEWAY MRS M
BYTHEWAY MRS M BYWATER MR J CABLE MS B CADBURY MR J CADBURY MRS J CADDEN MRS J CADDY MRS MARION CADENA ANDREW CADEY MR A CADMAN MRS A CADMAN MRS I CADNEY MR K CADOO MS R CAFFYN MS M CAHILL SIR ALBERT CAHN MR E CAHN MS K CAI MRS K CAIN MR
CAIRNS MISS B CAIRNS MS J CAKE MRS J CALAM MISS ANGELA CALDARA MR D CALDER MR I CALDER MR MICHAEL CALDER MRS P CALDER MR R CALDOW MR C CALDWELL MR M CALDWELL MR B CALEY MISS J CALEY MS H CALIN MRS E CALLAGHAN MR MICHAEL CALLAGHAN MR
CALLAGHAN MR A CALLAM MR ALBERT CALLAND MR G CALLANT MS L CALLENDER MR M CALLER MR P CALLER MR J CALLOW MR N CALLOW MS FRANCES CALMAN MR J CALVER MR R CALVER MR L CALVERT MR P CALWELL MR G CAMACHO MRS S CAMBRIDGE MISS H CAME MRS AN
CAMERON MS D CAMERON MR DUNCAN CAMERON MRS HELEN CAMERON MRS S CAMERON MR STUART CAMERON MRS JULIET CAMP MR R CAMP MRS BRIDGET CAMPBELL MR C CAMPBELL MR D CAMPBELL MRS E CAMPBELL MR F CAMPBELL MRS F CAMPBELL MR G CAMPBELL MR I CAMPBE
MS J CAMPBELL MR M CAMPBELL MS R CAMPBELL MS S CAMPBELL MISS D CAMPBELL-DUNLOP MR IAN CAMPBELL-GRANT MS P CAMPBELL-PARKER PROFESSOR G CAMPBELL-PLATT MR P CAMPBELL-PRESTON MRS J CAMPLING MRS E CANE MR LEIGH CANE MR R CANEPA-ANSON M
ROBERT CANEPA-ANSON MS P CANNELL MR P CANNING MRS A CANNON MR P CANNON MR C CANONICI MR P CANTER MR A CANTLE MRS M CANTOR MR B CANTRILL MRS M CAOUETTE MRS J CAPAS MRS C CAPEL BRADFORD MR H CAPLAN MS IRENE CAPLAN MR & MRS H CAPLAN MR D CA
MR P CAPP MR J CAPPS MISS N CAPRON MRS CAPSTICK MS D CAPTAININO MR ALAN CARDASH MR C CARDEN MISS P CARDIS MR GAVIN CARDY MS P CARDY MRS SUSAN CARDY MR W CARDY MR J CAREFORD MR D CARESWELL MS ELISABETH CAREW HUNT MR PATRICK CAREY MISS MAR
CARILLO MR G CARLE MS S CARLETON MS M CARLILE MRS J CARLSON MRS GUNILLA CARLTON MRS EDITH CARNE MRS P CARNEGIE MR AND MRS CARO MISS SANDRA CAROSSO DR G CARP MRS B CARPENTER MS C CARPENTER DR CHRISTINE CARPENTER MR & MRS D CARPENTER MRS
CARPENTER MRS J CARPENTER MISS JEAN CARPENTER MR M CARPENTER MISS P CARPENTER MRS P CARPENTER MR R CARPENTER MS R CARPENTER MR A CARR MRS E CARR MRS K CARR MR N CARR MS ROSAMONDE CARR MS MANUELA CARRA MR MANUEL CARREIRA-ESPIDO MRS D CARRE
MR LINDSAY CARRICK MR A C CARRINGTON MR B CARRINGTON MRS J CARRINGTON MRS A CARRINGTON-BROOK MS M CARR-JONES MR P CARROL MR B CARROLL MR RODERICK CARROLL MR S CARROLL MRS S CARROLL MR ANDREW CARRUTHERS MR B CARRUTHERS MS DIANA CARSON MR
CARSON MRS T CARSON MR A CARSTAIRS MRS F CARSTENS MR A CARTER PROFESSOR ALEXANDRA CARTER MRS B CARTER MR C CARTER MRS D CARTER MRS DEBORAH CARTER MR E CARTER MRS E CARTER MS EDNA CARTER MR GEOFFREY CARTER MR J CARTER MRS J CARTER MRS JU
CARTER MRS KIM CARTER MR M CARTER MRS M CARTER MR MARTIN CARTER MR NICHOLAS CARTER MRS P CARTER MR PETER CARTER MR PHILIP CARTER MR R CARTER MS R CARTER DR S CARTER MS S CARTER MR STEPHEN CARTER LADY TERESA CARTER MS V CARTER MS V CARTER MR
VIVIEN CARTER MRS P CARTER-SHAW MR MALCOLM CARTLEDGE MR D CARTLIDGE MR I CARTWRIGHT MS MIRIAM CARTWRIGHT MR R CARTWRIGHT MR RICARDO CARUNCHO MR PAVLOS CARVALHO MRS RENATE CARVER MRS A CARVILL MS JANE CARVILL MR STEVEN CARY MISS W CARY M
E CASALE MR M CASELLI MR EDWARD CASEMENT MS M CASEY MS REGINA CASEY MISS SUSAN CASEY MRS F CASH MR & MRS J CASH MR N CASH MS WENDY CASH MRS M CASHDAN MR O CASHER MR OMER CASHER MRS J CASS MR JORDI CASSANOVAS MR L CASSEL MR M CASSERLY M
BRIAN CASSIDY MR M CASSIDY MR S CASSIDY MRS P CASSIN MR M CAST MISS M CASTANHA MR L CASTELLI-GAIR MR A CASTLE MRS ANNE CASTLE MRS ISABELLA CASTLE MR J CASTLE MS M CASTLE KATHRYN CASTLES MR T CASTORINA MRS W CASWELL MR BRIAN CATCHPOLE MRS
CATCHPOLE MRS CHRISTINE CATER LADY ELIZABETH CATHERWOOD MRS J CATT MR J CATTELL SIMON CATTERALL MRS JEAN CATTON MR D CAUDLE MR FRANCIS CAUGHLIN MRS M CAULCOTT MRS S CAULDWELL MR D CAULFIELD MR I CAUSER DR ROGER CAUSON MR B CAUSTIN MRS
CAUSTON MRS C CAVALIER MR J CAVALLA MISS E CAVALLO MR MICHAEL CAVE MS R CAVE MS B CAVE MR R CAVILL MR N CAWOOD A CAWSON MS DEBORAH CAZALET MRS C CAZENOVE DESMOND CECIL MS LYNDA CECIL MS J CELESTIN MISS B CELILOGLU MR T CELNER MRS BER
CEPOLLINA DR D CERCCARELLI-HODEL MRS G CEREZCI MS M CERRONE MR G CERVENKA MRS A CHADHA MS D CHADS MR DAVID CHADWICK MR IAN CHADWICK MISS L CHADWICK MR A CHAKRABARTI MR S CHAKRABORTI MR P CHAKRAVERTY MS ALEXANDRA CHALDECOTT MRS E CHALFO
MR ANTHONY CHALK MR ERIC CHALKER MISS J CHALKLEY MR J CHALLEN MR J CHALLIS MS M CHALLIS MR PETER CHALLIS MS CONNIE CHALMERS DR D CHALMERS MRS JO CHALMERS MISS D CHAMBERLAIN MR JOHN CHAMBERLAIN MR L CHAMBERLAIN MRS L CHAMBERLAIN MS
CHAMBERLAIN MISS JOY CHAMBERLIN MR DAVID CHAMBERS MR E CHAMBERS MR GUY CHAMBERS MR K CHAMBERS MRS LIZ CHAMBERS MRS M CHAMBERS MRS P CHAMBERS MR R CHAMBERS MRS B CHAMPION MR ANTHONY CHAN MISS J CHAN MR G CHANA MS Z CHANCELLOR MRS N CHAN
MRS BARBARA CHANDLER MRS C CHANDLER MR F CHANDLER MS P CHANDLER MR R CHANDLER MR G CHANG MR T CHANG MRS J CHANNELL MRS M CHAN-REILLY MR MICHAEL CHANT MRS S CHANTAL MR N CHAPELLE MRS D CHAPLIN MRS I CHAPLINSKAYA MR A CHAPMAN MRS A CHAPM
MR B CHAPMAN MRS C CHAPMAN MR COLIN CHAPMAN MR DEREK CHAPMAN MRS E CHAPMAN MR H CHAPMAN MR J CHAPMAN MRS J CHAPMAN MRS JENNY CHAPMAN MR JEREMY CHAPMAN MR K CHAPMAN MRS K CHAPMAN MR KEITH CHAPMAN MRS M CHAPMAN MISS NATALIE CHAPMAN MI
P CHAPMAN MR PETER CHAPMAN MR P CHAPMAN MR R CHAPMAN MRS S CHAPMAN MRS P CHAPNESS MRS V CHAPPIN MR J CHAPPLE MR C CHAPRON MS I CHARALAMBOPOULOU MRS A CHARALAMBOU MS M CHARD MR R CHARD MR A CHARITY MRS GEORGINA CHARITY DR AND MRS J CHARKH
MR A CHARLES MS B CHARLES MRS D CHARLES MR E CHARLES MS GILL CHARLES MR & MRS K CHARLES MR M CHARLESWORTH MRS ENID CHARLEY MR JOHN CHARLICK D P CHARLTON MR J CHARLTON MR PETER CHARLTON MR R CHARLTON MRS TARA CHARLTON MRS P CHARLWOOD M
JUNE CHARMAN MR M CHARRINGTON MRS J CHARTERS MS J CHASE-GREY MR R CHASMAR MISS L CHASSELS MR A CHATER MRS D CHATFIELD MS S CHATTERJEE MRS P CHATTERS MR MATTHEW CHATTLE DR B CHATTOPADHYAY MRS M CHAUDHRY MISS S CHAUDHRY MR J CHAUHAN MR
CHAVANEAU MR LEONCE CHAVANNES MR PAUL CHAVE MS A CHAVEAU MISS S CHAWDA MS L CHAZEN MS P CHEAL MR KENNETH CHEALE MS M CHECKLEY MR A CHECKSFIELD MRS D CHEEK MRS A CHEESMAN MR C CHEETHAM MS I CHEETHAM MRS K CHEETHAM MISS L CHEETHAM MRS
CHELLEW MISS C CHEN MS K CHENEVIX TRENCH MR L CHERON MR IAN CHERRIE MR M CHERRIE MRS M CHERRINGTON MRS MERYLYN CHERRY MR DAVID CHESHIRE MRS E CHESHIRE MRS D CHESNEY MR JAMES CHESSELL MRS A CHESSON MR P CHESTER MRS P CHESTER MR M CHESTERFIE
MRS P CHESTERMAN PETER CHESTERS MRS CATHERINE CHETWYND MS LORNA CHETWYND MRS HEATHER CHEUNG MR KELVIN CHEUNG MS TERESA CHEUNG MRS V CHEVASCO MR W CHEVIS MRS J CHEW MR YUEN-WEI CHEW MISS M CHEYNE ANGELA CHICK MRS GAYNOR CHICK MRS J CHIDG
MS M CHIDGEY MRS P CHIGNELL MR R CHILCOT MRS K CHILDS MS L CHILDS MS NICOLA CHILDS DR PENELOPE CHILDS MR R CHILDS MRS J CHILLINGSWORTH MR STUART CHILLINGWORTH MR A Y CHIN MISS M CHIN MR MICHAEL CHING MR J CHINNERY MS DIANNE CHIPPERFIELD
IAN CHISNALL MRS K CHITA MS K CHITTENDEN MISS J CHITTLEBURGH MR J CHITTOCK MISS H CHIVERS MISS JOYCE MARY CHIVERS DR CHI-WING MRS A CHOATE MS S CHOHAN MRS H CHOLERA MR F CHOLERTON MR P CHOMET MR A CHONG MR I CHOONARA MRS TESSA CHOPPING
PATRICK CHORLEY MRS D CHOUDHURY MR & MRS C CHOWDHURY PAM CHOWHAN MRS E CHRIST MS I CHRISTENSEN MR K CHRISTIANE MS ROSSANNA CHRISTIANSON MR A CHRISTIE MR C CHRISTIE MISS JACQUELINE CHRISTIE MRS SARAH CHRISTIE MR I CHRISTMAS MR M CHRISTODOULID
MR S CHRISTODOULOU MR & MRS G CHRISTOFIDES MRS K CHRISTOFIDES MR M CHRISTON MRS J CHRISTOPHERSON MRS T CHRISTOU MR G F CHRONNELL MRS H CHRONOPOULOS MR THANOS CHRYSAKIS MR ANDREAS CHRYSANTHOU MRS E CHU MS K CHUA MS PAZ CHUAQUI MRS S CHUBB
P CHUCK MR MANGAL CHUDHA MS AMANDA CHUMAS MR E CHURCH MR H J CHURCH MR J CHURCH MR M CHURCH MR R CHURCH MRS T CHURCH MISS S CHURCHER KENNETH CHURCHILL MRS J CHURCHYARD MR P CHUTER MR GIUSEPPE CIARDI MR P CIMOVIC MR G CINAMON MRS S CITRO
MR A CIVIL MRS C CLAFEN MS N CLAIREBERT MRS B CLAMP MRS S CLAMP MR M CLANCEY MRS MARGARET CLAPHAM MS S CLAPP MR ALEC CLAPPERTON MISS J CLAPSON MRS K CLAPTON MR D CLARE MRS J CLARE MR K CLARE MS V CLARE MISS L CLARENDON MR L CLAREY MR
CLARIDGE MRS L CLARIDGE MRS A CLARK MR A CLARK MRS B CLARK MISS B CLARK MR B CLARK MR C CLARK MRS C CLARK MS C CLARK MISS C CLARK MRS CHRISTINE CLARK MS D CLARK MR E CLARK MISS F CLARK MR G CLARK MRS G CLARK MRS H CLARK MR IAN CLARK MISS IR
CLARK MISS J CLARK MR J CLARK MRS J CLARK DR L CLARK MS LINDA CLARK MISS M CLARK MRS M CLARK MR MALCOLM CLARK N CLARK MRS P CLARK MRS PATRICIA CLARK MR P E CLARK MR R CLARK MS R CLARK MR & MRS ROY CLARK MS S CLARK MRS SARAH CLARK SUSAN CLA
MR V CLARK MR W CLARK MR A CLARKE MRS A CLARKE MS A CLARKE MS ALISON CLARKE MRS A NGELACLARKE MRS C CLARKE MS C CLARKE MRS CATHERINE CLARKE MR COLIN CLARKE MRS D CLARKE MR DAVID CLARKE MRS E CLARKE MRS ELISABETH CLARKE MR F CLARKE MR
CLARKE MR J CLARKE MR & MRS J CLARKE MRS J CLARKE MR JAMES CLARKE MRS JANET CLARKE MRS JEAN CLARKE MR K CLARKE MRS M CLARKE MISS M CLARKE MR M CLARKE MS M CLARKE MS M S CLARKE MRS MAY CLARKE MS MIRANDA CLARKE MISS R CLARKE MR R CLARKE
RICHARD CLARKE MRS S CLARKE MS S CLARKE MRS VERA CLARKE MR BRYAN CLARKSON MRS JULIA CLARKSON MRS M CLASPER MR J CLAUSEN MR B CLAUSON MRS B CLAXTON DR E CLAY MR J CLAY MR R CLAY MS V CLAY MRS ANNE CLAYDEN MISS SUSAN CLAYDON MR A CLAYTON MI
C CLAYTON MR J CLAYTON MRS JUDITH CLAYTON MR M CLAYTON MS S CLAYTON MR S CLAYTON MR STEPHEN CLAYTON MR COLIN CLEAL MR F CLEAR MR A CLEARY MR B CLEAVE MR MARTIN CLEAVE MISS A CLEAVER MR OLIVER CLEAVER DR CHRISTOPHER CLEGG MR G CLEGG MR J CLE
MRS J CLEGG MR STUART CLELAND MR A CLEMENT MRS H CLEMENT MS ISABELLE CLEMENT DR M CLEMENT MS M CLEMENT MS E CLEMENT JONES MRS M CLEMENTE MS I CLEMENTS MS JANET CLEMENTS PROFESSOR DEREK CLEMENTS-CROOME MRS DEIDRE CLENET MR C CLERKE MR JO
CLEUR MR M CLIFFORD MR C CLIFT MS G CLIFTON MRS H CLIFTON MR MICHAEL CLINGO MS CAROL CLINTON MR D CLIPPINGDALE MR M CLONEY MR A CLOSE MRS S CLOSE-SMITH MR H CLOSS MR ROBERT CLOUGH MISS J CLOUT MRS P CLUDERAY MR G CLUETT MRS V CLUTTERBUCK
J CLYNE MRS GILL COATES MRS I COATES MR R COATES MR & MRS B COATSWORTH MS A COBB MR C COBB MRS F COBB MRS J COBB MRS M COBB MR P COBB MRS PATRICIA COBB MRS S COBBE MRS P COBHAM MRS J COBLEY MR I COCHRAN G COCHRANE MS SHEILA COCHRANE MS K CO
MR PHILIP COCKBURN MR A COCKER MR ANTHONY COCKETT MS B COCKETT MRS J COCKING MR P COCKLE MS S COCKLE MR ALAN COCKRAM MS L COCKRAM GEMMA COCKRELL MISS G COCKRELL DR R COCKRELL MRS KATRINA COCKS MR ROBERT COCKSHOTT MISS A COCKSHUT MR IAN CO
MR J CODD MS SUSAN CODLING MRS J COE MR K COE MISS Q COE MR STEVEN COE MONICA COFFEY MS WENDY COGGER MS C COGHLAN MRS M COGLAN MR A COHEN MRS B COHEN MR BERNARD COHEN MR D COHEN MR DAVID COHEN DENISE COHEN CHARITABLE TRUST MR E COHEN MR EDW
COHEN MR L COHEN MR LOUIS COHEN MR M COHEN MRS M COHEN MR N COHEN MRS PAM COHEN MR ROBERT COHEN MISS S COHEN MRS S COHEN MRS DELPHINE COKER MR P COKER MRS DAPHNE COLBEY MISS HELEN COLBORNE MRS EILEEN COLBURN MR M COLBURN MR JOHN COLDSTRE
MR ALAN COLE MR D COLE MRS D COLE MR DAVID COLE MRS G COLE MR JOSH COLE MRS L COLE MS MAUREEN COLE MR MICHAEL COLE MR NICHOLAS COLE MR P COLE MR SIMON COLE MS V COLE MR RONALD COLEE REVEREND COLEMAN MR BASIL COLEMAN MISS H COLEMAN MR
COLEMAN MS W COLEMAN MR G COLES MISS J COLES MR R E COLES MR C COLESHILL MR O COLIN LADY G COLIN-CAMPBELL MISS VALERIE COLIN-RUSS MISS M COLLAZOS MR ARTHUR COLLEN MR A COLLENDER MR G A COLLENS MR C COLLETT MR P COLLETT MS A COLLEY MS E
COLLEY MR J COLLEY MR A COLLIER MR J COLLIER MS P COLLIER MRS S COLLIER MS SALLY COLLIER MRS J COLLIN MR J COLLINGBOURNE MR R COLLINGBOURNE MRS A COLLINGRIDGE MS ELIZABETH COLLINGRIDGE MS ROMAYNE COLLINGWOOD MS A COLLINS MR BRIAN COLLI
MR BRYAN COLLINS MR C COLLINS MRS C COLLINS MISS D COLLINS MRS D COLLINS MRS G COLLINS MR H COLLINS MR J COLLINS MS JANE COLLINS DR J COLLINS DR & MRS JOHN COLLINS MR K COLLINS MR L COLLINS MR M COLLINS MS M COLLINS MRS M COLLINS MR MAURI
COLLINS MR P COLLINS MRS PAMELA COLLINS MRS RONA COLLINS MRS S COLLINS MR STEVEN COLLINS MISS VALERIE COLLINS MR D COLLINSON MR PETER COLLINSON MR J COLLIS MRS J COLLIS MS JANE COLLIS MR L COLLIS MRS P COLLIS MISS P COLLISON MR & MRS G COLL
MR A COLLYMORE MR B COLMAN MRS J COLMAN MR O COLMAN MR P COLQUHOUN MR N COLQUHOUNDENVERS MRS M COLUSSI MRS S COLVIN MR & MRS B W COLWELL MR J COLWELL MRS A COLWYN FOULKES MISS SUSAN COMB MRS ANNAMARIE COMBEN MRS COMBER MS GILLIAN COM
MRS J COMLEY DR WARWICK COMLEY MS P COMMANDER MR PAUL COMMERFORD MS C COMPAGNONI MISS A COMPER MR JOHN COMPTON MISS M COMPTON MR R COMPTON-BURNETT MR BURCU CON MR M CONACHER MRS M CONCANON MR B CONDON MR CHRISTOPHER CONE MS ANGE
CONERON MR D CONFREY MISS A CONGREVE MS N CONLAN MR MICHAEL CONLON MRS H CONN MS M CONN MR G CONNAUGHTON MR A CONNEL MS E CONNELL MR JOHN CONNELL MRS D CONNELLY MR BILL CONNER MS R CONNER MRS J CONNERADE MRS A CONNETT MRS HELEN CONNICK M
B CONNING MR B CONNOLLY MR BRENDAN CONNOLLY MR S CONNOLLY MRS S G CONNOLLY MR PETER CONNON MR JOE CONNOR MR P CONNOR MRS M CONRAD MR O CONRAD MRS NADINE CONRADI MRS C CONRICH MR B CONROY MR S CONROY REVEREND J CONRY MR J CONRY MR R CONSC
MR JOHN CONSTABLE MRS S CONSTANTI MISS A CONSTANTINE MS P CONWAY MR R CONWAY MISS T CONWAY MR BRIAN CONWAY-SMITH MR ALAN COOK MRS ANGELA COOK MR B COOK MR C COOK MR DAVID COOK MRS DOT COOK MRS E COOK MS FRANCES COOK MR J COOK MRS J COOK
JOHN COOK MRS JUDITH COOK MR M COOK MR & MRS M COOK MS M COOK MRS MICHELLE COOK MR N COOK MR R COOK MISS S COOK MRS SANDRA COOK MS Z COOK MRS B COOKE MR D COOKE MS D COOKE MRS G COOKE MISS JUDITH COOKE P M COOKE MR D H COOKSEY MR D COOKSEY
MARY COOKSEY MR M COOLE MS D COOLEY MR JOHN COOMBE MRS M COOMBE MRS EILEEN COOMBES DR M COOMBES MRS M COOMBES MR PETER COOMBES MRS C COOMBES-SMITH DR A COOMBS MRS A COOMBS MR G COOMBS MISS K COOMBS MRS M COOMBS MR F COOMES MRS ELIZABE
COONEY MR A COOPER B COOPER MR & MRS B COOPER MR BRIAN COOPER MR C COOPER MS C COOPER MR D COOPER MRS DIANA COOPER MRS E COOPER MR HUGH COOPER MISS J COOPER MRS J COOPER MS J COOPER MS JILLY COOPER OBE MR K COOPER MRS K COOPER MR L COOP
MR M COOPER MS M COOPER MRS MERILYN COOPER MRS P COOPER MR & MRS P COOPER MS P COOPER MR R COOPER MRS S COOPER DR STEPHANIE COOPER MRS T COOPER MS V COOPER MRS A COOTE MR J P COOTE MRS G COPE MRS F COPELAND MRS SONIA COPELAND MRS JOAN COPEM
MR A COPLAND MRS L COPLAND MS J COPLEY MR D COPP MRS IRENE COPPOCK MRS W COPSEY MS CELIA CORAM MR A CORBETT MR CHRIS CORBETT MRS S CORBETT MRS SARAH CORBIN MRS STELLA CORBISHLEY MS J CORBYN MS V CORCORAN MRS VICTORIA CORCORAN MISS M CORDE
ALVES MR K CORDEN MS C CORDERO MR M CORDERY MR A CORDINGLY MR C CORDINGLY MRS CELIA CORDLE MR F CORDON MRS V CORDY-SIMPSON MRS G H COREY MR IAN CORKER MR T CORKETT MRS L CORKLAND MR C CORLETT DR B CORLEY MS A CORNELL MR BRIAN CORNELL
CHRISTOPHER CORNER MR M CORNER MR R CORNES MR J CORNFORD MS ROSAMUND CORNFORD MR A CORNISH MR J CORNISH MR JAMES CORNISH MRS L CORNISH MR M CORNISH MS MARY CORNISH MR & MRS DAVID CORNWELL MR H CORONEL MRS H CORPS MR MATHEW CORRALL M
CORTES DR J COSGRAVE MR N COSIN MS M COSTA MS SANDRA COSTA MR PETER COSTAIN MS G COSTELLO DR M COSTELLO MR PETER COSTELLO MR J COSTELOE MR S COSTER MRS T COSTERTON MRS B COSTIDELL MR PATRICK COSTIGAN MR C COSTIN MR JOHN COSTIN MS H COTMORE
J COTTERILL MS C COTTON MR CLIVE COTTON MR D COTTON MS JANE COTTRELL MISS S COUFFIN MRS L COUGHLAN MR CHRIS COULCHER MRS D COULSTON MS P COULTEN MS A COULTER MS F COULTER MR M COULTER MR JOHN COULTHARD MR & MRS J F COUNSELL MRS KERRY COU
MS PENNY COUPE MR B COURT MISS C COURTENAY MRS E COURTENAY-STAMP MR SIMON COUSENS MR COUSIN MR D COUSSELL MS R COUTINO MRS J COUTTS MR S COUTTS MR ADRIAN COVA MRS C COVENEY MRS P COVENEY MS MARY COVENTRY MRS M COVER MS R COVER MISS R COL
MR S COVINGTON COLONEL COWAN MS ALEXANDRA COWAN MRS M COWAN MR R COWAN MISS VALERIE COWAN MRS D COWARD MR N COWDERY MR V COWDY MR AND MRS A COWELL MS A COWEN MISS F COWEN MR T COWEN MS ELENOR COWIE MR H COWIN MRS J COWLAND MS A COWL
MISS J COWLEY MR P COWLEY MRS SUSAN COWLEY MR H COWLING DR E COWNE MRS S COWPER MR A COX MRS B COX MISS C COX MISS D COX MR D COX MR G COX MR GEOFF COX MR & MRS H COX MRS I COX MR J COX MRS L COX MISS M COX MRS M COX MRS MAUREEN COX MISS P
MRS P COX MS P COX MRS S COX MR S COX MISS SARAH COX MS M COYTE MRS A CRABTREE MR E CRACK MRS G CRACKNELL MR M CRACKNELL MRS ESTHER CRADDOCK MR JACK CRADDOCK MRS M CRADDOCK PHIL CRADDOCK MR C CRAIG MRS FRANCES CRAIG DR G CRAIG MR GORDON CR
DR J CRAIG MS J CRAIG MISS S CRAIG MR P CRAIG-WOOD MS I CRAIK MR R CRAIK MRS E CRAINE MRS J CRAINE MR BRIAN CRAKER MS FIONA CRAMB MRS H CRAMER MR IVOR CRAMER MS J CRAMP MRS P CRAMP MR W CRAMPTON MR S CRAMPTON-HAYWARD MRS C CRANE MS HEL
CRANE MR P CRANE MS S CRANE MRS T CRANFIELD DR ROSS CRANSTON MRS E CRASKE MS V CRASKE MRS J CRAVEN MISS A CRAVITZ MISS B CRAWFORD MS G CRAWFORD MRS H CRAWFORD MR J CRAWFORD MRS J CRAWFORD MR JOHN CRAWFORD MR N CRAWFORD MRS P CRAWFORD
ROBERT CRAWFORD MISS RUTH CRAWFORD MR M CRAWFORD-PHILLIPS MISS G CRAWLEY MR JOHN CRAWLEY MR P CRAWLEY MRS D CRAWSHAW MR R CRAWSHAW MR MARTIN CRAXTON MRS P CRAY MRS A CREASY MS JUNE CREBBIN MRS W CREBER MR KEVIN CREED MS M CREESE M
CREIGHTON MS M CRELLIN MS S CREMER MS L CRESS MR JOHN CRESSWELL MR GEOFFREY CRETTIN MS J CREW MRS P CREW MR C CREWS MRS L CREWS MR R CRIBB MRS GAIL CRICHTON MISS K CRICHTON MRS S CRICHTON MS MARGARET CRICK MISS A CRICKETT MRS J CRIGHTON M
CRILLY MRS G CRIPPEN MS M CRIPPS MR K CRISELL JOHN CRISP MISS D CRISPIN MR C CRITCHLOW MR R CRITCHLOW MRS S CRITOPH MRS C CROCKER MS J CROCKER-MICHELL MRS M CROCKETT MRS R CROCKETT MRS W CROCKFORD MR O CROCOMBE MS ANNA CROFT DR B CROFT J CR
MS J CROFT MRS P CROFT MRS TERESA CROFT MRS D CROFTON MRS H CROFTON MISS C CROFTS MR M CROGGON MR J CROKER MR D CROMBIE MR B CROMPTON MRS KATHRINE CROMPTON MR MALCOLM CROMPTON MR D CRONIN MRS L CRONSHAW MRS C CROOK MR GEORGE CROOK MIS
CROOKALL MRS S CROOKS DR STEVE CROPPER MR A CROSBIE MS K CROSFIELD MRS A CROSS MR D CROSS MS E CROSS MR EDWARD CROSS MR J CROSS MS J CROSS MISS S CROSS MRS SHEILA CROSS MRS A CROSSLAND MR D CROSSLAND MRS G CROSSLAND MRS P CROSSLAND M
CROSSLEY-JACKSON MRS M CROUCHER MISS MARGARET CROUCHER MR P CROUCHER MR IAN CROUCHLY MARION CROUCHMAN MR GEOFF CROUGHTON MRS BARBARA CROW PROF R CROW MRS L CROWCROFT MISS FRANCES CROWE MRS M CROWE MRS E CROWHURST MRS C CROWLEY
MARGARET CROWLEY MISS S CROWN MRS E CROWTHER MRS MIRIAM CROZIER MR JAMES CRUDDAS MR T CRUDDAS MRS CAROLINE CRUFT MRS R CRUMP MR R CRUMPTON MRS E CRUTTENDEN MRS S CRYSTAL MRS K CSELEY MRS ELENI CUBITT MR D CUCKNEY MRS C CUCKOW MS R CUDDEF
DR LUIS GABRIEL CUERVO-AMORE MISS I CULHANE MR T CULLEN MR J CULLINGHAM MR A CULLUM MRS GILL CULVER MRS P CULVER MR R CULVERHOUSE MR R CULVERWELL MR MICHAEL CUMBERLIN ANNA CUMBERS MRS T CUMBO MR ANDREW CUMINE MR PATRICK CUMING MR
CUMMING MS J CUMMING MR J S CUMMING MRS J CUMMINGS MR L CUMMINGS MR PAUL CUMMINGS MR R CUMMINGS MRS R CUMMINGS MISS S CUMMINGS MS C CUMMINS MRS M CUMMINS MR MICHAEL CUMMINS MRS D CUNDY MRS J CUNIS MS DYMPHA CUNNANE MISS K CUNNEW M
CUNNINGHAM MRS A CUNNINGHAM MS B CUNNINGHAM MRS J CUNNINGHAM MS LISA CUNNINGHAM MRS M CUNNINGHAM MR TIM CUNNINGHAM MR M CUNNINGTON MS C CUOZZO MR JOSE CURA MR S CURL MRS A CURNOW MS A CURRAN MR A CURRIE MR D CURRIE MR J CURRIE MR T CUR
MRS E CURRIER MR J CURRIER MS N CURRY DR P CURRY DR S CURSON MS C CURTIN MRS ANNE CURTIS MR A CURTIS MS GERALDINE CURTIS MS HELEN CURTIS MRS L CURTIS MRS M CURTIS MS M CURTIS MS N CURTIS MR P CURTIS MR R CURTIS MRS RACHEL CURTIS MRS S CURTIS
N CURTISS MR B CURTOIS C CURZON MS D CURZON MISS GILLIAN CUSSEN MR P CUTHBERT MR JAMES CUTHBERTSON MR NICHOLAS CUTLER MRS S CUTLER MR JOHN CUTTING MRS VALERIE CUTTS MR A CZAYKOWSKI MR L DA COSTA MR FABIANO DA SILVA MRS JUNE DA SILVA MR L
SILVA MRS JANICE DABANOVIC MR J DABBS MS M DABESTANI MR J DACKINS MRS M DACOMBE MR ASHLEY DACOSTA MR MICHAEL DACOSTA MS S DACOSTA MRS P DADACHANJI MS G DAFNY JULIAN DAGGETT MRS P DAGNALL MS CAROLYN DAILEY MR ALAN DALE MRS BARBARA DALE L
G DALE DR NAOMI DALE MS N DALE MR R DALE MR G D'ALESSANDRO MRS LINDA DALEY MRS M DALEY MISS N DALEY MRS SUSAN DALEY MS SUSAN DALEY MRS M DALIAH MR MIKE DALIGAN LILIANA DALLA PIANA MISS M DALLING MR D DALLY MRS C DALTON MS J DALTON MRS J DALT
MS GAYNOR DALY MRS J DALY MR N DALY MR T DALY MS F DALZELL DR J DALZELL MRS R DAMSTRA MRS B DANAHER PATRICIA DANASWAMY MR NORMAN DANCE MISS K B DANCENEY MISS C DANDEKER MISS B DANDY MS A DANE MS S DANESHKHU MR J D'ANGELO MRS D DANIEL D
DANIEL MISS P DANIEL MR RICHARD DANIEL MRS B DANIELS MRS HELEN DANIELS MR MICHAEL DANIELS MISS SARAH DANIELS MR C DANN MRS D DANN MR JONATHAN DANN DR T DANN MR A DANSON MS D DAPERIS MRS A DARBY MRS G DARBY MR JAMES DARBY MR JOHN DARBY
TRUDI DARBY MR C DARE MS E DARE MR K DARE MRS A DARGAHI MR N DARGHOUTH MS S DARKING MR D DARLING MRS E DARLING MR P DARLING MR P DARLOW MS L DARNELL MRS M DARRACOTT MR A DART MS CAROLA DARWIN MRS Y DARWISH MRS A DAS DR B DAS MRS MARGARETE
MS MUKTA DAS MR P DAS MR A DASGUPTA DR S DASGUPTA MR D DASILVA MS S DASON MS S DATAR MR A DATERS MR M DATTA MR A DAVAGE MR R DAVAGE MR A DAVE DR T DAVE MR A DAVEY MR BRIAN DAVEY MR C DAVEY MR EDWARD DAVEY MR J DAVEY MR JON C DAVEY MRS K DA
MRS MARIA DAVEY MR FREDERIC DAVID MS P DAVID MRS S DAVID MRS ADELE DAVIDE MRS H DAVIDIAN MR R DAVIDS MR A DAVIDSON MISS C DAVIDSON MR F DAVIDSON MR J DAVIDSON MRS J DAVIDSON J DAVIDSON MR JOHN DAVIDSON MISS K DAVIDSON MR MEL DAVIDSON MR

IDSON MS SANDRA DAVIDSON DR SERENA DAVIDSON MR E DAVIE MR J DAVIE MR A DAVIES DR A E DAVIES MRS B DAVIES MR B DAVIES MRS BARBARA DAVIES MR C DAVIES MRS C DAVIES MS C DAVIES MRS C M DAVIES MISS CATHERINE DAVIES MR COLIN DAVIES MR D DAVIES MR
ALD DAVIES MS E DAVIES MR G DAVIES MISS H DAVIES MS ISABELLA DAVIES MR & MRS J DAVIES MR J DAVIES MR & MRS J M DAVIES MRS JANET DAVIES MR JOHN DAVIES MRS JOSEPHINE DAVIES MRS K DAVIES KAREN DAVIES MR KEITH DAVIES MR L DAVIES MRS L DAVIES
S LINDA DAVIES MS LISA DAVIES MS LYN DAVIES MISS M DAVIES DR MARK DAVIES MISS MONICA DAVIES MRS N DAVIES MISS O DAVIES MRS P DAVIES MR P DAVIES MR PATRICK DAVIES MR PETER DAVIES MISS R DAVIES MR R DAVIES MR RICHARD DAVIES MR ROBERT DAVIES
S S DAVIES MR S DAVIES MS S DAVIES MR STANLEY DAVIES MR T DAVIES MRS V DAVIES MS V DAVIES MR W S DAVIES MRS C DAVIES FOSTER MRS JOAN DAVIN-LOOBY MR A DAVIS MRS A DAVIS MS A DAVIS MISS B DAVIS MRS CHRISTIANE DAVIS MS C DAVIS MS E
IS MRS EDNA DAVIS MR GEOFFREY DAVIS MRS H DAVIS MR J DAVIS MR K DAVIS MRS K DAVIS MR M DAVIS MRS M DAVIS DR MARK DAVIS MR MICHAEL DAVIS MR N DAVIS MS R DAVIS MR R DAVIS MRS ROSEMARY DAVIES MR S DAVIS MISS SUSANNAH DAVIS MR T DAVIS MR WILLIAM
IS MRS Y DAVIS MS ELIZABETH DAVISON MR J DAVISON MR ALAN DAVTER MRS M DAVY J DAVYS MS J DAVYS MISS I DAW MS E DAWBER MR A DAWE MR A DAWES MRS Y DAWES MR LEO DAWKINS MRS S DAWKINS MR T DAWKINS MRS Y DAWOOD MR A DAWSON MISS ANNE DAWSON MR
AWSON DR H DAWSON MR J DAWSON MRS J DAWSON MS J DAWSON MR JEREMY DAWSON MR P DAWSON MS REBECCA DAWSON MR R DAWSON MR THOMAS DAWSON MRS WANDA DAWSON MISS L DAWSON JONES MRS PATRICIA DAWSON-LLOYD MRS BETTY DAY MR C DAY MR D DAY MRS J
J MRS JEANNE DAY MR J DAY MR L DAY MRS L DAY MRS M DAY MRS P DAY MR RICHARD DIGBY DAY MR STEPHEN DAY MR T DAY MRS C DAY MS S DAYBELL MR G DAYSON MS A D'COSTA MRS L DE ARIAS MRS M DE BLANK MRS M DE BOO MR R DE BUSSCHER MR D DE-COBAIN MR L DE
DOVA MRS V DE GIORGI MR SPENCER DE GREY MRS M DE HAAN MR C DE HALL MS INGE DE JONG MR MARC DE JONGH MR T DE LACY SARAH DE MATTOS MR W DE MENDONCA MISS A DE MESTRE MR MICHAEL DE MOWBRAY MR S DE PINNA MR LEOPOLD DE ROTHSCHILD CBE RD VICTORIA,
Y DE ROTHSCHILD MS C DE RYSKY MISS M DE SARAM MRS S DE SILVA MRS S DE VERE MR JOHN DE VEULLE MR D L S DE VILLIERS MRS P DE VILLIERS MR STEPHAN DE VOS MRS M DE WET MRS K DE WITT MR S DE WOLFE MRS SARAH DE MATTOS MR A DEACON MR ALAN DEACON MRS
EACON MR E DEACON MRS J DEACON MR L DEACON DR MAX DEACON MR RICHARD DEACON MRS SHIRIN DEACON MR RICHARD DEAG MR RAY DEAHL MS A DEAN MR D DEAN MRS H DEAN MS J DEAN MR JOHN DEAN MRS M DEAN MRS N DEAN MR P DEAN MRS C DEAN MR JOHN DEAR MR C
RING MR J DEARNER MRS B DE'ATH MISS J DEATON MR S DEBATTISTA MRS H DEBCZAK-DEBSKI MR R DEBNEY MARTIN DEBOO MR JEAN-MARC DEBRICON MISS G DEBRY MR JOHN DEBY DE-CONSTRUCT MISS N DECORT MISS S DEEB MISS M DEEBANK MRS M DEEDS MS S DEEKEN MR E
LEY MR AND MRS C P DEERING MR DOUGLAS DEETER MR SIMON DEFRIEF MRS K DEFTY MR L DEGAVINO MRS R DEGAZON-JOHNSON MR RICHARD DEGEN MR J DEGENHARDT MRS S DEHGHANIAN MS H DEIGHTON MR A DEL FABBRO MS J DELMAR MS PAULINE DEL MAR MS ISABEL DEL
MRS SANDRA DELAHOY MRS A DELAHUNTY MR D DELANEY MRS D DELANEY MRS B DELBRIDGE MRS N DELENDA MS V DELIUS MR J DELL MRS M DELL MRS M DELLER MRS M DELL'OSSO MS C DELMAN MR A DELOGU MRS E DEMBINSKA MS K DEMETRIOU MRS M DEMETRIOU MS R
METSOPOULLOS MR J DEMONT MR A DEMPSY DR PAUL DEMUTH MR JOSEPH DENBY MRS P DENBY MRS CHRISTINE DENCER MR D DENCH MRS D DENHAM MR GRAHAM DENHAM MR TREVOR DENHAM MR P DENHOLM MRS V DENLEY MRS DOROTHY DENNANT MRS H DENNE MISS JOAN DENNE
S P DENNETT MR BRIAN DENNEY MRS M DENNING MR S DENNING MR ALBERT DENNIS MRS ANN DENNIS MRS D DENNIS MR J DENNIS MR M DENNIS MR MARK DENNIS MR ROBERT DENNIS MR V DENNIS MS T DENNISON MRS B DENNY MRS C DENNY MISS D DENNY MRS C DENOVAN-SMITH
S C DENROCHE MS A DEPIANO MS COLETTE DEPLA MRS G DERBYSHIRE MR GARETH DERBYSHIRE MR G DERRIMAN DR ELIZABETH DESBOROUGH MRS J DESMOND MRS P DESOUZA MRS V DESOUZA MISS VALERIE DESPRE MRS M DESSAIX MR S DESSLOCH MR FREDERIC DESTIN K S DESVAUX
I DE-UJFALUSSY MS K DEUSS MR R DEVANEY MRS SHOBANA DEVANI MS CAROL DEVAUGHN MRS M DEVENA MR D DEVERELL MR J DEVERELL MS G DEVEREUX MR K DEVEY MRS E DE-VISE MS A DEVLIN MR & MRS D DEVONS MRS H DEVRIES DR CATHRYN DEW DR J DEW MRS ZALINA
AN MR ARTHUR DEWAR MR M DEWAR MR A DEWEY MR DEWEY MISS MARGARET DEWHIRST MRS D DEWHURST MR J DEWHURST MS S DEWSBERY MS S DEWSNAP MRS J DEY MRS M DEY GHATAK MS M DEYES MR M D'EYNCOURT MR A DHAIRYAWAN MR A DHANANI MR P DHANGAL MISS M
NSAY MS R DHAR MRS D D'HAYER SYVIA, LADY DHENIN MISS R DHESI MRS S DHOT MRS D DI CARCACI MISS B DI CORPO MRS KAREN DI LORENZO MR ROBERTO DI NAPOLI DR L DI SILVIO MRS P DIACK MRS B DIAMOND MRS E DIAMOND MRS J DIAMOND MR C DIAS MS ROSA DIAS MR
IAS MRS E DIBB MR N DIBB MISS MADELINE DIBBEN MS P DIBBIN MS A DI-BENEDETTO MR J DIBLEY MRS G DICK DR JAMES DICK MR MICHAEL DICK MR R DICK MR JOHN DICKENSON MRS V DICKENSON MS KATE DICKER MR M DICKINSON MR M DICKINSON MR R DICKINSON MISS S
KINSON MRS VINA DICKINSON MR F DICKS MRS F DICKSON MS G DICKSON JANE DICKSON MS SUSAN DICKSON MR W DICKSON MISS ANN DIETRICH MR BRIAN DIFFEY MS FRANCIS DIFFLEY MR G DIFILIPPO MR C DIGGENS MRS C DIGGINES MRS DIANA DIJMARESCU MRS L DILKS MR
DILLEY MISS NITA DILLEY MRS M DILLMAN MISS CLAIRE DILLON MR R DILLON MRS VIVIENNE DIMANT MR M DIMARCO MISS R DIMMOCK MR G DIMOCK MR G DIMON MRS D DIMOND MRS C DIMOU MR L DIN DR ROBERTO DINA MS J DINES MR A DINGWALL MISS K DINIZ MRS T DINNIS
J DINSDALE DR R DINSDALE MR T DINSLEY MRS K DINSMORE DR R DINWIDDIE MRS A DIONISI MR P DIONISIO MRS P DIPALMA MRS L DIPPLE MRS JUDITH DI-PRETORO MISS A DIPROSE DR F DISCHE MISS C DISERENS MS SUE DISLEY MRS M DITCHFIELD MRS J DITHERIDGE MR C
ER MR J DIVER MS P DIVES MR M DIVVER MS C DIWELL DR M DIX MRS B DIXON MS CAROL DIXON MR G DIXON MS J DIXON MS K DIXON MRS M DIXON MRS P DIXON MR P DIXON MISS R DIXON MR & MRS J DIXON MRS S DIXON-GREEN MR DIMITRI DJURIC MR B DOAR MS K DOBBIN MS
OBBS MS M DOBBS MR ROB DOBELL MRS D DOBRIN MR A DOBSON MISS H DOBSON MRS M DOCEMO MR A DOCHERTY DR H DODD MR L DODD MR LUKE DODD MS S C DODD MS DIANA DODDS MR B DODGE MR G DODGE DR DAVID DODGSON MRS JANE DODGSON MR B DODHIA MR R DODSON MR
ODSWORTH MR M DODWELL MR R DODWELL MRS NORA DOERFEL MS ANNA DOGGART MR G DOHERTY MR PAUL DOHERTY MS R DOHMEN MRS T DOICIN MRS M DOKELMAN MRS E DOKOPOULOU MRS JEAN DOLAMORE MRS J DOLBY MRS J D'OLIER MRS P D'OLIER MS I DOLLIN MISS E DOLMAN
E DOLMAN MRS FIONA DOLOUGHAN PROFESSOR RICHARD DOMB MRS DIANA DOMINGO MS JAQUELINE DOMINY MR P DOMINY MISS G DONA MR J DONALD MR S DONALD MR CHRISTOPHER DONALDSON MISS K DONALDSON MR GEORGE DONATH MR P DONE MR R D'ONFRIO MRS E DONNELLAN
S CAROL DONNELLY MRS D DONNELLY MS V DONNELLY MISS M DONOHUE LADY DONOUGHUE MRS ELIZABETH DONOVAN MR J DONOVAN MRS P DONOVAN MRS R DONOVAN MS K DOOBAY MS CAROLE DOOLEY MR GERARD DOOLEY MR MARK DOOLEY MRS B DOOLIN MR P DOON MRS OLIVIA
RN MS S DORAN MS SABINE DORAN MRS Z DORDI MR R DORE REVEREND T DOREY MRS M DORFFMAN MR D DORKINGS MR A DORMAN MRS C DORNER STEVEN DORNER MRS J DORNING MS C DORRALL MR R DORRINGTON MS A DOSHI MS V DOSHI MR H DOSSETT MRS V DOTTRIDGE MR ALEX
UBLE MRS G DOUBLE MRS B DOUGALL MS J DOUGHTY MS M DOUGHTY CHRISTOPHER DOUGLAS MR G DOUGLAS MISS JANE DOUGLAS MR JUSTIN DOUGLAS MS SUSAN DOUGLAS MS V DOUGLAS MR DAVID DOUGLAS-MORRIS MR I DOUGLASS MR P DOUGLASS MRS V DOUMAS-ALAFOUZOS MRS
OUST MS V DOUST MR AND MRS A DOVE MR D DOVE MRS G DOVE MRS SUSAN DOVE MS J DOVER MISS K DOVER MR L DOVER MRS JOSEPHINE DOVEY MISS J DOW MR R DOW MR S DOW MR M DOWD MR S DOWE MISS F DOWKES MS S DOWLATSHAHI MS J DOWLE MISS S DOWLE MISS H
LING MISS E DOWMAN MR B DOWN MR D DOWN R DOWN MR W DOWN MRS C DOWNARD MR M DOWNER MR R DOWNER MS C E DOWNES CATHERINE DOWNES MRS E DOWNES MS J DOWNES MR P A DOWNES MRS SANDRA DOWNES MISS V DOWNES MR H DOWNEY MR R DOWNEY MR A DOWNHAM
K DOWNIE MRS ANDREA DOWNING MR R DOWNING MR P DOWNS MR J DOWSETT MRS C DOWSON MR C DOYLE MS E DOYLE MISS MARY DOYLE MRS P DOYLE MR ROBERT DOYLE MR T DOYLE MR D DRABBLE MR F DRAGE MR M DRAISEY MR A DRAKE MR J DRAKE MR R DRAKE MR R DRAKEFORD
KENNETH DRAPER MS LUCY DRAPER MR M A DRAPER MRS M DRAPER MR N DRAPER MR P DRAPER MRS R DRAPER MR AND MRS C DREW MR R DREW MR J DREWITT MS S DREXLER MR KURT DRICKAMER MR I DRING MISS P DRINNAN MRS P DRION MR DRISCOLL MR I DRISCOLL MRS V
SCOLL MR A DRIVER MR B DRIVER MRS C DRIVER MR M DRIVER MARTIN DRIVER ROLF DRIVER MRS M DROBKA MRS P DROMGOOLE DR JOHNATHAN DRONSFIELD MR N DROUGHT MRS A DROWN MR A DRUCE MR DOUGLAS DRUSE MR L G DRUCE MS M DRUE MR J M DRUMMOND MR JOHN
MMOND MR A DRUMMOND-MURRAY MR E DRURY MR F DRURY MISS M DRURY MR STEPHEN DRURY MS HELEN DRYER MRS M DRYSCH MRS NATASHA DSILVA MRS C D'SOUZA MRS D'SOUZA-LIEBERMAN MRS M DU PLESSIS MR AND MRS M DU PRE MS M DUANE MR NEIL DUBBER MISS H DUBE
S B DUBS MS JENNIFER DUCE MISS M DUCE MS S DUCHEMIN MRS L DUCHINSKY MRS A DUCKER MR J DUCKER RUTH DUCKER MRS SHIRLEY DUCKER MISS JOSINA DUCKETT MRS A DUCKWORTH MR G DUCKWORTH MRS A DUDDRIDGE MRS E DUDLEY MRS P DUDLEY MS S DUDLEY MS J DUDMAN
UDZIEC-MABASI MR K DUESBURY MR C DUFF MR GRAHAM DUFF MR CHRISTIAN DUFFIN MRS M DUFFIN MR G DUFFUS MISS A DUFFY MS B DUFFY MR J DUFFY MR JOHN DUFFY MISS M DUFFY MRS S DUGAL MR J DUGDALE MR CHRISTOPHER DUGGAN MRS S DUGGAN MS D DUGWELL MRS
UHIG MRS S DUIC MR J DUKE MS M DUKE MR R DUKELOW MS S DULAY PAM DULLAGE MRS RAQUEL DUMANI MR M DUMBLETON MR N DUMMETT MR PAUL DUMONT DR H DUMOULIN MR STEFAN DUNATOV MRS F DUNBAR MR S DUNBAR MISS ROBERTA DUNBAVAND MR IAN DUNCALF MR B
CAN MR I DUNCAN MS I DUNCAN MR J DUNCAN MS K ANNE DUNCAN MR K DUNCAN MR P DUNCAN MISS H DUNCANSON MRS V DUNCKLEY MR WILLIAM DUNCUMB MR C DUNDAS MISS J DUNGAY MR D DUNKERLEY MR RICHARD DUNKERLEY MRS S DUNKERLEY MRS A DUNKLEY MRS J DUNKLEY
IAN DUNLOP DR CAROLINE DUNMORE MRS M DUNMORE MR J DUNN MRS J DUNN MRS JUDITH DUNN MR MICHAEL DUNN MR P DUNN MS PATRICIA DUNN MR R DUNN MR STEPHEN DUNN MRS SUSIE DUNN MR B DUNNAGE MRS R DUNNE MS SUSAN DUNNE MRS V DUNNE MR B K DUNS MRS M
STALL MR R DUNSTAN LESLEY DUNWOODIE DR R DUPE MISS K DU-POESSIS MS LESLEY DURANT MRS J DURHAM MS KAREN DURHAM-DIGGINS MS HILARY DURMAN MR G DURRANT MS W DURRANT MR K DURY PROFESSOR RICHARD DUSCHI MR & MRS J DUSSEK MR T DUSSEK MISS SANDRA
FIELD MR JOHN DUTHIE MR PIYUSH DUTT MRS S DUTT MR A DUTTA MR C DUTTON MS L DUTTON PETER DUTTON MR B DUTTSON DR GERARD DUVEEN MS E DUVOISIN MS IDA DYAN MRS P DYCKHOFF MS A DYE MRS CAROLYN DYER MRS D DYER MRS G DYER MISS J DYER MR JUSTIN DYER MRS
YER MR P DYER MR R DYER MRS S DYER MISS Y DYER MR JOHN DYKE MR H DYLAG MR D DYSON MR H DYSON MR JOHN DYSON MRS V DYSON MR M DYTKO MISS JOANNA EADE M EADIE MR R EAGLE J EAGLEN MR GARTH EAGLESFIELD MISS A EAMES MRS G EARL MRS P EARL MS J EARLE
H EARLE MR ROBERT EARLE MR M EARLES MR T J EARLEY MR E EARLY MR DAVID EARNSHAW MR J EARTHY MR P EASDOWN MR D EASMAN MR H EAST MS MARION EAST MRS MILLICENT EAST MRS PAULA EAST MISS R EAST MRS V EAST MISS B EASTER MS C EASTMAN MR R EASTMAN
R EASY MRS B EATON MRS F EATON MR R EATON MRS A EBBERSON DR A EBBUTT MISS C EBILAH MRS D EBLETT MRS M EBORALL MR VINCENT EBRAHIM MRS F ECCLES MRS M ECCLES MR B ECCLESTONE MR B ECKER MS R ECKERSALL MR BRYAN ECKERSLEY MS C ECONOMOU MR A
ICOTT MS V EDDINGTON MISS E EDDY MR B EDE MR M EDELSHAIN MRS H EDERER MR DAVID EDGAR MRS D EDGAR MRS P EDGAR MRS KATHERINE EDGE MISS PAT EDGE MR S EDGE MRS J EDGECOMBE MS MARIE EDGECOMBE MR PATRICK EDGE-PARTINGTON MS F EDHOLM
A EDKINS MRS S EDKINS MR LAURENCE EDMANS MRS G EDMISTON MS MARY EDMOND MRS PEGGY EDMOND MR BEN EDMONDS MR J EDMONDS MR P EDMONDS MR RICHARD EDMONDS MR ROBERT EDMONDS MS S EDMONDS MR S EDMONDS MR TIMOTHY EDMUNDS MR ROBIN EDMUNDSON MS
AH EDNEY MR D EDWARD MR A EDWARDS MRS A EDWARDS MS A EDWARDS MRS ALISON EDWARDS MR ANDREW EDWARDS MISS ANN EDWARDS MR B EDWARDS MS C EDWARDS MR CLIFFORD EDWARDS MR D EDWARDS MRS E EDWARDS MS E EDWARDS MR G EDWARDS MR GRAHAM EDWARDS
T EDWARDS MISS J EDWARDS MR J EDWARDS MRS J EDWARDS MS J EDWARDS MR K EDWARDS MRS L EDWARDS MISS L EDWARDS MISS M EDWARDS MRS M EDWARDS MISS NICOLA EDWARDS MR P EDWARDS MR P G EDWARDS MR PHILIP EDWARDS MR R EDWARDS MR S EDWARDS MR W
ARDS MRS A EDWELL MR G EDY MRS M EEDLE JUSTIN EELES MRS GILLIAN EELEY MR & MRS N EELEY MS I EFENDIEVA MR T EFFENDOWICZ MRS DOROTHY EFREMIDIS BABAK EFTEKHARI MRS R EGAN MRS V EGAN MRS C EGBE MR ROSS EGERTOM MISS HELEN EGFORD MS EILEEN
INGTON MISS J O EGGLETON MS B EGLES MRS H EHLERS MR D EHN MISS H EHRENBERG MR K EHRKE MRS F EHRLICH MRS R EHRLICH MISS H EICHELTER MR WALTER EIFLER DR NOEMI EISER MISS Z EL MIKATTI DR D ELBOURNE DR B ELCE MISS R ELCOMBE MR & MRS MARK ELDER
MARK ELDER MR STEPHEN ELDER STEVE ELDER MISS A ELDERTON MR JOHN ELDON MR C ELDRED MS D ELEAZAR MRS P ELEFTHERIOU MISS M A ELEFTHERY MISS JOANNE ELFORD MRS S ELGHANIAN-KRAYEM R ELGIE MRS JOAN EL-HUSSEINY MR B ELIAS PROFESSOR W ELKAN MRS
LKINS MR S ELLAHI MRS O ELLALASINGHAM MRS P ELLARD MR DAVID ELLEN MR M ELLENBOGEN MS SUE ELLENBY MR J ELLERDON MRS J ELLEY MR ANDREW ELLIOT MRS C ELLIOT MR CLINTON ELLIOT MR G ELLIOT MR HARVEY ELLIOT MR A ELLIOTT MR B ELLIOTT MS B ELLIOTT
S EMMA ELLIOTT MS JOAN ELLIOTT MRS JUDITH ELLIOTT MS K ELLIOTT MR KEITH ELLIOTT DR M ELLIOTT MRS M ELLIOTT MR RICHARD ELLIOTT MR ANDREW ELLIS MR C ELLIS C ELLIS MR D ELLIS MRS EMMA DAVID ELLIS MRS G ELLIS MR H ELLIS MRS H ELLIS MRS K ELLIS MR L ELLIS
L ELLIS MRS M ELLIS MS M ELLIS MR N ELLIS MR R ELLIS MRS R ELLIS MR ROGER ELLIS MR S ELLIS MR V ELLIS MR W ELLIS MRS C ELLIS-JONES MR R ELLISON MR TIM ELLISON MR A ELLISON-MACARTNEY MRS L ELLISTON MRS P ELLMORE MS ANN ELLSON MISS J ELLWOOD
RODERICK ELMER MRS C ELMHURST MS L EL-MINYAWI MR C ELRINGTON MRS G ELSEGOOD MRS E ELSEY MS N EL-SHATOURY MR L ELSTEIN MR MICHAEL ELSTONE MS R ELSY MR BRIAN ELTON MRS E ELTON MR JOHN ELTON MRS MAUREEN ELTON MR H ELVERSTON MRS M ELVIN MS
IA ELWES MR K ELWOOD MISS J ELY MRS F EMAD MRS C EMANUEL MR AND MRS EMANUEL MR P EMBLING MR BERNARD EMEGBOR MRS J EMERTON MRS S EMERTON MRS J EMERY MR M EMERY MR P EMERY MR A EMETT MS E EMLING MR N EMM MR H EMPSHALL MR R EMSLIE VALERIE
NDERBY MRS YOSHIKO ENDO MS KATHRYN ENGINEER MS ANN ENGLISH MISS B ENGLISH MISS D ENGLISH MS G ENGLISH MRS H ENGLISH MS HILARY ENGLISH MR M ENNEVER MRS M ENNIS MS D ENRIGHT MR J ENRIGHT MRS J ENRIGHT MR R B ENSELL MISS RITA ENSING MS R
WISTLE MISS J EPISCOPO MR NORMAN EPSTEIN MRS T EPSTEIN MR J EPTON MRS M EPTON MRS P ERASMUS MRS MARY ERAUT MS W ERINGA MR M ERISMANN MR C ERRIDGE MRS J ERRIDGE MS J ERSKINE MR ROGER S ERSSER MRS DIANA ESCUDERO MR M ESKI MR G M ESLAND MRS
SPEJO MR S ESSAM MRS T ESSAYAN MR S ESSEX MS K ESSON DR MIKE ESTEN MS NANCY ESTERSON MR JUAN ESTEVEZ-BRETON ROGER ESTOP MRS A ESTRUCH MISS MARGARET ETALL MRS M ETCHELL MRS A ETHERIDGE MS A ETHERIDGE MS C ETHERIDGE MS M ETHERIDGE MRS D
ERINGTON MS Y ETHERINGTON MS JASMIN ETMINAN MISS K ETOE MR C ETTINGER MR P ETTINGER MRS M ETTRIDGE MR P ETZEL MS A EUSTACE MR DAVID EVA MR A EVAN MRS J EVAN MRS A D EVANS MR A EVANS MRS A EVANS MR ANTHONY EVANS MR B EVANS MRS B EVANS B EVANS
C EVANS MR EVANS MRS EVANS MS CAROLAN EVANS MRS CATHERINE EVANS MR D EVANS MISS D EVANS D EVANS MR DAVID EVANS DOROTHY EVANS DR FELICITY EVANS MR FRANCIS EVANS MR G EVANS MRS GLENYS EVANS MR H EVANS MRS H EVANS MISS H ADAMS MRS I EVANS
IVOR EVANS MISS J EVANS MR J EVANS MRS J EVANS MS J EVANS MISS KAT EVANS MS KATE EVANS MRS M EVANS MRS M E EVANS MR N EVANS MRS P A EVANS MRS P EVANS MS P EVANS MR PETER EVANS MR R EVANS MRS R EVANS MS R EVANS MR S EVANS MRS S EVANS MRS SUSAN
ANNAH EVANS MR T EVANS MS V EVANS MRS MARGARET EVE MR J EVELYN MR G EVENDEN MR G EVENNETT MRS H EVERETT MISS J EVERETT MRS M EVERETT MR RAY EVERETT MR DAVID EVERITT MRS M EVERITT MR SIMON EVERITT MRS M EVERS MR PETER EVERSDEN MRS ROSEMARIE
RSHED MR DONALD EVERSON MRS PAM EVERTON MR B EVISON MS EWING MS J G EWING MISS L EWING MR P EWING MRS S EWING MR JOHN EWINGTON MR AYMERIC EXMELIN MS JOYCE EYNON MRS H FA MRS G FABBRI MISS G FABBRICOTTI MR B FABER MS T FABRE MR R FACER MR
H FACEY MR G FACKS-MARTIN MR RICHARD FADER MRS A FAGAN MS CERI FAGG MS J FAGG MR P FAHEY MISS R FAHIE MRS A FAHIM MRS AMAL FAHMY MS P FAHNESTOCK MRS L FAHOUM MR P FAHY MR S FAHY MRS S J FAHY MR AND MRS B FAIDHI MR COLIN FAIRBAIRN MR GUY
BAIRN MR JAMES FAIRBAIRN MRS V FAIRBRASS MS I FAIRBROTHER A FAIRBURN MS BARBARA FAIRBURN MS A FAIRCLOTH MRS A FAIRCLOUGH MR B FAIRCLOUGH MS B FAIRGRIEVE MR B FAIRHALL MR RICHARD FAIRHEAD MR M FAIRHURST MR J FAIRMAN MS F FAIRMANOR MRS S
AIRSERVICE MRS ANNE FAIRSTON MR GERARD FAIRTLOUGH MS J FAIRWEATHER MR P FAIRWEATHER MRS C FAITHFULL MR T FAKAHANY DR H FALK MR P FALK MR R FALK MR PIERS FALLOWFIELD-COOPER MRS Z FAMILI MS Z FAMILY MR T FANCOURT MRS L FANE MR R FANEKER MRS
E. FANTINI MR H FARAGALLA MRS H FARAGE PROFESSOR RICHARD FARDON MRS S FAREBROTHER MS FARAH FAREGHI MR D FARENDEN MRS J FAREWELL MR LUKE FAREY MRS MAUREEN FARGHER MRS D FARLEY MR D FARLEY MRS NORMA FARLEY MR OLIVER FARLEY DR D FARMER
D FARMER MR DAVID FARMER MR & MRS I FARMER MRS SHEILA FARMER MISS V FARMER MRS J FARMER-MOMBRU MS NICOLA FARNON MRS S FARNSWORTH MS A FARQUHAR MR D FARQUHARSON MR J FARQUHARSON DR CAROL FARR MR D FARR MRS MARY FARR MR RICHARD FARR MR
RRA MRS S FARRANT MRS S FARRAR MRS O FARRAWAY MRS P FARRELL MS V FARRELL MS E FARRELLY MR R FARRER MR N FARRIES MR G FARRINGTON MRS YVONNE FARRINGTON DR ALEXANDRA FARROW MRS C FARROW MR P FARROW MR C FARTHING MS J CARTY MR A FASSATI MR
THERS MRS M FAUGUST MS R FAULDER MRS CLARE FAULKES MR ALAN FAULKNER MISS ANN M FAULKNER MR C FAULKNER MISS CLAIRE FAULKNER MRS J FAULKNER MS J FAULKNER MR M FAULKNER MR MIKE FAULKNER MS V FAURE MR G FAUX MR A FAWCETT MR G FAWCETT MRS
H FAWCETT MRS P FAWCETT MR J FAWCETT WILSON MRS B FAWCITT MISS JOYCE FAY MS M FAYINKA MR R FEAKIN MR R FEARN MR H FEATHER MRS SALLY FEEHAN MRS B FEGARTY MISS P FEIHER MR R FEIRN MR DAVID FELD MR TOM FELDBERG MRS J FELDMAN MISS SARAH
GATE-CATT MRS E FELIX MS LIDIA FELIX MR DENIS FELSENSTEIN MRS C FELSTEAD MRS H FELTHAM MR K FELTON MRS M RITCHIE MR C FENDICK MR T FENEMORE-JONES MS E FENLEY MR COLIN FENN MRS J FENN MS ROSEMARY FENN MR JOHN FENNER OBE CBE MRS V FENNER-
NES MR E FENNESSY MRS C FENTON MR DAVID FENTON MRS L FENTON MISS S FENTON DR S FENTON MS STELLA FENTON MR D FENWICK MR P FENWICK MS S FENWICK MR F FEREBEE MR A FERGUSON MS C FERGUSON MRS E FERGUSON MS EMMA FERGUSON MS G FERGUSON MRS
LIAN FERGUSON JANE FERGUSON MRS M FERGUSON MR M FERGUSON MRS MARGARET FERGUSON MR R FERGUSON MR N FERNANDES MS A FERNANDEZ MRS ANOJA FERNANDO MRS H FERNANDO MR D FERNBACK MRS E FERNIE MR R FERNLEY MS CRISTINA FERRAIOLI MR P FERRARI MS
ERRARO STEVE FERRE AND JENNY DOCTOR MS J FERREE MR A FERRELL MRS Y FERRER MISS A FERRIER MRS T FERRON MRS J FERRY MR ALESSANDRO FESTA DR J FEUCHTWANG MISS G FEUZI MS LAURA FEW MS E FEWINGS MRS AMANDA FEWTRELL MRS K FFOULKES MR S FFOULKES
M FICKEN MR P FIDEL MRS D FIDGE MISS M FIDGE MR T FIEDLER MISS I FIEG MRS BETSY FIELD MRS DAPHNE FIELD MR G FIELD MRS J FIELD MR J FIELD MRS L FIELD MR R FIELD MR W FIELD MR F FIELDER DR R FIELDHOUSE MRS A FIELDING MS M FIELDING MRS P FIFOOT
S P FIGGINS MR CARL FIGUEIREDO TAMAR FILE MR & MRS K FILLERY MR BARRY FILLINGHAM MR P FILMER MRS S FILSELL MRS A FINCH MS A FINCH MR BRIAN FINCH MR D FINCH MR H FINCH MRS H FINCH MS M FINCH MR P FINCH MRS S M FINCH MR M FINCHAM MR J FINDER
A FINDLAY MR A FINDLAY MS S FINDLAY MR V FINDLAY MRS M FINER MR S FINESTER MISS M FINGERHUT MS K FINGLETON MR C FINIGAN MR J FINKLER MR D FINLAY MS D FINLAYSON MRS S FINLAYSON MR B FINN MRS G FINN MRS S FINN MRS MARGOT FINNIE MRS P FINNIGAN
FINNIS BRENDAN FINUCANE MRS MAUREEN FINUCANE MR S FIORINI MR P FIREBRACE MRS A FIROUZI MR M FIROUZYAR MRS FIRTH MRS L FISCHER MRS CAROLINE FISH MRS F FISH MR L FISH MS A FISHER MRS CHRISTINA FISHER MR D FISHER MR E FISHER MRS ELIZABETH
IER MR H FISHER MR GRAHAME FISHER MS HILDA FISHER MS J FISHER MS K FISHER MRS K FISHER MRS M FISHER MRS MARIKA FISHER MR MATTHEW FISHER MR PETER FISHER MR ROGER FISHER MISS S FISHER MR TODD FISHER MRS W FISHER MR WILLIAM FISHER MRS E
POOL MRS J FISK MR STEPHEN FISK MR R FISZER MS A FITCH MRS M FITZELL MRS B FITZGERALD MRS C FITZGERALD MR D FITZGERALD MRS J FITZGERALD MRS P FITZGERALD MRS M FITZPATRICK MR & MRS PETER FITZSIMONS MR T FIVAZ MRS PAMELA FIXTER MRS I FLAHERTY
FLANAGAN MRS B FLANAGAN MISS I FLANAGAN MRS D FLANDERS MR STEPHEN FLASH MS A FLATH MR B FLATMAN MISS MARGARET FLATMAN MR MICHAEL FLATMAN MR B FLAVELL MS W FLAX MS Z FLAX MR D FLAXEN MRS G FLEET DR F FLEISCHER MR A FLEMING MS C FLEMING
S D FLEMING MS ELIZABETH FLEMING MR I FLEMING MR J FLEMING MR S FLEMING MS CLARE FLENLEY MR ANGUS FLETCHER MR GRAHAM FLETCHER MS KAREN FLETCHER MS L FLETCHER MR AND MRS C FLETCHER H FLETCHER-ROGERS MS K FLIGELSTONE MR D FLINDERS MR P
T DR J FLOOD MS M FLOOK MR P FLORY MR D FLOWER MR A FLOWERS MRS R FLUSS MRS ANNA FLYNN MRS ICHIKO FLYNN MR J FLYNN MRS J FLYNN MR JOHN FLYNN MR N FLYNN MISS ALEXANDRA FLYTZANI MR M FODEN MRS Y FOGARTY MRS JENNY FOGDEN MISS M FOGG MR NIGEL
GAN MR G FOGWILL MR T FOLAN MR ROBERT FOLLEN MR AND MRS K FOLLETT MRS C FONG MS V FONSS MISS J FONTAINE MRS P FONTAINE MRS W FOO MR GEOFFREY FOOKS MRS L FOORD MR C FOOT MR GEOFFREY FOOT DR JOSEPH FOOTITT MRS A FORBES MR C FORBES MS D FORBES
E FORBES MRS A FORD MS BRYONY FORD MRS C FORD MR D FORD D M FORD MR E FORD MRS ELIZABETH FORD MS HELEN FORD MS J FORD MR M FORD MS P FORD MS PAMELA FORD MRS PATRICIA FORD MR RICHARD FORD MR S FORD MR J FORDE MS SUE FORDER MRS JULIE FORDHAM
JULLIAN FORDHAM MISS M FORE MRS C FOREMAN MRS I FORESTER MR L FORINO SIR DENIS FORMAN KT OBE & LADY FORMAN MISS G FORNAI MRS MARGARET FORREST MR P FORREST MR RICHARD FORREST MR W FORREST MR D FORRESTER MR R FORRESTER MR P
SDICK MRS M FORSDYKE MR J FORSHAW MR DAVID FORSTER MRS E FORSTER MS I FORSTER MRS M FORSTER MRS D FORSYTH MS ELINA FORSYTH MR I FORSYTH DR R FORSYTH HON SIR ROCCO AND LADY FORTE MRS N FOSKETT MRS M FOSS MRS L FOSSEL MS LYNN FOSSEY MRS M
SICK MISS A FOSTER MR ALFRED FOSTER MISS BERYL FOSTER MR BRYAN FOSTER MISS D FOSTER MR D FOSTER MS D FOSTER MRS DILYS FOSTER MRS FELICITY FOSTER MR I FOSTER MRS J FOSTER MR JON FOSTER MISS K FOSTER MISS KAREN FOSTER MR & MRS L FOSTER MR P
ER MRS P FOSTER MR PAUL FOSTER MR AND MRS R FOSTER MR R FOSTER MR RAYMOND FOSTER MR ROBERT FOSTER MS ROSEY FOSTER MS RUTH FOSTER MR S FOSTER MS SUSAN FOSTER & MS CATHERINE MALLYON MS VENETIA FOSTER MR JOHN FOUDY MR RICHARD FOULKES MR J
LEY MR M FOULSER MR H FOUNTAIN MR E FOURNIS MRS B FOWARD MRS M FOWKES MRS E FOWLER MR G FOWLER MS H FOWLER MR P L FOWLER MS S FOWLER MR A FOX MS C FOX MR C FOX MRS J FOX MRS JENNY FOX MISS JILLY FOX MRS M FOX DR M FOX MR R FOX MR R FOX MS
X MR C FOXALL MRS M FOXEN MR M FOXLEY MRS RUTH FOXMAN MR J FOXON MRS S FOXTON MRS M FOY MRS M FOYSTER MR A FRAKE MRS D FRAME DR PHILIP FRAME MR ROBERT A FRAMPTON MS A FRANCE MR R FRANCE R FRANCESCATO MR MARCO FRANCESCONI MR BRIAN FRANCIC
MRS M FRANCIS MRS G FRANCIS MR H FRANCIS MRS KATIE FRANCIS MR M FRANCIS MISS N FRANCIS MRS P FRANCIS MS S FRANCIS MRS SANDRA FRANCIS MS T FRANCIS MS T FRANCOMBE MR CAREL FRANK MR JEFF FRANK MR P FRANK MS ANNIE FRANKEL MRS
STINE FRANKEL MISS J FRANKL MR C FRANKLAND MR M FRANKLAND MISS C FRANKLIN MR DONALD FRANKLIN MR E FRANKLIN MR M FRANKLIN MRS P FRANKLIN MR CHARLES FRANKLYN MRS K FRANKS MRS C FRANZMANN MS J FRAPE MRS C FRASER MISS E FRASER MRS ELAINE
SER MS HYACINTH FRASER MS J FRASER MRS J FRASER MRS K FRASER MRS L FRASER MR M FRASER MRS M FRASER MR P FRASER MESSRS FRASER-ARMSTRONG & BEAUMONT MR L FRASER-MACKENZIE MRS M FRAYSSE MRS S FRAZER MRS G FREDERICK MS SUZANNE FREEDA AMELIA
EDMAN MR C FREEDMAN MS HANNAH FREEDMAN MRS R FREEDMAN MR S FREEDMAN MR ELLIOT FREEMAN MR GREGORY FREEMAN MRS S FREEMAN MISS SHIRLEY FREEMAN MRS T FREEMAN MR W FREEMAN MR A FREER MISS K FREER MR G A FREESTONE MRS E FREI MS E FREILICH
S V FREMANTLE MR C FRENCH MR DOUGLAS FRENCH MR J FRENCH DR L FRENCH MS M FRENCH MR PETER FRENCH MRS S FRENCH MRS J FRENDO MR LOUIS FRENKEL MRS P FRESHWATER MR P FRETTEN MR TONY FRETTON M FREYHAN MRS SUSAN FRIBBENS MR A FRICK MRS CORDULA
EDLANDER DR L FRIEDLER MRS H FRIEDMANN MISS C FRIEDRIECH MR K FRIEL MS L FRIELICH MRS HILARY FRIEND MR P FRISTON MRS S FRITH MS B FRITZSCHING MR J FROGGATT MISS MARGARET FROOD MR S FROSH MR CHRIS FROST MR D FROST MR H FROST MR K FROST MR M
ST MR STEPHEN FROST MS C FROUD MS ANTHEA FRY MS D FRY MR EDGAR FRY MR J FRY MRS JOAN FRY MR L FRY DR PATRICIA FRY MRS S FRY MR D FRYER MRS J FRYER MR WOLFGANG FUCHS MRS F FUDGE MR K FUDGE MR LUIS FUENTES MRS V FUHRER MS MICHELE FUIRER MS
E FUJIHARA MR TORU FUJII MR KAZUHISA FUJISHIRO MR Y FUKUSHI MS E FULCHER MR H FULDA MR M FULFORD MRS D FULLBROOK MR C FULLER MS L FULLER MRS P FULLER PETER FULLER MR R FULLER MRS Y FULLER MR J FULTON MR P FULTON MISS R FULTON MR T FULTON
S M FUMAGALLI MS F FUNG MS S FUNG MR E FUNNELL MISS G FUNNELL MRS A FURBER MS M L FURBERG MR H FURLONGE MRAND MRS HORACIO FURMAN MISS S FURNEAUX MS R FURNESS DR A FURNHAM MISS K FUROMOTO DR V FURST MISS TAKA FURUHASHI MR YUZURU FURUTA
B FUSSELL MRS B FUSSEY MRS M FYSH MS D GABER MRS S GACHES MRS H GADD MR MICHAEL GADD MRS A GADNEY MRS GILLIAN GADSBY MRS J GAGE MRS S GAHAGAN MISS H GAIN MR L GAIN MR T GAINS DR A GAITATZIS MS BEATA GAJEK DR B GAJJAR MS L GALASEAN MRS M
INSKI MISS A GALE MS B GALE BERYL GALE MRS D GALE MISS H GALE MR J GALE MR R GALE MISS V GALE MS E GALEA MISS SHARON GALER MISS D GALEWSKI MS A GALL MRS H GALL MR GEORGE GALLACCIO DR SIMON GALLACHER MRS K GALLAGHER MRS MARY GALLAGHER MR
ICK GALLAGHER MRS E GALLERY MR GEOFFREY GALLEY MR A GALLIMORE MISS JOAN GALLOGLY MR A GALLOP MS A GALLOWAY MR C GALLOWAY MRS J GALPIN MR D GALSWORTHY MS SUSAN GALT MR J GALTON MR J GALVIN MR PAUL GAMBACCINI MS K GAMBELL MR THOMAS
BLE MR E GAMBLING MRS B GAME MRS S GAMINARA MR M GAMLEN MS J GAMLIN MR A GAMMAGE MRS S GAMMERMAN MR M GAMMON MR R GANDERTON MR MOHAN GANDHI MR R GANDY MS H GANIARIS MISS CORA GANT MR IAN GANT MS L GANT MR W GANTHER MS R GARAVAGLIA MR J
RAT MR L GARBER MRS J GARBUTT MS WENDY GARBUTT MS R GARCHA MRS ELIZABETH GARCIA MR LUIS GARCIA MRS S GARCIA MRS B GARCIA ELORZA MR E GARDEN MR P GARDEN MR C GARDENER MR FRANCIS GARDENER MR ROGER GARDENER MS SUE GARDENER MR ANDREW GARDINER
D GARDINER MS KATHERINE GARDINER MR C GARDNER MISS E GARDNER MR F GARDNER MR FRANCIS GARDNER MS JILL GARDNER MR JOHN GARDNER MR K GARDNER MS M GARDNER MRS P GARDNER MR R GARDNER MR T GARDNER MR PAUL GAREL-JONES MRS FAITH GARFIELD MS R
GAN MRS ANNE GARLAND MRS M GARLAND MR MARK GARLAND MR W GARLAND MRS E GARNER MRS J GARNER MRS L GARNER MRS J GARNETT MRS VALERIE GARNHAM MR & MRS H GARRARD MR ANDREW GARRATT MR P GARRATT MR ANDREW GARRETT DR CHRISTINE GARRETT MR G GARRETT
FESSOR J GARRETT MR RAYMOND GARRETT MR P GARRETTY MR R GARROW MISS S GARRUSH DR PETER GARSIDE MR R GARTLAND MS PETRA GARTZEN MRS H GARVEY MR J GARVEY MRS J GARVEY MR S GARVEY MRS S GARVEY MRS D GARVIN MS D GARVIN MR D GARWOOD MISS E GARWOOD
GARWOOD MRS J GARWOOD MR J GASCOIGNE MISS A GASKELL MRS B GASKELL MISS D GASKELL MR R GASKELL MR SYLVAN GASKIN DR C GASS DR L GASTER MS ANNA GASZEWSKA MR MICHAEL GATES MR J GATISS MISS A GAUKROGER MRS D GAULD MRS CAILLIE GAUNTLETT MR P
ON MR G GAVAZZI MRS MADELEINE GAVIN MS I GAVRIELIDES THE ROBERT GAVRON CHARITABLE TRUST MISS ALISON GAWITH MR LESLIE GAWN MR JONATHAN GAY MRS V GAY MRS MERLYN GAYE MR J GAYLER MR D GAYLOR MR R GAYLOR MARTINE GAYNA MR DARREN GEDDES MS H

GEDDES MS J GEDDES MR M GEE MRS M GEE MR MICHAEL GEE MR S GEE MR STEWART GEE MR F GEEN R A GEESON MISS JANE GELDER MRS R GELERNTER MS C GELLING MR G GEMIN MR A GEMMELL MRS A GEMS MRS C L GENDLER MR D GENNINGS DR N GENTILLI MR M GENTLE MR
PENELOPE GEOGHEGAN MR ADRIAN GEORGE MR D GEORGE MR A GEORGE MR E GEORGE MRS PATRICIA GEORGE DR S GEORGE MR S GEORGE MS S GEORGE MS W GEORGE MRS Z GEORGE MS E GEORGEIOU MR C GEORGIADES MRS P GEORGIADES MRS S GEORGIOU MRS J GERA MRS L GERADIN
MRS J GERAGHTY MISS ANNELIES GERBER MS CAROL GEREN MRS S GERMON MR A GERODIMOS MR P GEROULANOS MR D GEROW MS A GERRON MS J GERRY MS E GERSCHEL MR M GESTHUYSEN MR N GHANSAH DR S GHATAK MRS C GHEORGHE MR J GHIS MR JOHN GHRAL MR M GIBB MR
GIBBINS MRS F GIBBON MRS N GIBBON MR CHRISTOPHER GIBBONS MR DONALD GIBBONS MS ELIZABETH GIBBONS MS K GIBBONS MRS M GIBBONS MRS M R GIBBONS MS MARION GIBBONS MR P GIBBONS MR S GIBBONS MRS S GIBBONS MRS DIANA GIBBS MR EDWARD GIBBS MS J GIBB
MR W GIBBS MRS B GIBSON MS CAROLINE GIBSON MR D GIBSON MRS FRANCES GIBSON MR G GIBSON MRS J GIBSON MS L GIBSON MR M GIBSON MS P GIBSON MR R GIBSON MRS S GIBSON MR T GIBSON MRS M GIBSON SHEPHERDLY MR R GIDOOMAL MRS K GIELGUD-KILLICK MR AL
GIFFORD MRS C LECOUNT MRS LOUISE GIGG MRS M GILANI MRS B GILBERT MR D GILBERT MR KENNETH GILBERT MR LEO GILBERT MRS M GILBERT MISS N GILBERT MRS S GILBERT MRS SYLVIA GILBERT MR J GILBIN MRS A GILBOYNE MR A GILBY DR EDITH GILCHRIS
MRS R GILCHRIST MS S GILCHRIST MISS SUSAN GILDER MRS E GILDING MRS P GILDON MRS J GILES MS J GILES MR K GILES MS C GILKES SUE GILKES MS A GILL DR B GILL MRS CHRISTIANA GILL MRS E GILL MR & MRS D GILL MRS M GILL MISS NAOMI GILL MR P GILL MR S GI
MR T GILL MR J GILLARD MR JONATHAN GILLBANKS MISS A M GILLESPIE MS K GILLETT MR R GILLETT MRS J GILLETT-SMITH MR AMBROSE GILLHAM MS S GILLIBRAND MRS K GILLIES MS S GILLILAND MR L GILLOT MR P GILLOTT MRS P GILL-PEDRO MS N GILMAN MR COLIN GILMOR
MS A GILMOUR MS HEATHER GILMOUR MRS JUNE GILMOUR MR M GILMOUR MS S GILPIN MRS R GILTROW MISS S GILZEANE MR G GIMBLE MRS R GIMBLE MRS S GIMBLETT MR F GINGER MS D GINN MRS P GIOVANELLI MS D GIRARDINI MRS G GIRDLESTONE MR F GIRLING MRS J GIRLI
MS M GIRLING MR M GISSING MS D GITTENS MRS BRENDA GLADDEN MRS A GLADSTONE DR K GLADSTONE MRS MARY GLADSTONE MR D GLADWELL MR DAVID GLADWELL MR J GLANCY MR CHARLES GLANVILLE MRS SHEILA GLANVILLE MRS J GLASER DR KAREN GLASER MR SEAN GLASGO
MS F GLASMAN MR J GLASTONBURY MR S GLAZIER MS A GLEADHILL MR D GLEAVE MRS J GLEAVES MRS KYOKO GLEDHILL MISS CELINE GLEESON MISS M GLEESON MRS M GLEESON MR P GLEESON MISS P GLEESON MS T GLEESON MR DAVID GLENCROSS MR MICHAEL GLENDINNING MIS
A GLENISTER MR H GLENNERSTER MR H GLENTON MR FRANCIS GLIBBERY DR ANGELA GLIDDON MR BRENDAN GLOVER MS CAROLINE GLOVER MRS D GLOVER MR PETER GLOVER MS S GLOVER MR P H GLUCKSMANN MS NICOLA GLUECK MR D GLYNNE MR B GOATER MR PAUL GOBEY MRS
GOCHEZ MR MICHAEL GODBEE MR JAMES GODBER MS G GODDARD MISS J GODDARD MS M GODDARD MS V GODDARD MR GODES MS A GODFREY MRS B GODFREY MS BARBARA GODFREY MRS D GODFREY MR GRAHAM GODFREY MISS H GODFREY MR J GODFREY MRS JANE GODFREY MR N GODFRE
MR R GODFREY MISS T GODFREY MS KAORU GODOY MRS Y GODSAVE MRS I GODSELL MRS C GODWIN MR DAVID GODWIN MISS G GODWIN MRS J GOEHR BIRGIT GOETERMANN MRS J GOFFEE MS L GOH MS Y GOHIL MS SELMA GOKCEN MRS B GOLBERG MR J GOLD MS M GOLD MRS S GOLD MR
C GOLDBART MR P GOLDBART MR A GOLDBERG MRS J GOLDBERG MR N GOLDBERG GOLDEN BOTTLE TRUST MR M GOLDENBERG MRS R GOLDENBERG DR RUTH GOLDER MRS D GOLDFOOT MR J GOLDHILL MR AND MRS T GOLDIE MR COLIN GOLDIN H J GOLDING JOHNNY GOLDIN
DR LESLIE GOLDING MR P GOLDING MS P GOLDING MR T GOLDING MR GERALD GOLDMAN MS H GOLDMAN MR M GOLDMAN MR CHARLES GOLDRING MS J GOLDSBROUGH DR SHIRLENE GOLDSBROUGH MRS C GOLDSMITH MISS H GOLDSMITH MS J GOLDSMITH MR MATTHEW GOLDSMITH MR
GOLDSMITH MRS P GOLDSMITH MS PAM GOLDSMITH MR R GOLDSMITH MRS A GOLDSTEIN MR G GOLDSTEIN MR J GOLDSTEIN MR R GOLDSTEIN MR G GOLDSTONE MS PATRICIA GOLDSTONE MISS M GOLDSTRAW MRS J GOLDSWORTHY MR S GOLDTHORPE MRS A GOLESTAN MR R GOLLMEIER M
A GOMIS MS E GONCALVES MR F GONSALVES MISS C GONZALEZ MR J GONZALEZ MISS N GOOD MRS C GOODALL MS J GOODALL MRS SUSAN GOODALL MRS E GOODCHILD MR N GOODDEN MR PAUL GOODE MS L GOODENOUGH MS C GOODESS MR T GOODEY MR W GOODFELLOW DR LIONE
GOODHARDT MR J GOODIER MRS C GOODING MR ANTHONY GOODMAN MR B W GOODMAN MISS ELIZABETH GOODMAN MRS GOODMAN MR J GOODMAN MRS JUDITH GOODMAN MISS M GOODMAN MS J GOODRICH MRS RUTH GOODSIR MISS CATHERINE GOODWIN MR D GOODWIN MR F GOODWIN M
G GOODWIN MRS LINDA GOODWIN MR MARTIN GOODWIN MISS S GOODWORTH MS CAROL GOODWRIGHT MR R GOODYER MRS T GOOGAN MS E GOOLD MRS S GOONEWARDENE MR K GOOZEE MR P GOOZEE MR J GOPAL MRS M GOPAUL MR RAMJI GORASIA MRS S GORDAN MISS F GORDEN MR
GORDON MRS A GORDON MS C GORDON SIR DONALD GORDON MR G GORDON MR GRAHAM GORDON MRS H GORDON MRS HANNAH GORDON MR IAN GORDON MR H GORDON MR J GORDON MR JOHN GORDON MR KENNETH GORDON MISS P GORDON MISS PATRICIA GORDON RODERICK GORDON MR
RUTH GORDON MRS S GORDON MR W GORDON MRS C GORDON-WILSON MR A GORE MR G GORE LADY P GORE-BOOTH MRS A GORHAM MR DON GORMAN MISS S GORMAN MS OONAGH GORMLEY MR P GORTON MR H GORVY MRS S GORWALA MISS A GOSLING MR E GOSLING MS S GOSLITSKI P GOSHE
MISS A GOSS MR MARK GOSSAGE MRS O GOSTWICK MRS L GOTHARD MS A GOTTHELF MS SYBIL GOTTLIEB MRS GILLIAN GOUDGE MRS A GOUGH MRS D GOUGH MISS A GOULD MR A GOULD MISS C GOULD MS IRENE GOULD MRS J GOULD MRS M GOULD M GOULD MR N GOULD MR P GOULD M
PETER GOULD MS S GOULD MRS SALLY GOULD MR TERRY GOULD MS M GOULDEN MS C GOULDER MR I GOURLAY MISS J GOURLIE MR E GOVEIA MS E GOWER MRS HELEN GOWER MRS C GOWERS MS E GOWING MR J GOWING THE RT HON THE EARL OF GOWRIE AND LADY GOWRIE MS P GRABI
MRS M GRABINER MRS P GRACE MS D GRACE-JONES MRS E GRACEY MR J GRACIAS MRS CARMEL GRADENWITZ ADAM GRAFF DR A GRAHAM MR A GRAHAM MISS ALISON GRAHAM MR D GRAHAM MRS E GRAHAM MS E GRAHAM MRS G GRAHAM MRS H GRAHAM MISS L GRAHAM L GRAHAM MR
GRAHAM MRS P GRAHAM MS P GRAHAM MR SEAN GRAHAM MR S GRAHAM MRS T GRAHAM MR V GRAHAM MRS BARBARA GRAHAME MRS S GRAMBAS MR F GRAMMENOPOULOS MR D GRANDORGE G K GRANDWOOD MRS J GRANELL MS C GRANERE MRS E GRANGE MR TIMOTHY GRANGE MR A GRA
MRS A GRANT MR ALAN GRANT MR C GRANT MRS C GRANT MR D GRANT MR EDWARD GRANT MS ELIZABETH GRANT MR I GRANT MRS I GRANT JUDITH GRANT MRS L GRANT MR M GRANT MS M GRANT MRS MARILYN GRANT MRS P GRANT MR PHILIP GRANT MRS S GRANT MRS J GRANTHAM MS JUL
GRANVILLE MR M GRANVILLE MRS R GRANVILLE MS S GRAOVAC MR ROBERT GRASSIE MRS H GRATZER MR B GRAVES MS EMILY GRAVES MRS KATRINA GRAVES MR L GRAVES MR D GRAVETT MRS A GRAY MS A GRAY MR ANDREW GRAY MS ANITA GRAY MR C GRAY MRS DIANA GRAY DR D GR
MRS E GRAY MS I GRAY MR INNES GRAY MR IVAN GRAY MRS J GRAY MS J GRAY MRS K GRAY MRS KAREN GRAY MR L GRAY MRS M GRAY MR P GRAY MR RICHARD GRAY MR S GRAY MS S GRAY MR T GRAY MRS V GRAY MRS V GRAY MISS J GRAYDON MR J GRAYSON MR B P GRAZIANO MR PA
GREATBATCH MRS J GREATOREX MRS P GREATOREX MISS H GREAVES MRS I GREAVES MRS IRENA GREAVES MR M GREAVES MR ALAN GREEN MR B GREEN BARRY GREEN MR CHRISTOPHER GREEN MR D GREEN MRS D GREEN MS D GREEN MR DAVID GREEN MR G GREEN MRS H GREEN MRS
GREEN MR JOHN GREEN MR K GREEN MRS K GREEN MS L GREEN MRS N GREEN MS N GREEN MR NEVILLE GREEN MR P GREEN MRS P GREEN MR PAUL GREEN MISS R GREEN MR S GREEN MRS S GREEN MRS S V GREEN MR STEPHEN GREEN MRS W GREEN MISS D GREENAWAY MR R GREENAW
MR J GREENBERG DR R GREENBERG MR R GREENBERG MRS V GREENBERG MRS C GREENE MRS E GREENE MR MICHAEL GREENE MS TERESA GREENER MR G GREENFIELD MRS JACKIE GREENGLASS MRS S GREENHALL GREENHILL & CO. INTERNATIONAL LLP MR P GREENHILL MS
GREENHOUGH MR GUY GREENHOUS MR JOHN GREENING MBE MRS S GREENING MR ROBERT GREENISH MISS B GREENLAND DR D GREENSLADE MR W GREENSLADE MR G GREENSMITH NICOLAS GREENSTONE MISS GILLIAN GREENWAY MRS CHRISTINE GREENWOOD MR J GREENWOOD MISS
GREENWOOD MRS KATHLEEN GREENWOOD MR ROIN J GREENWOOD MS S GREENWOOD MR M GREER MR A GREGORY MISS B GREGORY MRS C GREGORY MR C GREGORY MR D GREGORY MRS D GREGORY MRS EVA GREGORY MR H GREGORY MS M GREGORY MR P GREGORY MISS S GREGORY MS
GREGORY MRS V GREGORY MISS F GREIG MRS M GRESHAM MS SUE GRESTY MR C GREY MRS DIANA GREY MRS H GREY MRS M GREY MR P GREY MS S GREY MRS L GREY-TURNER MR H GRIBBEN MR M GRIBBLE MRS CYNTHIA GRICE MR R GRIERSON MRS J GRIEVE MR J GRIEVES MRS C GRIFF
MR D GRIFFIN MRS E GRIFFIN MR F GRIFFIN MISS H GRIFFIN MR P GRIFFIN MS RUTH GRIFFIN MR T GRIFFIN MR DAVID GRIFFITH MS K GRIFFITH MR W GRIFFITH A J GRIFFITHS MS B GRIFFITHS MRS C GRIFFITHS MRS E GRIFFITHS MR G GRIFFITHS MR J GRIFFITHS MS J GRIFFIT
MR K GRIFFITHS MISS L GRIFFITHS MRS M GRIFFITHS MRS O GRIFFITHS MRS P GRIFFITHS MR PAUL GRIFFITHS MRS R GRIFFITHS MR T GRIFFITHS TIM GRIFFITHS MISS M GRIGGS MRS HOORIK GRIGORIAN MS ROMAYNE GRIGOROVA MS SUE GRIMDITCH MR H GRIMES MRS H GRIMES
C GRIMSEY MRS M GRIMSHAW MR NEIL GRIMSHAW MR R GRIMSHAW MRS R GRIMSHAW MR D GRIMWOOD MRS JOAN GRIMWOOD MR M GRIMWOOD MISS W GRINSTED MRS E GRINTER MRS A GRIPARI MR J GRIST MR J GRITTEN MS J GROGAN MS J GROHE MR J GROMAN MR GUY GRONQUI
MRS PATRICIA GRONVOLD MEYER MR TREVOR GROOCOCK MRS E GROOM MR M GROOM MR B GROOMBRIDGE MS G GROSS MR S GROSS MR K GROSSFIELD MR STEFAN GROSSKOPF MR R A GROSSKURTH MS C GROSSMAN MR ERWIN GROSSMAN MRS FRANCES GROSVENOR MISS P GROSVENOR M
G GROUT MS J GROUT MS A GROVE MS P GROVE MRS TESSA GROVER DR H J GROVES MRS H GROVES MRS J GROVES MR J GROVES MRS P GROVES MR P GROW MR K GRUBB MR COLIN GRUDZ MRS MAUREEN GRUFFYDD-JONES MRS JUNE GRUN MISS A GRUNBERG MS M GRUNDBERG MR A GRUN
MS I GRUNMANN MS S GRUSS-SANGL MRS L GRZYBEK MS TANYA GUADALUPE MR C GUBBINS MRS D GUBERTINI MS D GUCK MRS J GUDKA MRS T GUDKA MS BARBARA GUELFF MS YVONNE GUERRIER MS I GUERTLER MRS A GUEST MR CHRISTOPHER GUEST MR J GUEST MR WILLIAM GUE
MRS P GUGENHEIM MR S GUILD MR XAVIER GUILLEN MR A GUINN DR S GUIOLI MR E GUITAR MS P GULABIBALA MR A GULFARAZ MRS E GULLICK MR MARK GULLIDGE MRS C GULLIFORD MRS L GULLIVER MR C GUMMER MR K GUMMER MR A GUNN MRS J GUNN DR A GUNNING MR G GUNNI
MRS J GUNNING MR G GUNSTONE MS SUZANNE GUNTON MRS J GUNTRIP DR B GUPTA MR B GUPTA MR KAMAL GUPTA MR P GUPTA DR ROBERT GURD MRS PAMELA GURMIN MR & MRS R GURNEY MR T GURNEY MRS C GURRY MRS S GURY MS ULLA GUSTAFSSON MRS B GUTHRIE MR F GUTHRIE M
J GUTHRIE MR K GUTHRIE MRS R GUTHRIE MS ANTONIA GUTMAN MR DAVID GUTMAN MISS H GUTTERIDGE MR W GUTTMANN MRS G GUY MISS HELEN GUY MR J GUY MS R GUY MS C GUYON MR ANTHONY GWYN-JONES MR P GWYNN-JONES MR DANIEL GYSIN MR J GYSIN MISS H HAASE MRS
HAASTRUP SONUGA MR A HABLUTZEL MRS BETTY HACKER MR H HACKER MS S HACKER MR D HACKING MR R HACKMAN MRS G HADDAD MR PETER HADDEN MRS H HADDON MR M HADDON MRS MARGARET HADDON MS MARGARET HADDRELL MS S HADI MR ANGELOS HADJINICOLAOU MR JO
HADLER MR G HADLEY MRS J HADLEY MR JAMES HADLEY MR R HADLOW MR GEOFF HADWICK MR G HADWICK MS P HADZIPANI MRS N HAEMMERLE MS M HAFFEN MRS R HAFFENDEN MRS B HAFTER MR NICK HAGGARD WILLIAM HAGGARD MR D L M HAGGER MR T HAGGER MRS M HAGGIE
P HAGON MS YERAS HAGOPIAN MRS A HAGUE MS JUDY HAGUE MR PETER HAGUE MRS D HAHN DR MICHAEL HAHN MR P HAHN MS I HAHNDEL MS N HAIDAR MR B HAIGH MS H HAIGH MS LISA HAIGHT MR ANDREW HAILEY MR D HAILEY MRS JANE HAILSTONE MRS E HAIM MS C HAINES M
HAINES MR K HAINES MS L HAINES MR M HAINES MR ROY HAINES MR DAVID HAINSWORTH MR I HAJI MISS J HAKEN MR MORDECHAI HAKLAY MRS I HALBERSTADT MR A HALDANE MR A HALE MR D HALE MRS JANE HALE MRS S HALE MS S HALE MR TONY HALE MS S HALES MR ANDRE
HALEY MS J HALEY MR J HALEY MR J HALIFAX MRS A HALL MR ANDREW HALL MRS B HALL MS BETTY HALL MR C HALL DR D HALL MR D HALL MS FIONA HALL MR G HALL G HALL MS GEORGINA HALL MRS HAZEL HALL MR AND MRS J HALL MR J HALL MRS J HALL MS J HALL JERE
HALL MR JEREMY HALL MRS K HALL MR K HALL MRS L HALL LESLEY C HALL MR M HALL MARTIN HALL MR N HALL MRS N HALL MR P HALL MRS P M HALL MR PATRICK HALL MR R HALL MRS R HALL MRS T HALL MISS V HALL MR W HALL MRS S HALLAM MS P HALLARD MR MICHA
HALLAS A HALLE MS S HALLET MS ELIZABETH HALLETT MR G HALLETT MS JANET HALLETT MR N HALLETT MISS C HALLINAN MR J HALL-MAY MRS V HALLOWS MRS J HALLPIKE MR A HALLS MR P HALLS MR W HALON MRS K HALPENNY MR J HALPER MR A HALPIN MRS C HALSEY
DOUGLAS HALSEY MR L HALSEY MRS M HALTON MISS P HALY MISS J HAM MR O HAMAD VISCOUNTESS HAMBLEDEN MRS DOROTHY HAMBLETON MRS K HAMBLETON-GREY MRS V HAMBLIN E R HAMBROOK MR F HAMBROOK MR H HAMBROOK MISS A HAMEED MRS CAROLE HAMILTON MRS
HAMILTON MRS ELIZABETH HAMILTON MRS G HAMILTON GEORGE HAMILTON MR & MRS HAMILTON MS M HAMILTON MR P HAMILTON MR AND MRS THOMAS HAMILTON MR W HAMILTON MS JANE HAMILTON-MUTCH MR D HAMLEY MR T HAMLIN MR I HAMLYN MS L HAMLYN MR M HAMLYN
SHEILA HAMM MR W HAMM MR M HAMMANT MR J HAMMER MR K HAMMER MRS ANNETTE HAMMOND MS BRENDA HAMMOND MRS C NUTTALL MR DAVID HAMMOND MS J HAMMOND MRS JUDICAELLE HAMMOND MR NORMAN HAMMOND MR T HAMMOND MS V H HAMMOND MRS WINIFRED HAMMOND
B HAMMOND-GIBBS MS R HAMNER MR I HAMPSON MRS Y HAMPSON MRS A HAMPTON MS D HAMPTON DR J HAMPTON MR T HAMPTON MR P HAMSHARE DR C HANBIDGE MRS J HANCOCK MISS MARGARET HANCOCK DR R HANCOCK MS Y HANCOCK MRS PATRICIA HAND MRS B HANDA REBEC
HANDLER MR T HANDLER MR DEREK HANDLEY MS PATRICIA HANDLEY MR D HANDS MR M HANDYSIDE MR N HANDYSIDES MRS V HANINGTON MR A HANKS MS B HANN H HANN MS SYLVIA HANNA MRS I HANNAH MISS M HANNANT MISS DEIRDRE HANNIGAN MS ANNE HANRAHAN MRS VIVIEN
HANRECK MRS D HANSEN MRS I HANSEN MS P HANSEN MISS S HANSLOT MR B HANSON MISS F HANSON MR G HANSSEN MS K HAPGOOD MR S HAR EVEN MR D HARALAMBIDIS MRS MARIKO HARANO MR J HARARI MRS ZOE HARBEN MS SUE R HARBOR MR C HARBORD MR TIMOTHY HARBORD
GWYLIM HARBOTTLE MRS H HARBRON MR A HARDEN MR E HARDEN A HARDIE MRS EMMA HARDIE MRS P HARDIE MR R HARDIE MRS ANN HARDING MS E HARDING MISS G HARDING MRS J HARDING MS J HARDING MR J HARDING MRS JOY HARDING MR R HARDING MRS S HARDING MS
HARDING MR B HARDMAN MR NICK HARDS MISS SUSAN HARDS MISS J HARDWICK MRS J HARDWICK MS M HARDWICK MR ALLEN HARDY MR G HARDY MR J HARDY MRS J HARDY MS AMANDA HARE MR J HARE MRS J HARE MR M HARE MRS JANET HARFIELD MR H HARGRAVE MR BENJAM
HARGREAVES MRS E HARGREAVES MRS JENNIFER HARGREAVES MR JOHN HARGREAVES MR RICHARD HARGREAVES MR MASATOMO HARIGAYA MR K HARIHARAN MRS N HARIRI MR J HARKNESS MRS MARIA HARLAN MS J HARLAND MRS M HARLAND MR W HARLOWE MR K HARMAN MR P HARM
MR R HARMAN MS R HARMASZ MR H HARMS MR C HARMSWORTH MR D HARMSWORTH MR N HARNACK MR P HARNBY MR J HARNESS MISS DIANA HAROUN MRS V HAROUTUNIAN MR C HARPER MRS CAROL HARPER MR G HARPER MRS H HARPER MS J HARPER MRS M HARPER MR CHARLES HARP
MR & MRS R HARREX MRS K HARRIES MRS L HARRIES DR RICHARD HARRIES MR M HARRIMAN MRS B HARRINGTON MRS E HARRINGTON MR J HARRINGTON MRS J HARRINGTON MS R HARRINGTON MRS A HARRINGTON-HAWES MR A HARRIS MRS A HARRIS MS A HARRIS PROFESSOR A HARR
MISS C HARRIS MR C HARRIS MRS C HARRIS MS CANDIDA HARRIS MISS D HARRIS MR D HARRIS MRS D HARRIS MRS E HARRIS DR F HARRIS MRS H HARRIS MRS HERMIONE HARRIS DR I HARRIS MISS J HARRIS MR J HARRIS MRS J HARRIS MS J HARRIS MRS JANET HARRIS MS JAN
HARRIS MR K HARRIS MS K HARRIS MR L HARRIS MRS L HARRIS MR M HARRIS MRS M HARRIS MR NEVILLE HARRIS DR NIGEL HARRIS MRS P HARRIS MS P HARRIS MR PAUL HARRIS MRS PAULINE HARRIS MR R HARRIS R HARRIS MRS ROSEMARY HARRIS MRS S HARRIS MRS SARAH HARR
MR STEVE HARRIS MRS V HARRIS MS V HARRIS MRS ZOE HARRIS MR A HARRISON MISS C HARRISON MR DAVID HARRISON MISS H HARRISON MS J HARRISON MS L HARRISON MISS M HARRISON MS P HARRISON MRS PENNY HARRISON MR R HARRISON MR S HARRISON MS S HARRIS
MR STEPHEN HARRISON MR WILLIAM HARRISON MS M HARRISS MS K HARROLD MR T HARROLD MISS B HARROP MR S HARROP MS A HART MRS A HART MS C HART MRS D HART MS E HART MRS HEATHER HART MRS H HART MRS HILDA HART MRS J HART MR J HART MRS JANE HART MISS
HART MRS K HART MS K HART MRS L HART MR M HART MRS MELANIE HART MISS P HART MRS P HART MR R HART MRS S HART MR E HARTE MRS M HARTE MR A HARTER MR K HARTFIELD MRS D HARTIGAN MS A HARTLEY MR C HARTLEY MR P HARTLEY MS R HARTLEY MS S HARTLEY M
HARTMANN MR R HARTMANN MR M HARTNALL MRS T HARTHELL MRS M HARTRIDGE MR M HARVERSON MR ANTHONY HARVEY MS C HARVEY MR D HARVEY PROFESSOR D HARVEY MS E HARVEY MR AND MRS I HARVEY MR J HARVEY MRS J V HARVEY L HARVEY MR M HARVEY MS M HARVEY
P HARVEY MS PAULA HARVEY MR R HARVEY MS S HARVEY MR C HARVEY PIPER MR JAMES HARVEY-BROWN MR C HARVEY-KELLY E HARWOOD MRS E HARWOOD MRS F HARWOOD MR J HARWOOD MR WALTER HARWOOD DR A HASELDEN MR DAVID HASELL MR H HASENSRAUCH MRS NANA HASH
MRS PRISCILLA HASHMI MR K HASKELL MR S HASKELL MR C HASKETT MISS JANE HASKIN MRS M HASKINS MR T HASKINS MS J HASLAM MRS KIM HASLAM MR R HASLAM MISS RUTH HASLAM MR JAMES HASLER-WINTER MR A HASLEWOOD MS AMINA HASSAM MR J HASSAN MRS J HASS
MS S HASSAN MRS M HASSELL MS M HASSON MR JOHN HASTIE MRS D HASTINGS MR G HASTINGS MR J HASTINGS MR M HASTINGS MR S HASTWELL MRS K HATCH MRS M HATCH MR R HATCH MS J HATCHER MRS M HATCHER MS J HATELEY MS ANNE HATHAWAY MR B HATHAWAY MR GLE
HATHAWAY F HATHERALL MRS A HATJOULLIS MR DIETRICH HATLAPA MISS R HATLEY MS N HATRY MRS B HATT MR T HATTEMORE MR M HATTINGH G HATTON MR S HATTON MR CLIFFORD HATTS MS I HATZOPOULOU MR J HAUDE MR JAMES HAUGH MR P HAUGHTON MR A HAUKE MR C HAUKE M
GILLIAN HAUHTON MS E HAUPTMAN MRS L HAUSER MRS N HAVARD MRS S HAVERCAN MR G HAVERCROFT E HAVILAND MISS E HAWES MR P HAWES MR R HAWES MISS B HAWKER MRS HEATHER HAWKER KEITH HAWKER MR A HAWKES MISS C HAWKES MRS I HAWKES MR J HAWKES MRS
HAWKES MR PETER HAWKES MS V HAWKES MR B HAWKINS MR D HAWKINS MR F HAWKINS MISS GEMMA HAWKINS MISS J HAWKINS MR M HAWKINS MS MARGARET HAWKINS MISS PAMELA HAWKINS DR R HAWKINS MS S HAWKINS MISS E HAWORTH MRS G HAWORTH MS L HAWORTH MR
HAWTHORN MRS J HAWTHORN MRS MARGARET HAWTHORNE MR A HAXTON MR P HAXTON MR K HAYCOCK MRS L HAYDEN MR P HAYDEN DR S HAYDEN MS E HAYDON MRS A HAYES MS ANGELA HAYES MR B HAYES MISS C HAYES MRS G HAYES MISS J HAYES MS KIM HAYES MISS M HAYES
M HAYES DR N HAYES MS PHILIPPA HAYES MRS R HAYES MR R HAYFIELD MRS T HAYHOE T HAYLES MRS G HAYLETT MR J HAYLETT MS G HAYNES MR J HAYNES MRS L HAYNES MR M HAYNES MRS M HAYNES MR N HAYNES MR J HAYNS MRS J HAYSOM MR KEITH HAYTON MR R HAYTON M
HAYWARD MRS C HAYWARD MRS J HAYWARD MS JENNIFER HAYWARD MRS M HAYWARD MR P HAYWARD MS GORDON HAYWOOD MR K HAYWOOD MR W HAYWOOD MRS S HAYZER MS J HAZAN MRS D HAZELL MR P HAZELL MRS E HAZLE STEFF HAZLEHURST MR A HEAD MR B HEAD MR P HEAD
W HEAD MR R HEADLAND MRS M HEALD MR J HEALEY MR GEOFFREY HEALING MRS S HEALTH-DOWNEY MR P HEALY MS D HEANY MS P HEARD MR M HEARN MR N HEARN MR SIMON HEARN MS V HEARN MR I HEARNDEN MR P HEARSON MRS F HEASLIP MR K HEASMAN MR A HEATH DR ANTHO
HEATH DR DAVID HEATH MR G HEATH DR IONA HEATH MR J HEATH MR JOHN HEATH MRS L HEATH MRS M HEATH MR R HEATH MRS W HEATH MRS M HEATHCOTE MR R HEATHCOTE MR A HEATHER MS J HEATON MR OLIVER HEATON MRS R HEATON STELLA HEBBARD MR E HEBBELMANN DR
HEBBORN MR M HEBRON MR MICHAEL HEBRON MRS H HECKER MR NEAL HECKFORD MR P HEDBERG MR MARTIN HEDEMANN-ROBINSON MISS S HEDGER MRS MAUREEN HEDGES MRS P HEDGES MR F HEDIN MRS ANN HEDLEY MRS J HEED MR S HEELER MRS M HEERY MISS OLGA HEGEDUS
E HEIBERG MR PATRICK HEIDE MR T HEIDEMAN DR THOMAS HEIL DR BJORN HEILE MRS B HEILLER MR T HEINEMANN MR W HEINRICHS DAME DRUE HEINZ DBE MS M HELAL MRS A HELFET MR P HELLEN MRS L HELLER MRS B HELLMAN MISS KARIN HELLMER MR MILES HELLON MR A HE
MR F HELM MRS BRIGITTE HELMICH-KEMP MR H HELY-HUTCHINSON MRS A HEMEON MR MARK HEMMINGS MS N HEMMINGS MR A HENDERSON MR ANDREW HENDERSON MR F HENDERSON MISS J HENDERSON MR J HENDERSON MR L HENDERSON MR N HENDERSON MR P HENDERSON MR RONA
HENDERSON MR R HENDRA MR N HENDRICKSE MRS JACKIE HENDRY MS L HENDRY MRS M HENEGHAN MR D HENFREY MRS A HENLEY I HENLEY MISS PATRICIA HENLEY MRS M HENMAN MR A HENNESSEY-BROWN MRS ASTRID HENNESSY MR G HENNING MISS A HENRI MR S HENRICH M
HENRIQUEZ MISS J HENRY MR J HENRY MRS N HENRY MR P HENRY MISS SARAH HENRY MISS DORA HENSCHEL MISS P HENSHAW MR ROBERT HENTY MRS SHEILA HENWOOD MR SIMON HENWOOD MRS J HEPBURN MRS V HEPBURN MRS MRS HEPPEL MISS SHELLEY HEPPOLETTE MRS
HEPWORTH MR PETER HERATY MRS M HERBERG MISS A HERBERT MR I HERBERT MRS J HERBERT MISS JEAN HERBERT MS P HERBERT MS M HERCOD MISS S HERD HERITAGE OF LONDON TRUST MRS D HERKE MISS S HERMAN MRS J HERMANS MR D HERMELE MR E A HERMITAGE MISS
HERNANDEZ MR JOHN HERON MS SUSANNA HERON MISS G HERRING MISS V HERRINGTON MR THOMAS HERRMANN MR CHARLES HERRON MRS J HERSHON DR E HERST MR FRANCIS HERVE MR A HERWIG MS K HERZINGER MR R HESLOP MR A HESS MR KEITH HESTER MS G HETHERING
PROFESSOR G HEUMAN MRS J HEWANICKA MRS J BRONWEN HEWER MISS C HEWERDINE MRS MARGARET ADOCK MISS A HEWITT MISS D HEWITT MR D HEWITT MRS D HEWITT MR J HEWITT MR & MRS J HEWITT MR M J HEWITT MR PETER HEWITT MR PHILIP HEWITT MR RICHARD HEWITT
A HEWLETT MRS M HEWLETT MR E HEWSON MRS G HEXT MR SICCO HEYLIGERS MR D HEYNES MR G HEYS MRS B HEYWOOD JONES MR JOHN HEYWORTH MR D HIBBERD MR J HIBBERD MR K HIBBERD MR MARK HIBBERD MS S HIBBERD MR BARRY HIBBERT MS E HIBBERT MR F HIBBERT SI
HIBBERT MRS CLARE HIBBET MRS S HIBBINS MR M HICHENS MR JOHN HICK MR P HICKEY MRS B HICKLIN MR C HICKMAN MR JAMES HICKMAN MR CLIVE HICKS MR D HICKS MR J HICKS MRS J HICKS MR L HICKS M HICKS MISS P HICKS MR STEVEN HICKS MRS S HICKS MS B HICKS
MS R HICKSON MR R HIDDERLEY MISS J HIECKEL MRS SHIRLEY HIGGENS MS J HIGGIN MRS B HIGGINS MR E HIGGINS MRS E HIGGINS MRS IRENE HIGGINS MRS J HIGGINS MR L HIGGINS MR N HIGGINS MRS P HIGGINS MISS S HIGGINS MRS S HIGGINS MRS S HIGGINS
MR A HIGGS MRS H HIGH MR N HIGHAM MRS H HIGUCHI DR T HIGUCHI MRS BETTY HIJAZI MRS MARY HILDYARD MR PETER HILEY MR A HILL MISS ASHLEY HILL MR B D HILL SIR BRIAN HILL MS C HILL MRS CAROLINE HILL MISS F HILL MR G HILL MS G HILL MISS H HILL MRS
HILL MISS J HILL MR JOHN HILL MRS L HILL MR M HILL QC MR M HILL MRS M HILL MRS MARGARET HILL MR NIGEL HILL MR R HILL MR S HILL MRS S HILL MR T HILL MR AND MRS HILL MISS THERESA HILL MRS V HILL MR W HILL MR K HILLARY MR RON HILLEL MS A HILLEN
COLLETTE HILLER MR A HILLIER MRS C HILLIER MR F HILLIER MR G HILLIER MS J HILLIER MR W HILLIER MR W HILLIER-FRY MISS E HILLION MR ANTHONY HILLMAN LIZ HILLMAN MR S HILLMAN MS A HILLS MR B HILLS MR C HILLS MISS G HILLS MRS I HILLS MRS J HILLS M
HILLS MRS M HILLS MR STEPHEN HILLS MISS VANESSA HILLS MR DAVID HILTON MRS G HILTON MR J HILTON MR M HILTON MS M HILTON MS MICHELE HILTON MR R HILTON MR S HILTON MS SUSAN HILTON MR P HINCKLEY MR D HIND MISS P HIND MR R HIND MR MARTIN HINDLE M
KAREN HINDLEY MR E HINDS MS JENNY HINDS MISS MICHELLE HINDS MR R HINDSON MRS S HINE MR J HINES MR STEPHEN HINES MR GRAHAM HINETT MR D HINGIS MRS A HINGLEY MRS D HINKS MR J HINKS MS L HINSHELWOOD DR DAVID HINTON MR DAVID HINTON MRS K HINTON M
JULIE HIPPERSON MRS R HIRAI MRS I HIROE MR A HIROSAWA MR G HIRSCH S M HIRSCH MRS J HIRSCHKORN MR M HIRSCHL MR J HIRST MS J HIRST MR M HIRST MR PAUL HIRST MRS B HISCOCK MISS J HISCOCK MR P R HISCOCK MRS J HISCOCKS MR G HISKETT MS C HITCH MRS
HITCHCOCK MRS A HITCHIN MR PETER HITCHING MR G HITCHINS MR D HITEL MRS A HITMAN MRS P HITT MR S HIVES MRS TERESA HO MR B HOARE MR C HOARE MRS C HOARE MR RICHARD HOARE MR J HOATH MR J HOBAN MISS MARIA HOBBERT MISS H HOBBIGER MR D HOBBS MR G HOB
MR J HOBBS MRS J HOBBS PROFESSOR J HOBBS MISS VIVIEN HOBBS MISS J A HOBBY MISS J HOBDAY MS S HOBDAY DR J HOBRO MR A HOBSON MR J HOBSON MS M HOCHBERG MR J HOCKIN MRS RENA HOCKNEY MR DOUGLAS HODDER MRS H HODES MR PETER HODES MISS A HODGE M
H HODGE MR P HODGE MS V HODGE MR A HODGES MRS A HODGES MR G HODGES MR AND MRS S R HODGES MRS VIVIEN HODGES MR A HODGETTS MR I HODGKIN MR KEITH HODGKINSON MISS MARGARET HODGKINSON J H HODGSON MRS J HODGSON MS K HODGSON MR M HODGSON MRS
HODGSON MR PETER HODGSON MR R HODGSON MS S HODGSON MS L C HODSDON MR G HODSON MRS A HOELLER MR P HOEY MR ROYSTEN HOEY MISS S HOEY DR M HOFFBRAND MS CLAIRE HOFFMAN MR D HOFFMAN MRS M HOFFMAN MR S HOFFMAN MR JOCHEN HOFFMANN MR A HOFLAND
WOLFGANG HOFMANN MS L HOGARTH MS M HOGARTH MR B HOGBEN MR C HOGG MS C HOGG MR G HOGG MR M HOGG MRS PATRICIA HOGG MISS R HOGG MR R HOGG MR SIMON HOGG MRS S HOGG MR K HOGSON MRS MIRA HOINKIS MR P HOLBOURNE MR BARRY HOLDEN MR E HOLDEN MIS
HOLDEN MR J HOLDEN MR M HOLDEN MR R HOLDEN MRS A HOLDER MRS G HOLDER MRS D HOLDFORD MR A HOLDICH MISS H HOLDSWORTH MR M HOLDSWORTH MISS D HOLE MR DAVID HOLE MR M HOLFORD MR P HOLGATE MR J HOLL MISS A HOLLAND MR C HOLLAND MRS C HOLLAND M
I HOLLAND MR J HOLLAND MRS M HOLLAND MS M HOLLAND DR MICHAEL HOLLAND MR & MRS N HOLLAND MS P HOLLAND MRS SAMANTHA HOLLAND MRS W HOLLAND MRS WENDY HOLLAND DR D HOLLANDER MR M HOLLEY MRS M HOLLIDAY MR R HOLLINGHURST MRS D HOLLINGSWORTH M
F HOLLINGSWORTH DR ANTONY HOLLINGWORTH MRS J HOLLINGWORTH MR PETER HOLLINGWORTH MR T HOLLINS MR C HOLLIS MRS EVA HOLLIS MR & MRS L HOLLMAN MR COLLIN HOLLOWAY DR I HOLLOWAY MR S HOLLOWAY MR T HOLLOWAY MR J B HOLLYMAN MISS BARBARA HOLMAN
M HOLMAN MR R HOLMAN MS S HOLMAN MR ARTHUR HOLME MISS P HOLMEAR MISS A HOLMES MS CAROL HOLMES MR C HOLMES MISS E HOLMES MRS ELIZABETH HOLMES MR G HOLMES MR J HOLMES MS J HOLMES MRS L HOLMES MR LAURENCE HOLMES MR M HOLMES MRS M HOLMES
DR P HOLMES MRS P HOLMES MR PETER HOLMES MR R HOLMES MRS RITA HOLMES MR S HOLMES MR P HOLMES-JOHNSON DR M HOLMES-SIEDLE MISS V HOLMIA MRS M HOLNESS MRS S HOLROYD MR ALAN HOLT MR CHARLES HOLT MRS J HOLT DR LAURA HOLT MRS M HOLT MRS MARY H
MS MIRANDA HOLT MR A HOLYER MRS M HOMAN MR R HOMAWALA MS D HOMDEN MRS DEE HOME MS RACHEL HOMER MR A HOMERSHAM MR K HOMES MRS S HOMES MRS S HOMEWOOD MRS E HONE MRS M HONEY MS C HOOD MS D HOOD DR ELAINE HOOD MR GEORGE HOOD R C HOOD MRS H H
MRS A HOOK MRS J HOOK MRS M HOOK MR REG HOOK MR A HOOPER MRS E HOOPER MR K HOOPER MRS NINA HOOPER R HOOPER MRS B HOPE MRS HELGA HOPE MRS J HOPE MR JULIAN HOPE MR P HOPE MS PAT HOPE MR PAUL HOPE MR STEVEN HOPE MR E HOPEWELL-ASH MS C HOPK
DR D HOPKINS MISS G HOPKINS MR H HOPKINS MISS J HOPKINS MR L HOPKINS MR M HOPKINS MS M HOPKINS MR W HOPKINS MRS E HOPKINSON MR J HOPPIT MR D HOPWOOD MS R HOPWOOD MS S HORAN MR J HORDERN MR PAUL HORE MISS B D R HORGAN MRS J HORGAN MR HOR
MS ANDRE HORNBY MS K HORNBY MR ALAN HORNE MR D HORNE MR DAVID HORNE MR GERALD HORNE MRS MARGARET HORNE MR R HORNE MS S HORNE MISS D HORNEGOLD MR JOHN HORNSEY MR J HOROVITZ MRS A HORROCKS MRS F HORROCKS MS J HORROCKS MR A HORSBURGH MR
HORSEMAN MRS CONSTANCE HORSEY MR ANDREW HORSLER MS ANNA HORSLEY MR W HORSLEY MRS P HORSNELL MR P HORSWILL MS HELENE HORT MRS A HORTON MS B HORTON MR D HORTON MISS G HORTON MRS M HORTON MR PAUL HORTON MRS R HORTON DR A HORWELL MRS J
HORWOOD MRS M HORWOOD MR CHRISTOPHER HOSEGOOD MRS J HOSFORD MS J HOSIE MR & MRS J HOSKIN MRS ELIZABETH HOSKING MRS DINAH HOSKINS MRS MARY HOSKINS DR TREVOR HOSKINS MRS M HOSSEINI MISS T HOUDEK MRS S HOUGH MS SARAH HOUGH MS V HOUGHAM
DORIS HOUGHTON MR E HOUGHTON MR H HOUGHTON MS SARAH HOUGHTON MRS G HOUGHTON-JONES MR J HOULSTON MISS P HOUNSOM MR CLIVE HOUNSOME MS R HOURIHANE MISS J LE M HOUSE MRS P HOUSE MR S HOUSE MRS B HOUSTON MR H HOUMAN MR A HOWARD MR ALEXAN
HOWARD MRS AVRIL HOWARD MRS B HOWARD MR C HOWARD MR D HOWARD MRS E HOWARD MR J HOWARD MS J HOWARD REVEREND JOHN HOWARD MRS K HOWARD MR KIERON HOWARD MRS M HOWARD MS M HOWARD MR MICHAEL HOWARD MS N HOWARD MR PAUL HOWARD MR S HOWARD
EMMA HOWARD BOYD MRS E HOWARD-BAKER MISS S HOWARD-JONES MRS A HOWARD-TURNER MR A HOWARTH MISS J HOWARTH MRS MARGARET HOWARTH MR S HOWARTH MS PHILLIPA HOWDEN MR G HOWDLE MRS B HOWE MS HANNAH HOWE THE EARL HOWE MISS JOAN HOWE MRS LINDA HO

A Festival on the River

A FESTIVAL ON THE RIVER

THE STORY OF SOUTHBANK CENTRE

CHARLOTTE MULLINS

Penguin Books

Written and edited by Charlotte Mullins

Art direction: Anne Odling-Smee / www.o-sb.co.uk
Design assistance: Jo Glover
Research: Nicola Smyth
Picture research: Jane Lambert

First published in 2007 by
Penguin Books Ltd
80 Strand
London WR2R 0RL
England
www.penguin.com

Southbank Centre
Belvedere Road
London
SE1 8XX
020 7921 0600
www.southbankcentre.co.uk

British Library Cataloguing-in-Publication Data
A catalogue record for this book is available from the British Library.

ISBN: 978-0-141-03439-3

Printed and bound in Italy by Graphicom
Reprographics by Dawkins Colour

Proceeds from the sale of this book will support Southbank Centre's
artistic programme.

CONTENTS

THE SOUTH BANK

By John Agard

Where seagulls congregate for symphonies
a stone's throw from Mandela's profile

Where a living parrot once graced a gallery
but backed her feathers to the avant style
and even caused controversy

Where many elderly meet for warmth and tea and cake
and skateboarders were delinquent swans on a concrete lake

Where foyer music is free to all
whether your ear be chamber-tuned, orchestral, jazzy

Where a little walk across a hall
leads you to visual arts and living crafts
for does not driftwood sculpture come from a breathing sea?

Where at summer's freeing heights
a blitz of dance transforms a floor
to tap ballet kathak and more

Where a poetry library awaits you
with diverse verse from epic to haiku

Gone the days when winding walkways
formed an up and down maze
As a new piazza invites a river view
And ground-level entrances embrace a complex venue.

Walk in and be entranced. Do.

From John Agard's A Stone's Throw from Embankment:
The South Bank Collection, *1993, published by Southbank Centre*

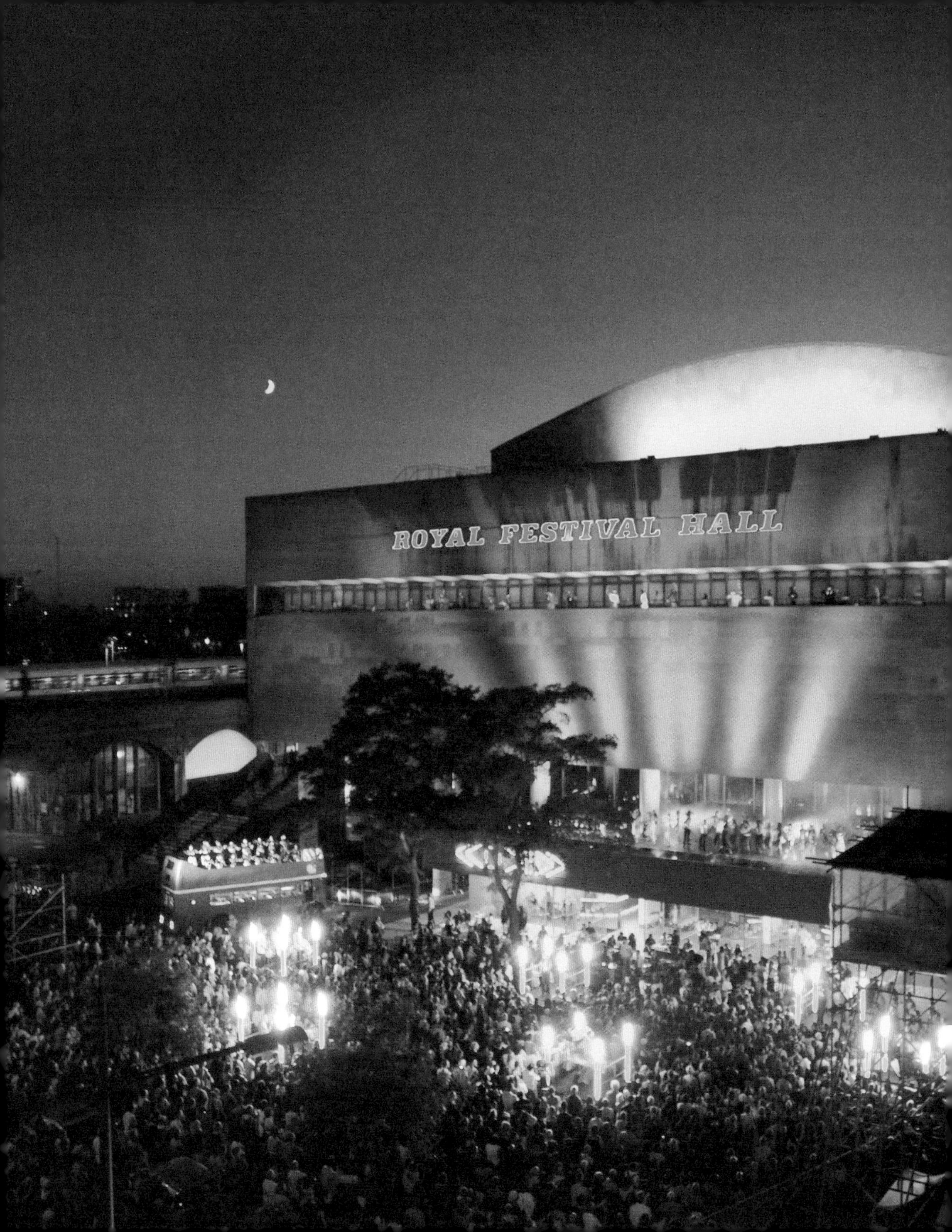
ROYAL FESTIVAL HALL

INTRODUCTION

What does Southbank Centre mean to you? It is certainly more than the sum of its buildings – the Royal Festival Hall, Queen Elizabeth Hall, Purcell Room, Hayward. It stretches from the London Eye to BFI Southbank (formerly the National Film Theatre) and includes a flagpole, a book market, cafés and restaurants, fountains and free foyer entertainment. But, most importantly, it is home to memories. Millions of memories. People who now live on the other side of the world met and fell in love on its terraces; dancers and musicians have begun their careers on its stages. Journalists have had their first break in its galleries – and bathrooms – and performers have got lost in the underground car parks trying to find the artists' entrances. Three thousand people sang The Clash's "London Calling" at the end of its Bollywood extravaganza "Escapade" in 2002, and 220,000 participants became temporary members of the Philharmonia thanks to PLAY.orchestra in 2006. Conductors and daleks have raced through its service tunnels, pensioners have danced on its roofs and Labour Party ministers have sung along to D:Ream's "Things Can Only Get Better" outside the Royal Festival Hall at the 1997 general election victory party.

As a venue, Southbank Centre has played host to many of the biggest names in classical music, from Otto Klemperer to Sir Simon Rattle, Maria Callas to Angela Gheorghiu. But it also attracts exemplary performers from all genres of music, dance and art, and past stars have included Louis Armstrong, Lou Reed, Radiohead, Bridget Riley, Dame Shirley Bassey, Fats Domino, Akram Khan and Patti Smith. (Many of those who have performed at Southbank Centre have contributed memories to this book.) Dame Edith Sitwell and Jean Cocteau narrated scores on stage, Mo Mowlam read from her memoirs and Bret Easton Ellis from his novels. Performers have danced along its terraces and Evelyn Glennie has used it as a giant percussion instrument. The gamelan has entertained outside as wayang and Kathak shows have unfolded in the halls.

Southbank Centre as it stands today grew out of the Festival of Britain's flagship exhibition, held on the south bank of the Thames in 1951. The Royal Festival Hall was designed and built within three years to

The very first visual encounter with the building itself was somewhat surprising. That concrete thing is the famous Southbank Centre? Southbank Centre had such a reputation and the Queen Elizabeth Hall sounded so *royal* that the engagement had caused me some sleepless nights. Not to mention the fact that I was presenting a premiere there [*Petrushka*, 2001]. After this first surprise, the next obstacle to overcome was to find the artists' entrance. Not an easy job. From then on, it was really a pleasure to dive in to this beehive of artistic activity. This house is such a cluster of powerful and inspiring energy.
Tero Saarinen, dancer and choreographer

Page 11: "Escapade" lights up
Southbank Centre in 2002.
Previous page: Southbank
Centre in 2006.
Below: The Royal Festival Hall
and South Bank Exhibition
under construction, before both
opened in May 1951.

ensure it opened at the same time. After years of bombing and rationing,
the South Bank Exhibition was an unprecedented extravaganza, filled
with new technology, art, design and colour. Eight-and-a-half million
people arrived by train, tram, bus, car and on foot to experience it. But
all too soon the exhibition was over. The flags were taken down and the
fountains switched off. One by one the pavilions were dismantled until the
Royal Festival Hall stood alone. Even the temporary pedestrian Bailey
bridge that linked the site to the north bank was taken away. The south
bank's proximity to central London was forgotten, and the hall had to
fight to survive.

The Queen Elizabeth Hall and Purcell Room were built alongside
the Royal Festival Hall in 1967, and the Hayward opened in 1968.
There were now more reasons to visit the south bank, but the new
network of pedestrian walkways that surrounded the halls and gallery
were windswept and alienating. Throughout the 1970s and early 1980s
the buildings looked in on themselves, embracing neither their riverside
location nor their proximity to each other. Only with the Greater London
Council's ambitious open foyer programme of 1983 did Southbank Centre
start to come alive. The Royal Festival Hall's foyers began to open during
the day, with live music presented in the bar and exhibitions on the
ballroom floor. In the 1980s the site started to be thought of as one

place, with performances and events happening beyond the safe-havens of auditoria and galleries. But during the 1990s a period of retrenchment set in, with budgets cut and morale at a low ebb.

In 2002, a new chairman, Lord Hollick, was appointed, shortly followed by a new chief executive, Michael Lynch. (Artistic director Jude Kelly started in September 2005.) They realized they had to ensure the fragmented site was connected back together again and rejuvenated. The Rick Mather masterplan for Southbank Centre, put in place by former chairman Elliott Bernerd, allowed work to be carried out incrementally when funds became available, and slowly things began to take shape. The Hayward's new foyer opened in 2003 and, to coincide with the opening of the Golden Jubilee pedestrian bridges that now flank Hungerford bridge, the Festival Stairs were added. While the final preparations were made to refurbish the Royal Festival Hall, shops and restaurants were built under the hall facing the river, timed to open just as the hall closed for two years. Staff members were relocated to Southbank Centre Building, a new purpose-built office block alongside the railway tracks, the first new structure on site for 38 years. Former offices, which had been squirreled away in makeshift spaces all over the Royal Festival Hall, were removed, freeing up 35 per cent of extra public space. Southbank Centre continues to develop, and plans are being discussed for Jubilee Gardens, the Queen

When I first came to Britain in the 1970s as a student, I was taken to see a Kathak performance at Southbank Centre on my very first night. It was a rather surreal way to be introduced to this country and to London in particular. Until then I had associated Wordsworth with the bridges over the Thames as the quintessential English experience but here was a very unexpected collision of textures and associations. I had no idea then that I would actually end up performing on, and then choreographing for, that very stage many years later.
Shobana Jeyasingh, choreographer

When I found out that my MoMA retrospective [New York, 1999] was going to the Hayward, I heard much about what a difficult space it was in which to show. I should have relaxed because I have always been enamoured by Brutalist architecture and had a great experience with the Whitney Museum – Marcel Breuer's Brutalist masterpiece – in a previous retrospective. These hard, cold, massive spaces of concrete and stone are surprisingly conducive to the contemplations of images of warm, soft flesh. Having exhibitions in both the Hayward and the Whitney are among my favourite experiences as an exhibiting artist.
Chuck Close, artist

Top: The Hayward in 1969.
Above: The Royal Festival Hall main bar in the 1950s.
Overleaf: the south bank at night, c.1993.

Elizabeth Hall and Purcell Room, the Hayward and the Belvedere Road Southbank Centre car park.

The 2005–07 Royal Festival Hall refurbishment required significant funding – £91m in total. Unusually, for a public arts centre, the majority of this money did not come from the government but was a straight split between public and private funding. The revenue from the new restaurants and franchises beneath the Royal Festival Hall and Southbank Centre Building contributed to the refurbishment, as did the money from the new 25-year lease taken out by the London Eye (which stands on Southbank Centre land). Major donors also came on board (see page 175), as did more than 18,000 individual donors who dedicated seats in the auditorium or sent cheques to help towards the fundraising campaign. Every single donor who gave money to the campaign (up to 1 January 2007) is listed alphabetically in this book, starting on the cover and running along each page.

The reason so many people contributed to the fundraising campaign, it seems, is their great affection for the Royal Festival Hall and Southbank Centre. This book builds on the memories of many of those who have donated and who have registered their recollections as part of "Love the Festival Hall", an ongoing database of living history. One such contributor, Rachel Curtis, explains why she chose to dedicate a seat in the auditorium:

My husband always admired the architecture of the south bank, especially the Royal Festival Hall. He remained interested in the renovation of Southbank Centre despite us living in Southampton. When we visited London we would always go to the Royal Festival Hall to relax, eat, enjoy the music and admire the magnificent landscape of London. When he was diagnosed with cancer at the age of 37 we were devastated, but he always maintained his enjoyment of architecture and music. When he died in 2004, I decided a fitting memorial would be to purchase a seat in his memory. He will now be able to hear as much music as he likes in the splendid surroundings of the Royal Festival Hall. I visit when I can and remember with fondness our special and happy times spent on the south bank. As soon as it reopens, I hope to attend a concert with friends. We are going to buy his seat and leave it empty and hope he is with us.

This book is for everyone who has similarly fond memories lodged within Southbank Centre's buildings and terraces, shops and restaurants, bathrooms and service tunnels, viewing platforms and gardens.

The south bank means a lot to me, since I too (born late 1951) was a product of Festival of Britain euphoria. To me the Royal Festival Hall stands for that unnegotiable principle: you can make the excellent popular, but that is not the same as saying what is popular is necessarily excellent. Hard also to imagine how daring the entire structure was at the time. A similar architectural bravura spread throughout the neighbouring south bank: I have always enjoyed the gritty, heroic massing of the Hayward. And it was here that my career as a writer began: dolefully and fraudulently attending the press view of an event when just out of university, Joan Asquith (the Arts Council's glamorous press officer of the day) strode up to me and demanded who I was writing for. I mumbled. She said "Oh, well nobody is here from *The Listener*. You'd better do it for them." So quite by accident I became the art critic of the BBC's weekly review. And, as someone said, all the rest was sociology.

Stephen Bayley, cultural commentator

1 MUD FLATS AND MARSHLAND

Top: Belvedere Road in 1930.
Above: Tenison Street being
demolished, 30 December 1948.
Previous page: A workman putting
the finishing touches to the Royal
Festival Hall in 1951.

*8 May 1945. Prime Minister Winston Churchill announces on the
radio that war has come to an end in Europe. He declares a national
holiday, and thousands of people head into London to celebrate,
clattering off trains at the Waterloo terminus, streaming over Waterloo
bridge, heading for London's heart – Trafalgar Square, Buckingham
Palace, Westminster.*

*A formal thanksgiving service for MPs at St Margaret's Church, next
to the Houses of Parliament, gives way to a cavalcade of Ministers and,
as dusk falls, Big Ben's remarkably unscathed face is illuminated and
public buildings are floodlit once more. Crowds throng Westminster,
dancing along Whitehall, Birdcage Walk, The Mall. But directly across
the Thames, on the south bank, it is a different story.*

*Lambeth Palace and St Thomas's Hospital were both bombed during
the war, and many of the wharves, factories and industrial buildings
that stretch between the palace and London Bridge, following the river's
curve, have been burnt-out or destroyed. County Hall has survived, but
the imposing nineteenth-century brewery that stood just a few hundred
yards downstream has been gutted. Terraces that ran behind the brewery,
on Belvedere Road and Tenison Street, appear abandoned.*

*It seems incredible to think that, in just six years, this down-at-heel
area of London will be transformed into a potent symbol of national
resurrection. It will become home to the ambitious South Bank
Exhibition, the centrepiece of the 1951 Festival of Britain.*

L ondon's south bank is now a vibrant cultural destination, with concert
halls and art galleries, performance spaces and libraries, theatres,
cinemas and museums, restaurants and bars. Entertainment is
in the south bank's blood – as far back as the sixteenth century it was the
home of theatres and bear-baiting arenas, with audiences ferried across
the Thames from the "safe" north bank to London's lawless fringe. Nearby
Bankes Side was home to Shakespeare's Globe theatre; it is even thought
that Roman gladiators fought in the area.

But the 27 acres that originally formed the Festival of Britain's South
Bank Exhibition, and which are now home to Southbank Centre, started
out as low-lying marshland. On a 1658 map of London, the riverside
brothels and inns around London Bridge peter out as the river twists
upstream. Only a solitary windmill stands on Lambeth Marsh, the
spot where the Royal Festival Hall will be built almost 300 years later.
Excepting the cluster of properties around Lambeth Palace and London
Bridge (the only solid river crossing until 1750), south of the Thames was

mainly fields. This was in sharp contrast to the north bank, where tightly packed houses stretched from Westminster to the Tower of London.

By the mid-eighteenth century much of Lambeth Marsh had been drained, and industry began to profit from the area's location. Timber wharves stretched from the new Westminster bridge towards Blackfriars, where the third river crossing opened in 1769. That same year, Eleanor Coade's Artificial Stone Manufactory started production nearby. Transport links with the north bank were strengthening all the time, but the City of London kept the south at arm's length, using it primarily as a place to locate unwanted industries. Once keen to ensure lewd behaviour was kept out of the City, now smelly manufacturers were similarly banished from London's centre. Hence vinegar distilleries, tallow factories and waterworks started to appear along the river.

In time, Victorian industry replaced many of the timber yards that lined the Thames. In 1826 a new 58-metre shot tower was erected to make twelve million lead pellets an hour for the army. A decade later the neoclassical Lion brewery became its neighbour, topped by a red stone lion, one of the last works made by Coade's before it closed in 1837.

Below: The south bank of the Thames, 17 December 1948. The shot tower stands surrounded by low-lying warehouses, and Big Ben can just be seen through the fog.

Right: Rocque's engraved map of London, showing both banks of the Thames in 1746. Much of the south bank was marshland.
Below: A lithograph of the shot tower and Lion brewery, published to celebrate the opening of the brewery in 1836.

The railways arrived, and Waterloo station expanded to accommodate new lines coming from the south in to London. In 1864, Charing Cross station opened on the north bank, and tracks were carried on viaducts from Waterloo across the new Hungerford railway bridge, which replaced Isambard Kingdom Brunel's original footbridge built twenty years earlier. The railways came to define the south bank, with an armature of viaducts carrying steam trains across roads and between houses (Hungerford bridge still bisects the site of Southbank Centre). The newly formed Metropolitan Board of Works endeavoured to clean up the sewers, but nineteenth-century observers continued to comment on the putrid smells – animal fat, fish, stale beer and chlorate of lime – that emanated from the streets around Waterloo station.

By the early twentieth century, the south bank finally gained its own embankment, but it only ran in front of Lambeth Palace and up to Westminster bridge. County Hall, built between 1911 and 1933 as a home for the London County Council (which replaced the Metropolitan Board of Works), had to wait until after the Second World War to see the embankment extended beyond its Edwardian Baroque façade to Waterloo bridge. Until the late 1940s, the southern banks of the Thames were a ramshackle medley of pontoons, wooden piles and floating decks, with tapering mud banks revealed at low tide.

The first London County Council plan of 1910 to redevelop the south bank hinged on the transformation of Hungerford bridge – then, as now, carrying trains to Charing Cross – into a road. Trains would no longer cross the river; in their place, cars would drive down a bridge lined with shops and the south bank would be given its own embankment and boulevards. Nothing came of this scheme, and it wasn't until 1943 that a new masterplan for the area was laid out in JH Forshaw and Patrick Abercrombie's influential *County of London Plan*. The Abercrombie plan called the south bank "depressing" and "lacking in dignity", and suggested the removal of all industry and the reinvention of the site as a cultural quarter, complete with swimming pool, theatre and concert hall.

Top: The shot tower and workshops in the 1940s.
Above: Barges at low tide on the mud flats of the south bank, in the shadow of the shot tower.

Proposing a concert hall was timely, for the Blitz had destroyed London's premier concert hall two years earlier. The Queen's Hall in Langham Place, home to the Proms, was destroyed on 10 May 1941. Malcolm Sargent had been conducting Sir Edward Elgar's *The Dream Of Gerontius* with the London Philharmonic Orchestra and Royal Choral Society that afternoon, and was horrified to learn that later that night an incendiary bomb had burnt the hall to the ground. This left only the Royal Albert Hall as a large-scale concert venue and, while the Proms quickly transferred there, many musicians were reluctant to follow because of its echoing acoustics and vast scale (it seats 6,000).

Despite the Abercrombie plan's suggestion for a new concert hall on the south bank, no immediate action was taken. Britain was at war, and London was under attack. The Blitz in 1940–41 killed 22,000 Londoners in eight months; when the V-bombs (or doodlebugs, as they were known) started falling on the city in June 1944, whole streets were destroyed. By the end of the war, 30,000 people had been killed by them, and 10,000 homes destroyed. Building work didn't entirely cease – a new Waterloo bridge opened in 1945 – but it wasn't until plans for the Festival of Britain were unveiled that the idea of a south bank concert hall was revived.

In 1943 the Royal Society of Arts first proposed marking the centenary of the 1851 Great Exhibition with an international trade fair, but not much was done about it until Gerald Barry, editor of the left-wing *News Chronicle*, took up the cause in 1945. He lobbied the Board of Trade to get a centenary exhibition off the ground and his persistence paid off, with the government putting the idea to committee.

Above: The interior of the 1851 Great Exhibition, held in Joseph Paxton's purpose-built Crystal Palace in Hyde Park, London.

Despite the Ramsden committee coming back in favour of a "Universal International Exhibition, to demonstrate to the world the recovery of the United Kingdom from the effects of the war in the moral, cultural, spiritual and material fields," and the appointment of Gerald Barry as director of the proposed exhibition on 1 April 1948, the Festival of Britain soon ran into problems. The committee proposed that it be held on the site of the 1851 Great Exhibition in Hyde Park, but the government was against the use of London's main green space. Sites were then considered at Osterley Park, Battersea Park and South Kensington, but costs, lack of space and lack of support deemed them all unsuitable. Meanwhile, the exhibition was scaled back from an international trade fair to a national show, which meant the Board of Trade was no longer interested in being involved and responsibility for it was handed to Herbert Morrison, the only government minister without departmental responsibility at that time.

What could have seemed like a run of bad luck actually worked in the Festival of Britain's favour. Morrison became an ardent supporter of Barry's vision for a festival that was "the people's show", and managed to persuade both sides of the House of Commons to support it, pushing through acts of parliament to ensure that regulations surrounding building rationing could be overlooked when it came to Festival matters. When the pound was devalued and all publicly funded projects were scaled back in 1949, Morrison managed to renegotiate the Festival's budget at £11 million, a reduction of less than ten per cent.

Morrison was a firm believer in the newly formed Welfare State and, as the former head of the London County Council, he was committed to access to the arts for Londoners. Following the general election in July 1945, when Clement Attlee and the Labour Party came to power, plans were set in place to ensure delivery of a social programme that saw health, education, housing and the arts as a right for all. The class system had been suspended as people fought side by side in the war, and there was a pervading belief that a better, fairer society had to result from that. The Festival of Britain was seen as a way to reflect this. The only problem was that the government had spent so much time prevaricating about where to

The most memorable moment I can recall during my four years residency at Southbank Centre was having the opportunity to do a project with ten women, aged between 40 and 81. I remember spending two weeks in the summer submerged in the Hothouse – the small makeshift studio at Southbank Centre – with these ten women, Hanif Kureshi, the writer, two of my company dancers and three musicians. Believe me, it was hot in there! But even through the constant complaints of not having enough air to work in, or that the studio was too small, or that some women were finding the movement material extremely difficult, beneath all this, there was a silent awareness that we were gradually forming a close community, even a family, over those ten days. Now, I can reflect that it was one of the few profound journeys I have experienced in my life. And that's how I will always remember Southbank Centre: a place where I felt people from all ages, cultures, religions could come together, and find similarities and – more importantly – differences, that we could celebrate through our art forms.
Akram Khan, dancer and choreographer

hold it that, by the time they had found a site, there were only three years left to plan, build and fill the Festival.

The south bank had initially been proposed as a venue for the Festival's flagship exhibition, but it had somehow been overlooked until the summer of 1948. The government then promptly earmarked £2m for the stalled London County Council concert hall, providing it could be ready in time for the opening of the Festival that would now surround it on the south bank. Robert Matthew, chief architect of the London County Council, was asked whether the hall could be built in under three years. He gulped (one imagines), and said yes. It would be the first concert hall built in London since the ill-fated Queen's Hall in 1893. The future of the south bank had finally been decided.

The South Bank Exhibition would be at the heart of the nationwide

Left: Shell of the 1893 Queen's Hall, Langham Place, London. It was destroyed by a bomb on 10 May 1941.

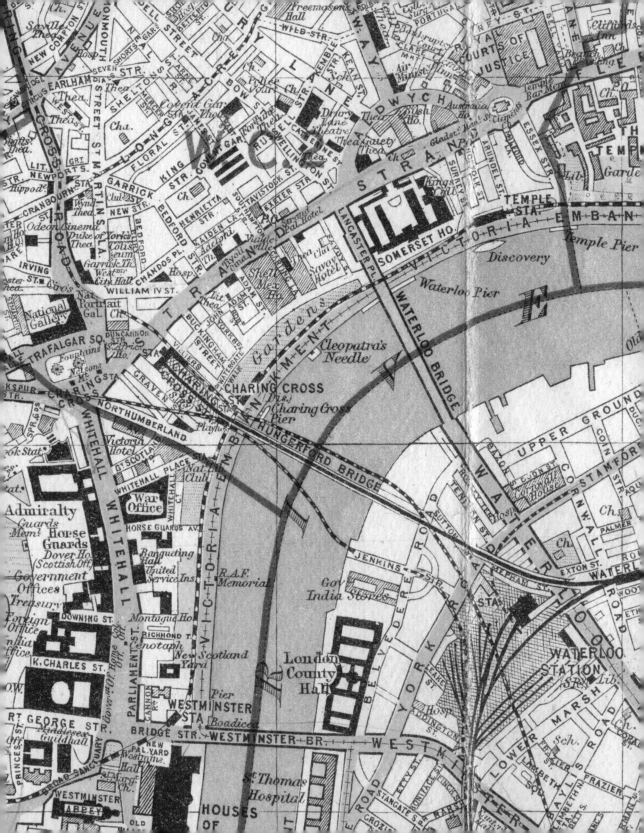

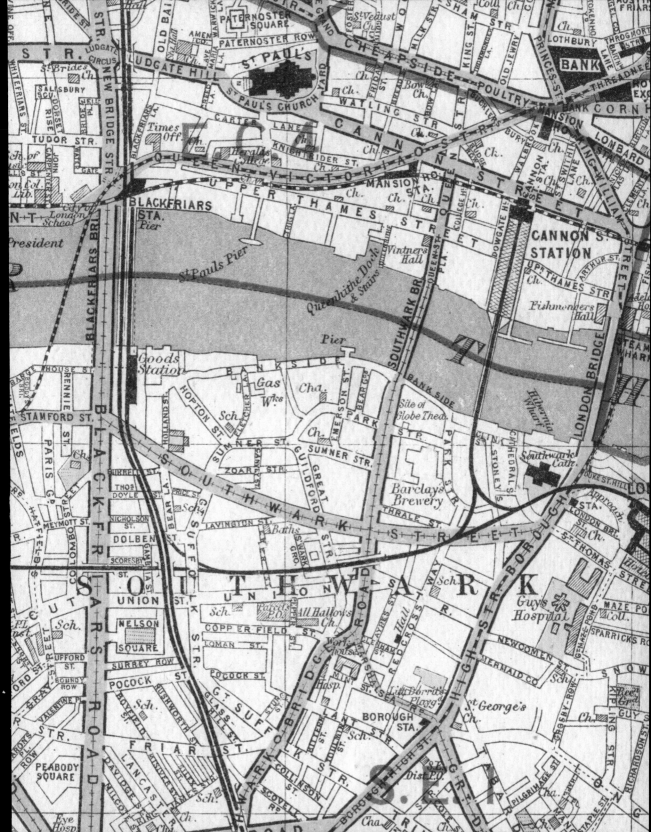

Above: The disused Lion brewery offered for let in 1930.
Previous pages: A detail from the Bartholomew map of 1947, showing the south bank prior to redevelopment.

Festival that showcased Britain's resilience. Barry didn't want it to have the "glorious assurance" of the Great Exhibition in 1851, which aimed to place Britain firmly at the centre of the world, but rather, Barry claimed, he wanted it to be "the people's show, not organized arbitrarily for them to enjoy, but put on largely by them, by us all, as an expression of a way of life in which we believe."

What the Festival of Britain did share with the Great Exhibition, during the early planning stages, was a desire to showcase the latest in science, technology, arts and industrial design. Barry recruited Ian Cox as director of science and approached the newly formed Council of Industrial Design (later to become the Design Council) to ensure design was integral to the Festival. The Festival was to be a "tonic to the nation", a chance to see the future in all its possibilities.

To help Barry realize his vision across the 27-acre exhibition ground in less than three years, he quickly appointed a design group led by 38-year-old architect and writer, Hugh Casson. Casson was in charge of commissioning the temporary pavilions that would dot the site, working alongside architects Misha Black and Ralph Tubbs, and designers James Holland and James Gardner. Black worked with Ian Cox to plan the architecture and theme of "The Land" – the Upstream half of the exhibition next to County Hall. Casson, meanwhile, worked with Mark Hartland Thomas, chief industrial officer at the Council of Industrial Design, on the Downstream site – "The People" – which incorporated the new concert hall.

As the youthful team of architects and designers hunched over drawing boards, hastily sketching modernist glass and steel pavilions inspired by Le Corbusier and Mies van der Rohe, preparations on site had already begun. The disued Lion brewery was torn down, with only the stone lions that had stood on its roof being saved at the behest of King George VI. While they were being repaired, prior to being installed on the Festival site, a small recess was discovered in one of the lion's backs. In it were found two William IV coins and an old green bottle, inside which was an advertisement for Coade's, the artificial stone-makers who had made the lions, and a note from the sculptor WF Woodington stating that they were completed on Princess Victoria's birthday on 24 May 1837. (One lion was moved to Waterloo station after standing for some years outside the Royal Festival Hall. It now stands on the corner of Westminster bridge near County Hall. The other is at Twickenham stadium.)

Along with the brewery and riverside wharves, whole terraces of houses were demolished and local residents were forcibly rehoused. Only the shot tower was left untouched. "Many people, myself included," Barry recalled, "at first thought that the shot tower should come down. It seemed to have little to say in terms of modern architecture, and to be in danger

> London was a kind of mythic city during the war. I first visited the Royal Festival Hall in 1951 and to discover such a hall immediately after the war, that was a great feeling of something new happening.
> **Pierre Boulez, composer and conductor**

Left: The hidden recess in the Coade lion is revealed. The lion had been removed from the Lion brewery for restoration in 1948.

Opposite: The south bank site on 17 May 1949, cleared for building work to begin. Only the shot tower remains.
Right: The foundation stone ceremony for the Royal Festival Hall, held on 12 October 1949.
Below: Clement Attlee laying the foundation stone.
Bottom: The architects responsible for designing the Royal Festival Hall.

of looking like an anachronism. I was quite wrong. I reckoned without the sentiment of the Londoner and without the tower's possibilities."
It stayed, a solitary structure on a vast muddy site. The creation of the Festival of Britain, and the concert hall, could begin.

The concert hall was planned to stand between the shot tower and Hungerford bridge, and an embankment was hastily being built to create a riverside promenade. Laying the concert hall's foundation stone, Prime Minister Clement Attlee said, in October 1949: "I believe that our old skill has not deserted us, that our old state and determination to serve our country and to serve the world is still strong and vigorous. And in our pride in the past, and in our hopes for the future, we can all – irrespective of any views we hold – be united." Through the concert hall, he continued, "we shall also show that we are not just a nation of shopkeepers, but a people who appreciate and practise the arts."

For Robert Matthew and his architectural team at the London County Council, this appreciation of the arts had them up against the ropes. Matthew had agreed that the architects' department could design and build an internationally reputable concert hall in under three years. There would be no time to launch a competition to choose an architect – the design had to be done in-house, and done fast. He immediately appointed Leslie Martin as the head of design. Matthew was aware that the concert hall was to be the first major public building commissioned since the end of the war, and he was keen to employ young architects to ensure that the finished design was modernist in its outlook.

DIARY OF AN ARCHITECTURAL STUDENT, 1949–50

In October 1949, Jean Symons decided to take a sabbatical from her studies at the Architectural Association and gain some first-hand experience of working on a building site. She was employed as a technical assistant by the London County Council, and prepared weekly progress reports on the construction of the Royal Festival Hall. The following are extracts from her site diary.

October 1949

The only evidence that the mass of concrete slabs and columns is to be a concert hall is a small pillbox under Hungerford bridge, the purpose of which is to test the principle of construction to be applied to the auditorium. It is a box within a box. There are two layers of concrete with an air space in between. Inside are hung layers of glass silk. With the doors shut one feels completely cut off from the world.

April 1950

The main internal staircases, which were purposely omitted earlier to prevent their being used as wheelbarrow runs, are under construction. Life has become easier, now that it is possible to use staircases, rather than climbing seven or eight ladders to reach the top of the building.

May 1950

The King and Queen visit the site and it is announced that the hall will be known as Royal Festival Hall. I am impressed by the detailed questions the Queen asks, and amused at the way she holds up the official procession to chat with the workers on the site. There is a sudden shower. Instead of waiting for umbrellas, the King and Queen hurry to shelter under Waterloo bridge with everyone else. The consternation on the faces of the police guard is a joy to behold.

July 1950

At the end of the month a party is given by the LCC for everyone working on the site, to celebrate the completion of the roof – or, to be precise, the inner skin of the roof. The first music emitted by the piano, especially installed for the occasion, is "Put Another Nickel In", and the first concert, after the meal, consists of traditional Cockney and Irish songs. There is a race up to the roof, to crack a bottle of beer over it and hoist the flags.

October 1950

Working on acoustic splitter-chamber between main ventilation plant room and auditorium, and in ducts. Several thin men have left the job after being asked to clean out the rubbish that has been allowed to drop down the twelve-inch cavity between the auditorium walls.

November 1950

In response to repeated requests, the contractors decided to clean out the cavity between the two leaves of the auditorium wall. There were some connecting bars to be burnt off, so a man set to work with an oxy-acetylene torch. He set alight the paper covering to the glass silk, which hung down into the cavity from the roof... Holes have to be drilled so that water can be played on to the blaze. The fire brigade are asked to be as sparing as possible in their use of water, as the fibrous-plaster auditorium ceiling has just been finished and painted, and some of the panelling has already been fixed... The damage is not very great but it could have been disastrous.

December 1950

Boiler-house control panel showing conditions in every part of the building is installed. Pipes are being painted in distinguishing colours: green for heating and ventilating, royal blue for cold water, turquoise for domestic hot water; cream for gas; crimson and scarlet for hydrants and sprinklers. The walls are light-grey with dark-grey ceilings and red-tiled floor. It must be one of the finest boiler-houses in England.

Martin took up his position in October 1948. The architectural brief stipulated that the new concert hall must seat 3,000, and must also include a smaller venue that could seat 750. Given the size of the site the hall had been granted, Matthew and Martin quickly realized that the entire floor space would be taken up by the auditoria, leaving no room for foyers, bars and restaurants, unless they somehow suspended the main auditorium and located everything else underneath it. And so the "egg in the box" concept – an auditorium suspended in the middle of the hall – came into being. (In recent years the concept has been credited to Martin, but drawings by Matthew completed shortly before Martin's appointment suggest that he had already come up with the principle of a suspended auditorium.)

To further complicate matters, the London County Council brief also stipulated that the concert hall should include ample rehearsal space for musicians, a large restaurant facing the river, meeting rooms and an art gallery. As such the brief encapsulated a new way of thinking – that buildings could be as democratic as the ideals behind them. The building's goal was to persuade people to spend hours there, eating, drinking, talking and viewing, and not just to turn up for a pre-booked concert then go away again.

If the brief had democratic ideals, then the hall – in terms of its design – more than fulfilled them. Martin's early sketch shows the importance placed right from the start on circulation, fair and shared access and transparency. There was no grand entrance, no portico with Doric columns designed to dwarf those entering. With the concert hall propped up above the foyer on pillars, the audience could circulate freely beneath it at a shared bar, or wander up any of the staircases into the auditorium, from where every audience member would have an unimpeded view of the stage and, acoustically, would hear the same concert. The "egg in the box" idea also helped in terms of the proposed acoustics. Locating a concert hall next to a busy railway line was not ideal but, by cocooning the auditorium in the middle of the building, an extra layer of architectural protection was provided. On top of that, the auditorium was designed with a double skin of concrete enveloping it, a cushion of air between the two providing further absorption of unwanted noise.

Martin appointed Peter Moro as the head of detail design development, and Edwin Williams, already an employee of the London County Council's architects' department, handled the contract coordination. By December 1948 the first detailed drawings had been produced by the architects and, in April 1949, the contract was put out to tender. A month later, Holland Hannen and Cubitts were chosen to construct the hall. There were exactly two years to go before it had to open – Holland Hannen and

There are many venues like this which are aimed just at specific types of music. The Royal Festival Hall is a place… it's not just a hall, not just a chamber – the whole environment is based in making music – it's a very creative place. I think music is very welcomed here, all styles of music. You could have Ravi Shankar playing here one night, the next night you could have Blur. This is a really special place.
Courtney Pine, jazz saxophonist

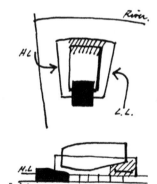

Above: Leslie Martin's first sketch for the Royal Festival Hall in 1948, showing the "egg in the box" and proposed second hall (dark section).
Opposite: Jean Symons (then Jean Layton) and Pat Dawburn at work on site in 1950.

Cubitts started moving their equipment on to site the following day.

Martin was keen that the auditorium wouldn't suffer from external noises filtering in, and he was equally keen to ensure that the acoustic quality of the hall was world class. He appointed Hope Bagenal, an experienced acoustician, to ensure that the auditorium offered the audience an excellent balance of definition and clarity from every seat. (Bagenal insisted that the hall was rectangular for this reason – only by allowing as many seats in a row at the front as at the back could the length of the hall be kept below 40 metres and therefore acoustic and visual integrity be maintained.)

But while Bagenal was an acoustic expert who had worked on concert halls across the world, there were no computer-simulated programmes he could rely on or models he could apply to the hall until it was physically there. While much was done by the architects to ensure that reverberation in the hall was kept to a minimum by designing every interior element to be absorbent (they were rather too good at this as it turned out), it was understood that the auditorium would need to be "tuned" once all the structural elements were in place. Acoustics were – and to a certain extent still are – an art form that couldn't be rushed. So the hall, or the auditorium at least, had to be finished months before the first concert was due to be performed to allow acoustic testing to take place.

In June 1949 work began on the foundations and, by the autumn, the concrete framework of the building began to appear. Martin and Moro met for lunch every day and began planning the interior finishes of the hall. Moro had recruited a dozen former architecture students of his to work on the fixtures and fittings, including Trevor Dannatt, as well as specialist designers such as Jesse Collins, Milner Gray and Robin Day. Because of the shortage of materials following the war, there were no catalogues of light sockets or chairs or music stands to flick through and order from. Quite simply, Moro and his team had to design and commission everything. When the initial architects' drawings were made, there was a shortage of steel but an adequate supply of timber. When the Royal Festival Hall was built this was reversed, and many aspects of Martin's designs had to be reworked to accommodate the constantly changing supply of core materials.

While the concert hall progressed, everything from strike action to the Korean war threatened to scupper the South Bank Exhibition and the Festival of Britain. The cost of the Festival was criticized by the right-wing establishment and the conservative press, with the *Evening Standard* referring to it as "Mr Morrison's multi-million pound baby" and "Morrison's Folly". The cold war, and the start of the Korean war in

Above: The Royal Festival Hall auditorium being built in September 1950.
Opposite: The first roof trusses being assembled in May 1950.

Above: A "topping out" dinner held for contractors in July 1950, to celebrate the completion of the roof.

Above: Workmen clad the Royal
Festival Hall roof in copper.

June 1950, caused committees and column inches to discuss whether the
Festival should be abandoned, as the newspapers speculated that a Third
World War was imminent. Even the Russians were against the Festival
going ahead – it was reported that they believed it was a complex disguise
for war preparations.

Following a site visit to the concert hall in May 1950 by the King
and Queen, when they agreed to be its patrons, it became known as the
Royal Festival Hall. Work continued day and night despite the freezing
conditions in the winter of 1950 and the wettest spring for decades in
1951, which saw the rest of the Festival site become a quagmire. But
not everything went smoothly for the Royal Festival Hall. A young
architecture student, Jean Symons, kept a diary of the fifteen months
she worked on site, and recorded everything that happened, from strike
ballots to an auditorium fire [see panel on page 34]. And, very early on in
the planning stages, Martin realized that the second concert hall and art
gallery would never be built in time. Plans were redrawn with the smaller
venue omitted, and a temporary facade was put in place on the Belvedere
Road side, with a view to the hall being added as soon as the Festival of
Britain closed. Hourglass light fittings adorned the asbestos cladding and

from the outside the building looked finished. But internally, the rehearsal spaces designed to fit around the second hall had not been built, and doors from the few dressing rooms that had been squeezed in would have opened into thin air behind the hastily erected screen had they been unlocked.

However, the decision to postpone work on the second hall meant that the main auditorium, foyer, restaurant and bars were finished on time and on budget, allowing for acoustic testing to be done in the spring of 1951. The first test inside the finished auditorium was made on 14 February. After an incredible effort on the part of the architects to ensure that everything from the empty seats to the wall panels were absorbent and so didn't create a reverberation echo, as can sometimes be found in big auditoria, it was found that the residual reverberation was too little – under the optimum two seconds they had been aiming for. While there were still things that could have been done to shorten reverberation, there was very little that could be done to extend it. Bagenal had a real task on his hands, trying to solve a seemingly insurmountable problem. And he had less than three months in which to do it.

Top: The staff entrance to the Royal Festival Hall on Belvedere Road in 1951, with its "grasshopper" awning.
Above: Women cleaning the floor of the Royal Festival Hall foyer prior to its royal opening.
Left: King George VI and Queen Elizabeth make a site visit in May 1950.

2 THE FESTIVAL OF BRITAIN

3 May 1951. It is a grey, cloudy day, but the rain has held off, and King George VI has insisted the ceremony still be held outdoors. The royal family, flanked by a dozen trumpeters and yeoman warders, wait for the King to declare the Festival of Britain officially open. The ceremony takes place not on the south bank, but outside St Paul's Cathedral. Gerald Barry, director of the Festival, had asked for the inauguration to be held at the Tower of London, so that the royal party could approach the Festival site from the river on the state barge, but the King refused, claiming that the Tower's bloody history would not be appropriate, and that anyway the barge leaked.

Instead, the King and family travel from St Paul's in open-topped carriages, waving to thousands of onlookers who line the City's streets. As they enter the gates of the South Bank Exhibition, 14,000 invited visitors crowd forwards to watch the royal party take the first guided tour. Winston Churchill greets them as they approach the vast Dome of Discovery, and they all glide up into the upper exhibition hall on long escalators. The day is spent looking at fountains and telescopes, gazing up at turbines and locomotives, with Queen Mary – the King's mother, who is well into her eighties – gamely completing the tour in a wheelchair. "We enjoyed it very much," the King tells Pathé News cameras, "and hope to come again."

By the evening, when the King unveils a commemorative plaque at the Royal Festival Hall and attends the inaugural concert, he wearily jokes that this is not the official opening of the Hall. "I opened the whole Festival of Britain this morning," he says. "I don't have to open anything else now, I am just attending the first concert."

The concert programme is a roll-call of rousing British works including Sir Edward Elgar's "Pomp and Circumstance No. 1" and Thomas Arne's "Rule Britannia", conducted by Sir Adrian Boult and Sir Malcolm Sargent and played by members of London's five symphony orchestras. With so much national pride being conjured, the King probably doesn't even notice that Gerald Barry, General Lord Ismay (chairman of the Festival Council), and the Lord Mayor and Lady Mayoress are fifteen minutes late and miss the beginning of the concert. Having had to take the goods lift up to the Ceremonial Box (and, allegedly, first being taken to the wrong floor) the King would no doubt have understood that lifts were the reason for their tardiness. Barry and company had watched the King unveil the commemorative plaque, then bundled into the passenger lift and overloaded it. It had to be hand-cranked down by engineers and the doors forced open. Perhaps wisely, the clerk of works for the Royal Festival Hall, who was also trapped in the lift, didn't inform the illustrious passengers of his day job.

G erald Barry was given three years and one month to create
the Festival of Britain. From working with one colleague in
April 1948, Barry went on to run an office of some 600 staff and
oversee a programme that stretched across the country and included
events in 17,000 towns and villages across Britain. An official touring
show moved between Yorkshire, Lancashire and the Midlands as the
Festival ship *Campania* toured Britain's ports, both adorned with the
Festival's iconic symbol (as designed by competition-winner Abram
Games). Every county swelled with festival spirit as new "Festival"
playing fields opened, trees were planted and schools extended. There
was even a druid's "Festival" pilgrimage to Stonehenge.

But London, with its hugely over-budget Festival pleasure gardens
in Battersea Park, a major science exhibition in South Kensington and
modern housing showcase in the east end, was at the centre of the Festival.
And the flagship show was the South Bank Exhibition, where the Dome of

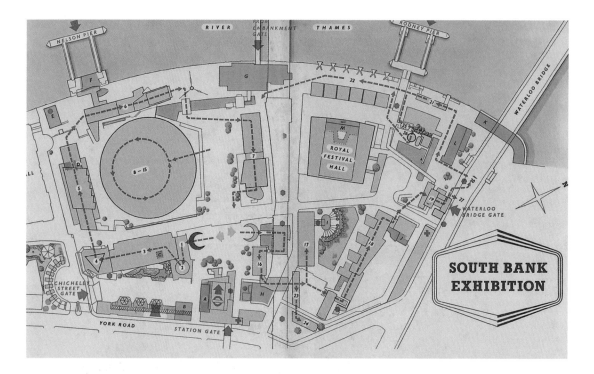

Above: The official Festival of Britain site plan of the South Bank Exhibition, 1951.

Discovery, the Skylon, the Royal Festival Hall, fountains and flags, open-air restaurants and dancing ensured that the eight-and-a-half million people who passed through its turnstiles during the summer of 1951 had a day (or night) they would never forget.

Barry had brought together a young team of international architects, designers and artists – not one over 45 and many living in Britain as refugees – and had set them to work to create something filled with "fun, fantasy and colour". For many, this offered the first opportunity to work on such a scale. As HT Cadbury-Brown, who designed many of the fountains, said: "There was a terrific feeling of optimism. It was joyous to work on the first big anything, after years of small exhibitions, alterations, and a little housing work... There was a real sense in which the Festival marked an upturn in people's lives... It was an event for a new dawn, for enjoying life on modern terms, with modern technology."

Because of the temporary nature of the exhibition pavilions, built to last just one summer, the designs could be more experimental and avant-garde than might otherwise have been possible. Building materials were still rationed, so the architects had to be inventive. To readers of magazines such as *The Architectural Review*, the buildings that did rise from this extraordinary commission had a lot in common with those previously seen on the continent – light, transparent structures with glass walls and cantilevered balconies. They were mini-palaces that paid homage to modernism and talked of the future, of weightlessness, linearity and possibility. While continental viewers and architecture experts may not have found them revolutionary, to Britons suffering from rationing, prefabs and greyness, they must have seemed incredible.

What was distinctly new about the exhibition was its layout. Unlike major temporary expositions in France and Italy, at that time the benchmark in exhibition design, the South Bank Exhibition didn't adhere to a strict grid of boulevards with pavilions ranging off left and right. The site didn't lend itself to this – there was an immovable railway bridge running right through the middle of it, for a start – but it was also felt that a more flexible layout would offer the visitor more of a sense of excitement, intimacy and surprise. Hugh Casson, the Festival's chief architect, explained in *Brief City*, a film made as the Festival closed: "The South Bank [Exhibition] had no processional way and no great vistas. On purpose, it didn't have the symmetry and repetitive grandeur of some other great cities and their exhibitions. It was planned intimately, like rooms opening one out of another. Each room or courtyard differed in size and shape, and colour, character and furniture."

The Hungerford bridge divided the exhibition site into two sections, named Upstream (towards County Hall) and Downstream (towards Waterloo bridge). Casson was aware that the site must embrace the river, and appeal to those on the north bank: "As the south bank is a part of London that people ordinarily don't go to very much, we must try somehow to link the south bank with the north bank and make it very easy to go from one to the other."

The Thames was a barrier that Barry, Casson and their team had to entice people over. So they built flagpoles along the new embankment, and cantilevered seating decks over the river. The Skylon was built on the river's edge, and they even commissioned a temporary footbridge, the Bailey bridge, constructed by the Royal Engineers and decorated by architect Misha Black, to run alongside the Hungerford railway bridge and to increase access to the site from the north bank.

While the site could be accessed from a number of gates – from Waterloo station, Waterloo bridge, County Hall and the river – it was the gate at the end of the Bailey bridge that was the most popular. Opening day was certainly one of the busiest, despite the driving rain that caused the newly surfaced walkways and squares to turn into shallow lakes. Long queues of people in hats and mackintoshes formed at each gate, waiting to present their five-shilling advance tickets. George Simner, now head of the

Above: The Chicheley Street entrance to the South Bank Exhibition.
Overleaf: An aerial view of the South Bank Exhibition with a key to all the pavilions.

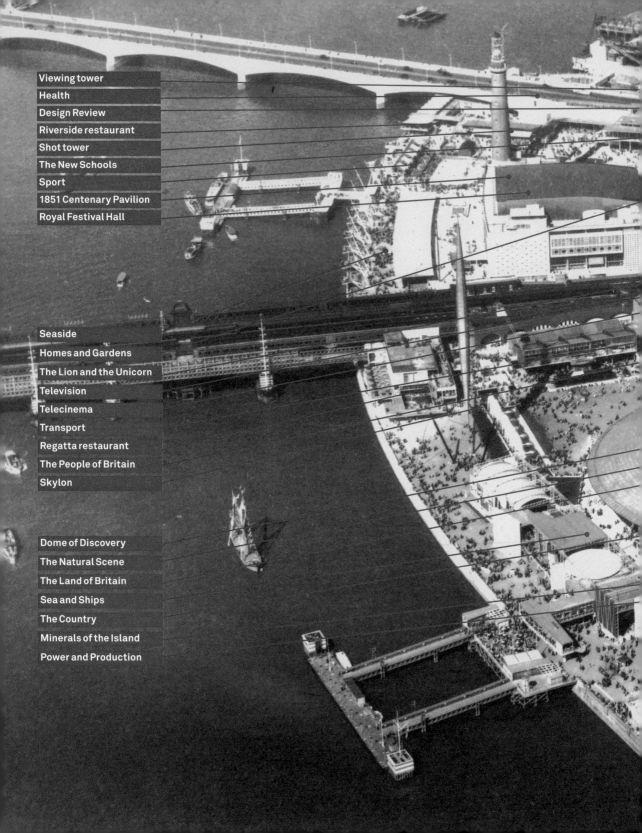

Viewing tower
Health
Design Review
Riverside restaurant
Shot tower
The New Schools
Sport
1851 Centenary Pavilion
Royal Festival Hall

Seaside
Homes and Gardens
The Lion and the Unicorn
Television
Telecinema
Transport
Regatta restaurant
The People of Britain
Skylon

Dome of Discovery
The Natural Scene
The Land of Britain
Sea and Ships
The Country
Minerals of the Island
Power and Production

Festival of Britain Society, distinctly remembers what it was like to enter
the exhibition's ground: "It was a whole new world. It was just amazing
after coming out of these dirty streets that had been bombed. It's hard to
describe now because colour is everywhere, but back then it wasn't."

The organizers had designed the two exhibitions to start from a shared
point just inside the station gate on York Road. Two curved entrances
– one red, one blue – located on the central piazza on the Fairway marked
the beginning of "The Land" and "The People". "The Land" explored
Britain's natural heritage, with areas dedicated to wildlife, agriculture,
minerals and raw materials. However, the biggest pavilions were given
over to how man had harnessed resources – Power and Production; Sea
and Ships; Transport. Scale-models of boats and engines were hung from
the ceiling; full-size turbines rotated on the Fairway. But the pavilion
that many people headed for first, and which included half the content of
"The Land" exhibition, was the impressive Dome of Discovery.

The Dome, the largest aluminium structure in the world when it was
built, had a diameter of 365 feet. (The Millennium Dome on London's
Greenwich Peninsula used the same calendar number scaled up to
metres.) Located on the land that is now Jubilee Gardens and designed
by Ralph Tubbs, part of Casson's team, it housed the story of Britain's
leading role in discovery and exploration. It was filled with the latest
technology, including a 74-inch telescope destined for an observatory
in Australia, as well as displays trumpeting Britain's past scientific
achievements and a polar theatre complete with a team of Huskies. There
was even a prototype for Jodrell Bank, a radio-telescope with its dish
aerial mounted at the top of the shot tower.

Right: The Fairway in the
South Bank Exhibition, with
the Transport pavilion behind.
Opposite: Ernest Race's iconic
Antelope chairs in front of the
Dome of Discovery provided a
welcome rest for visitors.

Right: A family gazes at the Dome of Discovery, while other visitors contemplate the Skylon, whose "legs" can be seen behind the fountain.
Below: At the Royal Festival Hall, Robin Day's orchestra chairs are stacked on Peter Moro's "net and ball" carpet.

Even though the Dome was packed with scientific wonders, the most iconic feature of the Upstream section was the Skylon, a 90-metre, 100-tonne conjuring trick. You could stand on a small brass plaque underneath it and look inside and wonder how this streamlined silver rocket stayed in the air. It was created by Philip Powell and Hidalgo Moya, and was the award-winning entry in a competition to design a "vertical feature" for the site. (Because of the time constraints, only two features of the entire site were put out to competition – the "vertical feature" and the '51 restaurant, won by Leonard Manasseh.) The name Skylon came later courtesy of poet Margaret Sheppard Fidler, who responded to Barry's appeal on the radio to find a name for it. For Sheppard Fidler, the word Skylon was a fusion of sky-hook and pylon. It also shared a phonetic similarity with nylon, still a relatively new material. The name stuck, and the Skylon became the motif of the Festival, and the victim of a popular joke that it was like modern Britain – it had no visible means of support.

Scientific development was perhaps the single most important theme running through the Festival. The colourful Abacus screen by Edward Mills looked like a giant atomic model; the "net and ball" carpet by Peter Moro in the Royal Festival Hall was based on oscilloscope waves. Ernest Race's Antelope chairs, made from recycled aeroplane metal, had atomic ball feet and a spindly linearity. Even the Regatta restaurant wallpaper, by William J Odell, was based on insulin crystallography diagrams. In the area of crystallography – a branch of science that looks at the structure of crystals and compounds – Britain was a world leader, and designers and artists across the site used the newly available images of microscopic patterns to inspire them. Mark Hartland Thomas, chief industrial officer at the Council for Industrial Design, even chose crystallography diagrams as the source material for his Festival Pattern Group. This partnership of designers and manufacturers used images of insulin, haemoglobin and other compounds to create fabrics, glassware, lampshades, wallpaper, furniture and cutlery, all inspired by the abstract loops and whorls of microscopic chemical structures. Many of the finished products ended up in Misha Black's Regatta restaurant, where even the ashtrays and menu cards were patterned with crystallography inspired designs.

The Regatta restaurant was split-level, with a large ground floor terrace. People could drink coffee and tea outdoors, something that was unheard of in Britain in 1951. Race's Antelope chairs clustered around *Cypress*, a slender abstract sculpture by Lynn Chadwick; the sculpture's linearity and structure echoed Race's chairs and the building's transparent design. Chadwick, along with Reg Butler, whose wiry anthropomorphic *Birdcage* stood nearby, would be dubbed "geometry of fear" artists the following year by critic Herbert Read, but at the South Bank Exhibition their attenuated forms appeared futuristic, even optimistic.

Art was an integral part of the South Bank Exhibition, and between the newly formed Arts Council – which commissioned Henry Moore, Barbara Hepworth and Jacob Epstein – and the Festival of Britain office, dozens of artists were asked to make ambitious murals, sculptures and fountains. At the Riverside restaurant, designed by Jane Drew, a large Ben Nicholson mural curved along one wall. Nearby stood Butler's *Birdcage*, Barbara Hepworth's *Turning Forms* – which slowly rotated – and a fountain by Eduardo Paolozzi. (A young Terence Conran, working on site as architect Dennis Lennon's assistant, remembers that Paolozzi's fountain was always breaking down.) Drew's building was one of the last to be constructed, dependent as it was on the new embankment being completed, and so it had to be built quickly. She had the roof made in sections in Bristol, and remembers: "We got the girls who made the aeroplane wings to come up and they took less than a week to assemble that roof. It was an aluminium surface, just like an aeroplane wing." Underneath it ran Nicholson's mural. Because it was curved, to act as a screen, it couldn't be glazed within Drew's budget. She installed a visual ha-ha in front of it, a channel of stones to stop anyone walking too close to it, but, she remembers: "He [Nicholson] said I only put those pebbles there to give the public some ammunition to throw at him! I pointed out that they were all cemented down."

Top: Lynn Chadwick's *Cypress* sculpture in the courtyard of the Regatta restaurant.
Above: The view from the Royal Festival Hall restaurant overlooking the Thames in 1951.

Downstream was dedicated to "The People". It was smaller than the Upstream site, and housed the Royal Festival Hall, which wasn't part of the exhibition, so the remaining pavilions were squeezed in around it. A Seaside pavilion ran between the Royal Festival Hall and the river, bringing sticks of rock and donkeys to the capital, and the Lion and the Unicorn pavilion – dedicated to showing how character and tradition had moulded the British way of life – was built behind it. The shot tower also stood Downstream, its now redundant height used to house the Dome's radio-telescope dish and a lighthouse lamp. The Sport pavilion stood nearby, which held sporting trophies including the Ashes, a Lonsdale belt and the first Derby cup. The 400-seater Telecinema (forerunner to the BFI National Film Theatre), with its glass-walled projection room, stood away from the river, and further pavilions dedicated to homes and gardens, schools and health were also slotted in. There was even a scale-model of Paxton's Crystal Palace at the foot of the shot tower, a last-minute addition to the site to remind everyone that the Festival of Britain was a centenary celebration of the 1851 Great Exhibition.

Visually, however, it was the Royal Festival Hall that dominated Downstream. Clad in Portland stone, with a copper roof that was shaped like a barrel, it faced the river with a gently curving facade cut through with long horizontal windows. Its main entrance was not from the riverside, but along its northern wall, facing Waterloo Bridge, where ground level glass doors gave on to a series of stairs that led all ticket holders up, across the ballroom floor and into the main bar. The scale of the

ROBIN AND LUCIENNE DAY

The designers Robin and Lucienne Day have a long-lasting relationship with the south bank, dating back to the Festival of Britain. They had met at the Royal College of Art in London in 1940 and married two years later. The war hindered their design ambitions – Robin wanted to make furniture and Lucienne to design furnishing fabrics – and by the time the war ended Robin was making a living as an exhibition designer and teaching at the Regent Street Polytechnic School of Architecture, alongside Peter Moro.

Robin continued to design furniture and, in 1948, won an international competition organized by the Museum of Modern Art in New York with a low-cost storage unit designed with Clive Latimer. This established Day's reputation as a furniture designer at exactly the moment the London County Council and the Festival of Britain team were looking for fresh new talent.

Robin was chosen by Peter Moro as the furniture consultant for the Royal Festival Hall, and was given the task of designing all the chairs. He created folding seats for the auditorium using steel tubing usually found in car manufacturing [right], and spindly-legged chairs for the orchestra with moulded plywood back rests that allowed men to put their coat-tails through them. He made chairs for the foyer – Lucienne calls them his Butterfly chairs – with armrests and seats made from one piece of moulded plywood, and a more restrained version with a cream leather seat for the restaurant. While the slender legs and bent ply were reminiscent of American designer Charles Eames's

furniture, Robin used technology that came of age in the war, and his complex, moulded-plywood designs were only possible thanks to the technological advances seen in the manufacture of Mosquito aircraft.

Meanwhile Robin was designing three room sets for the Homes and Gardens pavilion in the Festival's South Bank Exhibition that focused

on space-saving furniture, a key concern of the day. He furnished them with items from the Council of Industrial Design's approved design list, and included sculptures by Barbara Hepworth and Reg Butler. He also featured Lucienne's Provence wallpaper, and his own award-winning storage unit, which was now being produced by Heal's.

Lucienne designed the seating fabric for Wells Coates's Telecinema and a printed rayon Festival dress fabric, as well as three wallpapers and a new furnishing fabric called Calyx [above]. Calyx was her first major foray into furnishing fabrics, as they had been rationed until 1951 and consequently there was no market for new patterns.

Her designs grew from nature and in particular plant forms, but took account of abstract developments in art, particularly the paintings of Paul Klee and Joan Miro.

When Robin had asked her to design a fabric for the Homes and Gardens pavilion, she had pragmatically explained that without a client she couldn't produce anything. Then she came up with the design for Calyx and decided to take it to Heal's, hoping they would produce it for the Festival. The director of Heal's wholesale and export took one look at her design and told her bluntly that he didn't think it would sell, but for the sake of the Festival he would produce it and give her half the usual £10 fee. Just a year later Calyx, with its abstract flowers in citrus yellow, tomato and black on an olive background, won the American Institute of Decorators' highest award. Heal's duly paid Lucienne the rest of the fee, and Calyx is still being made today.

Top: The Royal Festival Hall and Festival flagpole during the Festival of Britain, 1951. Above: The rock garden in the foyer of the Royal Festival Hall, 1951.

hall unfolded before you. White columns rose from a marble floor and held the auditorium – at 10,000 tonnes, the same weight as the Eiffel Tower – above the heads of concert-goers as they moved freely about the vast foyer. Staircases with slender treads rose from the foyer and led to the auditorium.

Initial press reports on the hall's acoustics had been good. Not only had the architects succeeded in eliminating noise from the railway and roads outside, but, as Anthony Turner in the *Daily Mail* reported, the Royal Festival Hall was "the first in the world to be built round acoustic waves. Any sound, from a single whispered note to a great chord from choir, organ and orchestra will be reproduced in every part of it with exact tonal faithfulness."

Following the inaugural event, further concerts were held with a distinctly British feel, and almost everything written by Sir Edward Elgar and Vaughan Williams was performed. Every major regional orchestra was invited to perform two concerts, and a Festival of Britain "summer season" began on 10 May with a performance of Benjamin Britten's *Spring Symphony* by the London Philharmonic Orchestra.

Reporters such as Marjorie Proops, writing in the *Daily Herald* on the opening concert, were at pains to comment on the variety of dress on show. Tweed suits could be seen alongside tailed jackets; blouses and skirts next to dinner dresses. Proops even noted that, alongside all the finery, one man wore his working clothes. (Two hundred of the men who had worked on site, building the Royal Festival Hall, had been invited.) Everyone mingled together in the foyer before the concert, then ate roast duck and cold salmon and danced to Geraldo's Embassy Orchestra on the ballroom floor. It seemed that Martin's vision for a democratic hall had been achieved.

I am about twelve years old, lying on my back on the floor listening to a symphony orchestra in full swing, looking at neat modern geometric patterns on the wall, and thinking that I have just discovered the centre of the universe… it must have been 1967.

I had joined the National Youth Orchestra in 1966 as a tender eleven-year-old, and we were now at the Royal Festival Hall. We had arrived early and a professional orchestra was still rehearsing. For a brief time we were let loose in the building, awaiting our turn on stage, and I remember walking in and out of the boxes, exploring the spaces, and eventually lying down on the floor to listen to the sound of a "grown up" orchestra rehearsing. I think it was Eric Leinsdorf conducting Brahms, but now, almost 40 years on, the details are blurred, somehow incidental, and quite probably misremembered. What remains is the emotion; the sense of being at the centre of something rather modern, immensely powerful and tremendously vital. In that moment music and the act of being in a great communal space had somehow fused.

Marshall Marcus, violinist and former CEO of the Orchestra of the Age of Enlightenment, now head of music for Southbank Centre

Left: An interval crowd enjoying the level six terrace of the Royal Festival Hall in 1951.

But the reality was that the Royal Festival Hall was democratic only for the group of people who already went to concerts. Proops's comment that one man wore his working clothes to the opening runs counter to memories that men who worked on the hall and were invited to the opening didn't actually go because they didn't possess a dinner jacket (or even a lounge suit) that was the expected attire. Others remember walking around the South Bank Exhibition, looking at the men and women dining in the Royal Festival Hall restaurant overlooking the river, and knowing that their exhibition entrance ticket didn't allow them to even go inside the building. For the Royal Festival Hall had ushers on every door, and was only open a couple of hours prior to the evening concerts, and then for concert ticket-holders only. Even to find out about concerts, official Festival guidebooks suggested people looked in the newspapers; there was little information given on site. Consequently, the vast majority of visitors to the South Bank Exhibition never even made it across the threshold of the Royal Festival Hall.

In the end, though, this didn't matter. The Festival wasn't about classical concerts tucked away in a soundproof box. It was about hearing music outdoors, about discovering things around chance corners, about art and design cropping up everywhere, about science and new possibilities. It was about fountains and spectacle and drinking tea in the open air. It was about the atmosphere. It was about just being there.

So the Downstream exhibition "The People" wended its way along the river and politely bypassed the Royal Festival Hall. One of the most popular (and best remembered) pavilions on site was the Lion and the

Above: The Royal Festival Hall during the Festival of Britain. It was not part of the South Bank Exhibition, and was closed to all but concert-goers.

Unicorn, home to a display of what can only be called British eccentricity. Laurie Lee, later to be fêted for his childhood memoir *Cider with Rosie*, was the Festival's chief caption writer, and had asked people prior to the exhibition's opening to send him any oddities they came across for display in the pavilion. He was swamped with items, from shrouds and artificial limbs to collapsible rubber buses and functioning musical instruments made out of matchsticks. One manufacturer, he recalled, "sought permission to exhibit a model of the south bank made out of toilet rolls."

Audrey Russell, a radio commentator who had covered the opening ceremonies for the BBC, was particularly taken with the Lion and the Unicorn pavilion: "It was about our attitude to life, our love of free speech, our penchant towards eccentricity, and the ability of different social strata to be amused at the antics of each other." She recalled a flock of plaster birds flying across the ceiling, a symbol of the liberation of British spirit, as well as the cleverly juxtaposed objects on display. "I can remember a 365-day clock by Thomas Tompion," she said, "an original edition of Dr Johnson's *Dictionary*, an edition of Shakespeare, one of the Bible, a tailor's pinking scissors… and a corrected page proof of Winston Churchill's *History of the Second World War*." All these were displayed alongside masterpieces by Gainsborough and Constable. And, thankfully, there was no sign of the toilet-roll south bank model.

Coming out of the Lion and the Unicorn pavilion and striking off across a small piazza, the Homes and Gardens pavilion came into view, where room sets full of contemporary furniture and furnishings proved popular.

Right: The Lion and the Unicorn pavilion, with the Royal Festival Hall behind.
Opposite: Maurice Wilson's watercolour of the South Bank Exhibition at night, featuring the Royal Festival Hall and the Skylon.

Young designers Robin and Lucienne Day were major contributors [see panel on page 53], and even the teenage Terence Conran managed to create some chairs out of welded reinforcing rod – "about the only metal available to me at the time", he recalls.

A full tour of both Upstream and Downstream exhibitions would have been exhausting, but there were plenty of open-air cafés and restaurants at which to break your journey. And the long opening hours – 10.30–23.30 six days a week, with Sunday opening only slightly reduced to 12.30–23.00 – meant that you could stay as night fell and watch the site be transformed.

In the first week the Festival of Britain was open, the northern embankment had to be closed to traffic by police, as crowds stood and gazed at the floodlit dreamland on the other side of the Thames. Music could be heard across the water and, as people approached the site over the Bailey bridge, they inadvertently had smiles on their faces. If the South Bank Exhibition was a futuristic dream by day, it became other-worldly by night. The Skylon was lit from within and glowed like a blade of light against the night sky, while the Dome was lit from underneath so the aluminium carapace seemed to hover in mid-air. Light streamed from the Royal Festival Hall, whose roof was also floodlit, and giant masts ranked in front of it on the riverside walk were lit with incandescent bulbs. Boats moored on the Thames were strung with fairy lights, fountains were lit

with gas flames and the shot tower flashed a lighthouse beam across the river. Just a few years after blackout curtains had hung in every window, the south bank coruscated with light. It is not surprising that people spontaneously stood up and started dancing on the Fairway, despite the rain, or the fact that they were wearing heavy overcoats. Twice a week Geraldo's Embassy Orchestra would strike up and inhibitions would be thrown to the wind.

But while the Festival of Britain's flagship exhibition on the south bank seems to have been a popular success, its critics – and there were many – were vociferous in their damnation. The conservative press considered it a colossal waste of money, while Sir Thomas Beecham, who was to go on and conduct at the Royal Festival Hall, called it "a monumental piece of imbecility". Noel Coward, in a song called "Don't Make Fun of the Fair" from the 1952 Lyric Revue, wrote,

Take a nip from your brandy flask,
Scream and caper and shout,
Don't give anyone time to ask
What the hell it's about.

Even sympathetic observers such as Michael Frayn, looking back on the Festival in the 1960s, edged their praise with criticism: "The tone of the Festival was not unlike the tone of the *News Chronicle*, which he [Gerald Barry, director of the Festival of Britain] had edited for eleven years – philanthropic, kindly, whimsical, cosy, optimistic, middlebrow…"

In riposte to these and other critics, Dylan Thomas's words, written in 1951 after a visit to the South Bank Exhibition, sum up the Festival's triumph:

Perhaps you will go on a cool, dull day, sane as a biscuit, and find
that the exhibition does, indeed, tell the story of "British contributions
to world civilization in the arts of peace", that, and nothing else.
But I'm pleased to doubt it. Of course it is instructive; of course
there is behind it an articulate and comprehensive plan; it can show
you, unless you are an expert, more about, say, mineralogy or the
ionosphere than you may want to know. It's bursting its buttons, in
an orderly manner, with knowledge. But what everyone I know, and
have observed, seems to like most in it is the gay, absurd, irrelevant,
delighting imagination that flies and booms and spurts and trickles
out of the whole bright boiling.

Opposite: At night, everything from the Skylon and Dome to the fountains were illuminated in the South Bank Exhibition.

Everybody complained the Royal Festival Hall was too dry, it was too unfriendly, but I thought that the Royal Festival Hall was always at least honest, and that is more than I could say about some other halls.
Mitsuko Uchida, pianist

3

A LONE BEACON

30 September 1951. It's the morning after the night before. An official procession headed by a marching band is making its way through the South Bank Exhibition, towards the Festival flagpole. People line the route, singing rousing choruses of "Auld Lang Syne" and "Abide with Me".

The day before had been the last chance to gaze up inside the Skylon, to marvel at the 365-foot aluminium Dome of Discovery, to sit in the Regatta restaurant and eat from plates whose designs were inspired by the latest scientific thinking. It was the last time to see the giant radio telescope and the Huskies in the Dome, the plaster doves flocking over the eccentric displays in the Lion and the Unicorn pavilion. The fountains with their gas lamps were about to fall silent; the rotating sculptures were about to cease turning.

As dusk had descended, and more and more people crowded on to the Fairway, the site was illuminated for the last time. Where people had danced spontaneously in their raincoats throughout the particularly wet summer of 1951, they now stood shoulder to shoulder, struggling for a glimpse of the star turn who was set to close the Festival. Women sat on their boyfriends' shoulders; all eyes were turned towards the open-air stage. As Gracie Fields stepped up to perform, people fainted in the tightly packed crowd.

Those who stayed the course could be found lingering on the Fairway well after midnight, as if reluctant to go home and accept that the Festival of Britain was really at an end. Official guests stood around in the Royal Pavilion, drinking champagne and reminiscing. Ministers patiently listened to everyone's opposing views as to what should be done with the temporary pavilions.

Only in the clear morning light of Sunday, with the band progressing towards the flagpole, did the glorious dream of the future really seem over. The band struck up the National Anthem and the Union flag was lowered. As the crowds dispersed, the only decision left to be made was what should happen to the south bank site now.

Above: The South Bank Exhibition at night, with the shot tower and Royal Festival Hall illuminated.
Previous page: A new poster is pasted on to a billboard by the entrance to the Royal Festival Hall in the 1950s.

The first thing that had to be done was the return of the 15,000 exhibits. While they were being removed, and the fixtures and fittings auctioned off, government officials debated the future of the south bank site. All the buildings, with the exception of the Royal Festival Hall, had been designed to stand for a single summer. But, following the success of the exhibition, Gerald Barry, the Festival's director, hoped the pavilions might stand for another year or so. Herbert Morrison, the Minister who had been so instrumental in ensuring the

Festival went ahead in the first place, assured Barry that he would be similarly employed for the following year, and the Festival's executive committee supported the idea that a second South Bank Exhibition should be held in 1952.

Other suggestions were also put forward as to the future of individual pavilions. The London County Council discussed moving the Dome and the Skylon to Crystal Palace; a New York realtor offered to cover the $1m shipping costs to move the two structures to America. The Marquess of Bath fancied rebuilding the Skylon at Longleat, his ancestral home, and the Arts Council were interested in using the Lion and the Unicorn pavilion as an art gallery.

So it is perhaps surprising that by spring 1952 plans had been made for the entire site – excluding the Royal Festival Hall – to be razed to the ground. The reason? Politics. In October 1951 a general election saw the Conservative Party come to power. The new Minister of Works, David Eccles, went on a tour of the South Bank Exhibition site, and told Barry in no uncertain terms what was to go. His official reason was that he was "unwilling to become the caretaker of empty and deteriorating structures", but closer to the truth is that the Conservatives wished to wash their hands of an exhibition that was so closely affiliated with Labour and socialism. Despite the offers to relocate certain buildings, Eccles only offered a stay of execution to the Riverside restaurant and the Telecinema. Demolition of the Dome, the Skylon, and all the other pavilions began in March 1952.

By June 1953, the Queen's coronation, little was left of the South Bank Exhibition. Tennis courts had been laid over the site of the Transport pavilion; the Dome's imprint had become a circular patch of grass. The

When I was 16 [1968], my Mum brought me to see *The Nutcracker* at the Royal Festival Hall. It was a big deal for us to be up in London at all – it didn't happen that often – but, despite us being an unbookish household, Mum clearly had a sense that there was a need for these cultural things, a need to get them under your belt, even if you weren't going to make use of them later in life. I remember this sense of it being delightful and "other", the thrill of being in a magical and mysterious place.
Andrew Motion, Poet Laureate

Left: An aerial view of the South Bank Exhibition site in 1952. A grassy footprint is all that remains of the Dome of Discovery.

renamed South Bank Gardens – the site of the present Jubilee Gardens – was an incoherent mix of turfed areas where buildings had once stood alongside some of the original plantings. The riverside walk remained, linking the Upstream and Downstream sites, and the Royal Festival Hall stood next to the shot tower, with the scale-model of the Great Exhibition's Crystal Palace in its shadow. The Telecinema stood at the Waterloo edge of the site. Everything else had gone.

Following the destruction of the South Bank Exhibition, the Royal Festival Hall was dubbed the first modernist public building in Britain. This wasn't strictly true – the coastal De La Warr pavilion, designed by Eric Mendelsohn and Serge Chermayeff, had opened in 1935 – but in its own way it did reflect a new English interpretation of the international movement. The exterior of the Royal Festival Hall as we see it now, with its 1960s extensions on the riverfront and facing Belvedere Road, may be in keeping with the rigorous ideals of modernism and its eschewing of ornament. But the original design, with its small staircase windows that punched holes in blue-and-white tiled facades, its hourglass lights and glass-lens walls, showed a strong interest in surface and texture. These features were sadly obliterated in the 1960s, but while they lasted they were representative of a certain Festival style – a particularly English attention to detail and an interest in pattern and colour that couldn't totally be repressed despite the overall modernist thrust of the building.

Whatever you thought of the exterior of the Royal Festival Hall, chances are you would have been impressed by its interior. Bernard Levin, a young journalist in 1951, remembered how the Royal Festival Hall captured the happiness that pervaded the whole south bank site during the Festival of Britain. "At the end of a concert, the audience could not bear to leave, to

Opposite: South Bank Gardens in July 1957.
Above left: Concert-goers leaving the Royal Festival Hall at night.
Above right: The Hungerford Bar (now the Green Bar), 1950s.
Below: 1951 illustration of the Ladies' Powder Room at the Royal Festival Hall.

Below, opposite right and opposite below: 1951 illustrations showing the Royal Festival Hall auditorium, foyer and musicians in a practice room.

go from this beauty and opulence into the drab world of post-war Britain, still exhausted, shabby and rationed; we wandered about the corridors and walkways, clearly determined to remain there all night. After a few days of this the attendants, dressed for the opening month of the new hall in resplendent red and green tail-coated uniforms, improvised a solution; they went to the top of the building, linked arms, and moved slowly down from level to level, very gently shepherding us all into the main foyer, and thence, even more gently, into the reality outside."

Few visitors to the Royal Festival Hall during the summer of 1951 would have realized that the hall was far from complete. Facing Belvedere Road was a ribbed asbestos wall, covered in hourglass lights. This wall was in fact a screen, hastily erected when Leslie Martin realized that his designs for a second auditorium and art gallery would have to be put on hold if the rest of the building were to be finished in time. But the book that was published to mark its inauguration, *The Royal Festival Hall: An Official Record*, with illustrations by Gordon Cullen, Donald Dewar Mills, Pearl Falconer, FHK Henrion and Joseph Mayo, included descriptions of these additional spaces. There was to have been a 750-seat venue for music recitals and plays, a 670-square metre art gallery, an orchestral rehearsal room with full-size stage and individual practice rooms.

The Royal Festival Hall had been built as a democratic space, which would not only serve all types of visitor but would also offer the broadest programme of arts events possible. From the outset, it wanted to host opera and dance as well as classical music, to stage popular music nights alongside exhibitions, films and amateur dramatics performances. The curtailing of Martin's plans for a second auditorium and gallery drastically reduced the hall's ability to do this. And so, as the Dome and Skylon were

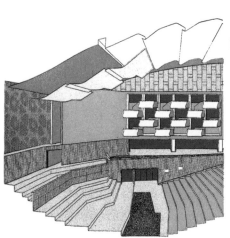

dismantled, Martin made plans to remove the temporary wall and finish the hall. However, there was to be no further building work on the south bank site for more than ten years.

Concerts at the Royal Festival Hall were a sell-out for the length of the Festival of Britain. But then the Festival was over. Ernest Bean, the hall's first general manager, remembered one critic summing up the venue's predicament: "Till now the concerts have been full," the critic opined. "But many seats have been sold to south bank visitors who merely wanted to sit down in comfort. What will happen now? The Festival closes tomorrow.

The hall remains, a giant, lone tree amid the waste."

Ernest Bean had reason to be worried by this critic's prediction. In the month after the South Bank Exhibition

closed, several concerts had to be cancelled due to poor ticket sales. The press picked up on this, and started seeing the Royal Festival Hall as a white elephant. Its location didn't help it, critics argued – who would cross from the "right side" of the river to hear any concert, no matter how good? Nowadays it is hard to imagine such watery prejudice holding sway, but the view of the south bank as being somehow "not London" was still prevalent in the 1950s. Bean, writing from the comfort of the 1960s when the Hall had proved it could draw one million people a year to its concerts, joked: "Could it be that the Hungerford bridge was the haunt of cut-throats and footpads? Were the waters of the Thames infested with Tsetse fly? Or were there more mundane explanations for the alleged immobility of the music-loving population domiciled in SW3?" The north-south divide was so firmly implanted in people's minds that advertisements and programmes emphasized the Royal Festival Hall's closeness to Charing Cross station on the north bank (the hall was nearer Waterloo) and carried the line "just across the Hungerford bridge".

Possibly to supplement its concert revenue in the early years, the Royal

Right: The queue for the Gas
Council's International Kitchens
Exhibition at the Royal Festival
Hall in November 1952.
Below, left to right: Royal
Festival Hall staff working in the
kitchens, box office, food stores,
wine cellar, front of house and
cashiers' office.

Festival Hall became a venue associated with temporary exhibitions
as well as classical performances. In November 1952, people queued for
hours to visit the Gas Council's International Kitchens Exhibition. Others
visited the hall to attend Wren reunions or fashion shows, corporate
functions or the Polish farmers' harvest ball. The ballroom – the largest
dance floor in London – was often in service, but the only thing it seems
you couldn't do on it with any regularity was dance. Excepting private
events and the annual New Year's Eve Ball, held until 1960, there was no
public dancing held in the hall at this time.

Only with the "Open Foyer" programme of 1983 did the dancing policy
change. For over twenty years the Royal Festival Hall has been open to
the public for at least twelve hours a day, seven days a week. But in the
1950s it was closed until 17.30 unless there was a special exhibition or
event being staged there. However, there were still plenty of staff on site
during the day, from the cashiers and box-office staff to the chefs and

kitchen workforce. The hall had its own four-strong fire crew, and a team of men who looked after the gas-fired boilers. There was even someone in the hall 24 hours a day, as the chief engineer had a flat on the top floor.

Everyone worked towards the few hours a night when audiences were in the building. The public arrived for everything from world premieres by Igor Stravinsky and Benjamin Britten to Festival Ballet seasons and Frank Sinatra nights, all experienced in the wood-panelled interior of the auditorium. Bernard Levin encapsulates what it must have been like to enter for the first time: "The glittering brightness of the Festival Hall, and the lavish use of space in its interior, the beauty of the shining new wood, metal, marble, the explosive shock of the brand-new auditorium, with those boxes that look like half-opened drawers and the pale beauty of the sycamore [sic] baffle over the orchestra – that experience has taken its place for me beside the first intoxicated tastings of the music itself."

Levin remembers that an "ethereal gong", tuned to concert-pitch A, enticed audiences into their seats. Chairs designed by Robin Day filled the steeply banked hall, and all offered a clear view of the open stage. The canopy above the orchestra gave way to a gently undulating plaster ceiling, both designed to enhance acoustics. Between the stalls seats and the stage a slate floor reflected sound into the audience, as did the wooden panels that lined the walls. Heavy red curtains hung behind the boxes, and doors of padded red leather ensured that sound seeped neither out nor in.

Some critics complained that orchestras sounded "dry" in the space, that there wasn't enough "fullness" to the tone. Ralph Downes, the Royal Festival Hall's organ consultant, attended an early acoustic test and recalled in his autobiography, "The experience was dire: timpani, played fortissimo, were almost reminiscent of those large, square Jacobs' biscuit-tins! Inwardly, though I groaned as a musician, I breathed a

Above: The impressive colour-coded boiler room.

fervent prayer of thanksgiving that it was not the organ but an orchestra that we had to hear first in this astounding ambience." The organ wasn't inaugurated until 1954 [see panel, right], and Downes continued to conduct his own acoustic tests with sample organ pipes throughout 1951 and 1952, but the hall had to open on time.

Publisher Victor Gollancz, an avid concert-goer, remembers his first visit in 1951: "The place seemed horribly raw; there was no atmosphere, no 'smell' (literally as well as metaphorically) about it…" Gollancz even said as much to Hope Bagenal, the hall's acoustician: "We told Hope Bagenal, who had been responsible for them [the acoustics], and whom my wife had known well when a student at the Architectural Association, that he ought to be ashamed of himself, or milder words to that effect. (For a first go, he had in fact done wonderfully.)"

Bagenal had made the best he could of an over-absorbent hall, but audiences complained of "dryness" and performers said they just couldn't

Right: The auditorium in 1966, with the organ pipes revealed.

It was my first ever concert, and it was in the Festival Hall. Seated with my parents, and aged about seven – it must have been 1967 – vivid recollections of that evening have stayed with me ever since. I had never before seen an orchestra and consequently the rituals of a concert were entirely new to me. I naturally assumed that the strange, complicated sound made by the musicians when they first appeared on stage was the opening piece, until it was explained to me that they were merely *tuning up*. I do recall, however, two actual works in that evening's programme. One was Bax's tone-poem "Tintagel", whose depiction of a storm excited me, but the other made a much deeper impression – Debussy's "L'après-midi d'un faune". The sound of that piece affected me almost physically, and I felt as if the temperature in the hall had risen several degrees.
George Benjamin, composer

THE ROYAL FESTIVAL HALL ORGAN, DESIGNED BY RALPH DOWNES

In 1948, Ralph Downes [right] was appointed as the Royal Festival Hall's organ consultant. He was renowned as an organist, and had previously been organ consultant at the Brompton Oratory, London's second-largest Roman Catholic church. He was also an advocate of Organ Reform, a movement which favoured the return of the seventeenth-century classical model, with its emphasis on clarity and brilliance of tone. It was worthy of being played as a solo instrument, Downes argued, unlike the Victorian organs with their broad, orchestral range that were currently in vogue. The Royal Festival Hall organ, designed by Downes, was to become the first example of Organ Reform in Britain.

Early on it was realized that the organ wouldn't be in place by 1951. With the shortage of materials, Harrison & Harrison – the Durham firm who had won the tender to build it – could not guarantee completion in time. Downes pushed on with his design [below right, his first sketch] for a sizeable organ that used controversial French-type reeds to ensure a natural, unforced sound. The pipes – 7,710 of them – were to be ranged across the entire width of the stage to compensate for the relatively low ceiling (compared to a church).

Downes's design had to change many times, and several uneasy compromises had to be agreed. With the addition of the orchestral canopy, Downes fumed that some pipes would have to be lopped in half or the whole thing rethought. Eventually he reordered the pipes and the canopy was raised.

It wasn't until 1952, when much of the organ had been built, that the frontage was agreed. Harrisons suggested covering up the pipes so they could be arranged the better to suit their tone. However Isaac Hayward, leader of the London County Council, wanted to see all the pipes arranged in decorative order (they had cost enough, he reasoned). Eventually the deadlock was broken by Leslie Martin, who designed a fantasy frontispiece of "fake" pipes. The functioning pipes were then laid out behind in tonal clusters. Stops on the organ's console controlled which pipes were used at any one time, with two blowers providing them with air.

The finished organ has five manual divisions – Great, Positive, Swell, Choir and Solo – controlled by four keyboards on the console, with a separate pedal keyboard played with the feet. It cost £51,500 – roughly £5m today – and was inaugurated on 24 March 1954 with a broad programme of Bach, Poulenc, Bliss, Handel and Elgar, played by André Marchal and Downes himself. Praised by most critics, the "King of Instruments" was played to packed houses every Wednesday evening until 1989. (The concerts were revived in 2000.) Its stand-alone quality led to an international series of recitals that attracted organists from all over the world, and it is regularly played to accompany orchestras.

The organ was included in the Royal Festival Hall's Grade I listing in April 1988, and was part restored by Harrison & Harrison in 2000, under the guidance of the current organ consultant, William McVicker. During the 2005-07 hall refurbishment, the organ chamber was cleared out and McVicker found a dusty pair of Downes's shoes tucked inside. While the organ was fine-tuned to ensure that it maintained its tone despite the changes being made to the auditorium's acoustics, McVicker kept the shoes in his desk drawer. They are now safely back in place, a tribute to the man who created such a unique organ.

hear each other on stage, which made it difficult to work together. Sir Thomas Beecham was very rude about the hall, saying it was "like a disused mining shack in Nevada. Frivolous and acoustically imperfect." However, this didn't stop him conducting in the hall many times before his death in 1961. Nor did it stop other giants of the conducting world such as Herbert von Karajan, Pierre Monteux and Otto Klemperer. Even Gollancz was left breathless after Klemperer's Beethoven performances with the London Philharmonia, saying, "I doubt whether they have been equalled in the whole history of musical interpretation."

The people who probably didn't worry about whether the sound quality was dry were those who attended the children's concerts. Costing half a crown, the Ernest Read and Robert Mayer children's concerts were held on Saturday mornings throughout the 1950s and 1960s. They were often broadcast nationally, and introduced a whole generation of schoolchildren to classical music.

Despite the early problems for orchestras in the auditorium, everyone agreed that chamber music fared much better there. One of the first concerts given in the hall, on 5 May 1951, was a sold-out violin sonata recital by Yehudi and Hephzibah Menuhin, in which the hall delivered such clarity that there wasn't a bad seat in the house. It was in the Royal Festival Hall that a thirteen-year-old Daniel Barenboim later made his debut as a pianist, in 1956, and where other pianists including Clara Haskil, Artur Rubenstein, Benedetti Michelangeli and Sviatoslav Richter chose to perform as part of world tours.

Despite its "dry" acoustics, many thought that the Royal Festival Hall was one of the best concert halls in the world. It hosted truly memorable

Above: Billboard posters advertising forthcoming concerts.
Right: A packed house for a children's concert in 1951.
Opposite: 1951 illustration of the Royal Festival Hall's cantilevered boxes.

Above: A Festival Ballet tutu is examined by the wardrobe mistress.
Below: Festival Ballet dancers prepare for a rehearsal at the Royal Festival Hall.

nights, such as when poet Edith Sitwell – dressed in her trademark flowing robes – recited the text she had written for William Walton's *Facade* in 1952, and when Stravinsky conducted his own *Oedipus Rex* in 1959 with Jean Cocteau, the work's librettist, as the narrator.

But the Royal Festival Hall wasn't only about classical music, and the 1950s and 1960s saw many jazz legends take the stage, including Louis Armstrong, Ella Fitzgerald, Fats Domino and Dave Brubeck. At a time when an album by these musicians could cost more than forty shillings, the seat price of twenty shillings meant these were sell-out concerts. Although the auditorium wasn't suitable for pop acts such as the Beatles (because anyone could climb on to the stage), other big names did sing there, including Maria Callas, Gene Kelly and Frank Sinatra. Sinatra would be driven to the artists' entrance at top speed, tyres screeching, and bundled in, bodyguards surrounding him, practising for only a matter of minutes in the small recital room on level five before performing. When Callas sang in 1962, the queue for tickets stretched right around the building. Gollancz remembers seeing her perform the waltz song from *La Bohème* with "such an outpouring of youthful vitality, such freshness and such warmth, that you might have been hearing it, not for the tenth or hundredth time, but as it came newly born from the heart and mind of its composer." On Callas's birthday on 2 December 1964, following her concert at the Royal Festival Hall, the orchestra struck up "Happy

Birthday" by way of an encore, and the entire audience sang to her.

In the summer months and over the Christmas period, all concerts would cease as the Festival Ballet (later called the English National Ballet) season opened. It would take four days to transform the stage to make it suitable for ballet, and even then the company had to work without the traditional proscenium arch, wings or fly tower (and therefore no vertical scenery changes). Because the second, smaller auditorium hadn't been built, during this time it was not possible to host concerts, or even allow orchestras to rehearse anywhere in the hall, day or night.

Leslie Martin continued to request permission to add the planned second auditorium to the Royal Festival Hall but, since the hall had opened, the road running alongside it, Belvedere Road, had been relaid, and this had reduced the size of the available plot. The hall couldn't be sunk into the ground as the Northern line ran underneath and, in addition to this, there was no money available. The London County Council had been relying on revenue from the government's Ministry of Works, who were to lease the Upstream site for new offices. But the Korean war and a change in leadership took the proposal back to the drawing board, with a deadlock on rates.

The London County Council then started to look around for new potential partners. British European Airways had already established themselves on the Upstream site, in the former Waterloo Gate building, where they had opened an express check-in service for customers flying from Heathrow. But this was small change – the London County Council needed someone who wanted acres of land, not a few square metres. And so negotiations opened with Shell. Shell not only wanted several acres of the Upstream site on which to build a 26-storey office block, they wanted part of the Downstream site too: the British Film Institute, currently occupying the Telecinema, would have to be rehoused (the National Film Theatre opened under Waterloo bridge in 1958). A deal was struck and, ten years after negotiations had begun, the Shell centre – built by Sir Howard Robertson and R Maynard Smith and home to 5,000 employees – opened in 1963.

Meanwhile, other arts venues were planned for the south bank. An opera house had been designed – first by Brian O'Rorke and then Denys Lasdun – to stand near the proposed National Theatre, but it was never realized. In 1966 a new site beyond Waterloo bridge was finally agreed upon for the National Theatre and Lasdun set to work on new plans, although it would be ten years before the theatre opened.

Leslie Martin left the London County Council a decade before the Queen Elizabeth Hall, the de facto second auditorium, opened in 1967.

One of my first jobs was at the COI, the Central Office of Information, which was just round the back of the Hayward site, just by Lambeth North railway station. I spent about six or seven years there cutting documentary films, so it was my sort of stamping ground for subject matter, and I think the very first film I ever made was looking out the back window of the COI over the south bank and watching the trains going in and out of Waterloo station [*Train*, 1966]. And I remember when the Hayward was being built, there was a big, big tree, abandoned – poor tree – squashed in among all the concrete, next to the Royal Festival Hall, and I think the second or the third film I ever made [*Tree*, 1966] was about this tree, about organic vegetation being crushed by ubiquitous concrete. So it was significant. In a sense, there was a prelude, in this curious location, concerned with "Spellbound" [an exhibition at the Hayward, 1996] because I used to know the area so very, very well.
Peter Greenaway, filmmaker and artist

Above: Workers improve facilities as the Royal Festival Hall is extended in 1964. Below: The newly extended Royal Festival Hall in October 1965.

The plan to extend the Royal Festival Hall had been reduced to enlarging the restaurant facing the river, and to replacing the temporary cladding facing Belvedere Road with a nine-metre extension that would finally provide adequate dressing rooms and rehearsal space for performers. The building's orientation was changed by moving the main entrance to the riverside walkway, with an entrance directly below for car passengers. The original entrance facing Waterloo bridge at ground level was partially blocked off, and a vital aspect of the 1951 design – the slow unfolding of the building – was lost.

Work began on the Royal Festival Hall expansion in 1962, and in June 1964 the building closed to the public for eight months to allow for it to be completed. The shot tower was demolished to make way for the Hayward, Queen Elizabeth Hall and Purcell Room (see chapters four and five) and hoardings surrounded the site. The south bank was a quagmire once again.

Slowly the extensions rose from the mud, windows on the original building were bricked in and Portland stone covered the joins. An all-day café was added at ground level, with direct access from the road beneath Riverside Terrace. This led to the closure of the Riverside restaurant, built for the Festival of Britain and the final piece of the South Bank

Exhibition to go. With the opening of the self-service cafeteria and the beginnings of an exhibition programme for the ballroom, the hall started to open up during the day. But access was limited, and irregular.

The opportunity to improve the auditorium's acoustics was taken and Hope Bagenal returned as acoustic consultant. Helmholtz resonators were placed in the ceiling to try to address the reverberation issues, and electro-acoustics were introduced. Richard Baker remembers holding a Helmholtz resonator in his hand as he reported on the reopening of the Royal Festival Hall for BBC Television, on 1 February 1965. The London Symphony Orchestra, conducted by Colin Davis and featuring the acclaimed pianist Rudolf Serkin, launched into an international mix of Wagner, Brahms and Berlioz. The programme featured no English composers – unlike the inaugural concert in 1951 – as if to assert that the Royal Festival Hall was now, finally, an international concert hall.

Much of the original design detail was lost during the 1962–65 refurbishment and expansion. Some original fixtures and fittings were taken out, many of Robin Day's chairs were replaced with ill-designed substitutes and Peter Moro's "net and ball" carpet was in part replaced by a dizzying swirling design. The new extensions added extra mezzanine levels to the hall, and reorientating the entrance meant the carefully planned opening up of the building had been lost. But the walkways surrounding the hall had been extended in line with the original plan for the building to separate pedestrians from vehicles, and the acoustics had, it was agreed, been improved.

Walkways continued to be built after the Royal Festival Hall reopened in anticipation of the Hayward, Queen Elizabeth Hall and Purcell Room. Eventually they snaked across the whole site, providing direct pedestrian access from Waterloo station and both the Waterloo and Hungerford bridges. While the iron and bronze lampposts erected on the riverside walk at this time harked back to the nineteenth century (faithful copies of the dolphin design that ran the length of the embankment further upstream), the walkways looked to the future. Boarded-concrete pillars with mushroom supports held up solid paths with thick concrete balustrades, and cast staircases linked them with the roads beneath. The original glass panels that lined the walkways in front of the Royal Festival Hall, allowing for the river to be seen from within the building, were replaced. The brutal power of concrete in all its raw natural glory was unleashed on the south bank.

Above: A Brutalist stairwell from 1967 that connected the new network of walkways around the Queen Elizabeth Hall with ground level.

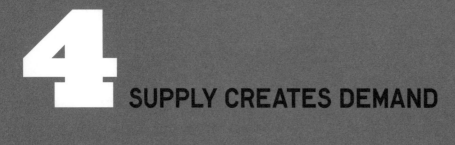

4 SUPPLY CREATES DEMAND

1 December 2006. The ten-minute bell rings in the foyer of the Queen Elizabeth Hall. The bar and café in the recently refurbished entrance are packed and, as the audience files in to the sharply raked auditorium, it is clear that the show is a sell-out. It's the final night of a nationwide tour of Revelations *by dance company Stan Won't Dance, artists in residence at Southbank Centre since 2004.*

Stan Won't Dance was founded by creative arts producer Ellie Beedham in collaboration with Liam Steel and Rob Tannion, two former DV8 dancers. Their first show, Sinner, *a small-scale work performed by the two men, was premiered at Southbank Centre in the Purcell Room in May 2004. It was an immediate success, with critics hailing Stan Won't Dance as the "best thing to happen to British physical theatre since DV8".* Sinner's *success – it toured for a year – led to* Revelations, *a more ambitious performance for seven dancers directed by Steel in the larger venue, the Queen Elizabeth Hall. It is six weeks since* Revelations *opened at Laban in London and embarked on a national tour. Despite mixed reviews, there is a crackle of excitement in the bar before tonight's performance. In Sarah Frater's review, in the day's* Evening Standard, *she says: "There are some fearsomely physical dance sequences, some excellent, as is the idea that a self-destruct impulse means we crush what we love."*

There's no curtain on stage, and the tubular set is already lit. Fragments of news stories play on a small television in a skewed kitchen that will soon see leather-clad apocalyptic angels burst out of the fridge and scuttle through the oven. A clock has stopped; the time is 6.06.

Getting to the Purcell Room is always something of an odyssey. The organizers usually send a car to pick up readers for Poetry International, but the drivers never know which door, or even which barrier, to head for. On at least three occasions I've had to get out on some poorly-lit service road and push through the wheelie bins looking for an entrance. I once bumped into Simon Callow who was trying to find the National Theatre. For all I know the whole complex might be littered with the skeletons of poets and actors who have become lost once and for all.

Simon Armitage, novelist and poet

Exposed lighting rigs hang over the audience. As at the Royal Festival Hall this is an open stage, with no wings, no proscenium arch, no fly tower. Because of this it is not a forgiving space to perform in but, for the audience, it means there's nothing to obstruct your view, wherever you sit.

The Queen Elizabeth Hall wasn't originally built to accommodate contemporary dance, and the stage was only modified to allow dance and operatic performances in 1987. Consequently, there's no wardrobe department, or proper scenery store. But this doesn't matter, as Tannion, Steel and five additional dancers acrobatically climb and swing their way over the set, singing, acting, pole-dancing and fighting for 90 minutes.

And then the performance is over. The audience make their way out into the bar. Some push through the heavy entrance doors and follow the brightly lit walkway in front of the Royal Festival Hall where artist David Batchelor's Christmas lights have just been switched on. The dancers are backstage, wriggling out of their leather costumes. It will be 1.30 before the Stan Won't Dance founders and production crew finish de-rigging the set, loading it into their cars for the last time. Already they are thinking about their next Southbank Centre commission, a complex outdoor piece for the following summer.

Opposite: Sonja Perreten and Rob Tannion in *Revelations* by Stan Won't Dance, directed by Liam Steel.
Previous page: Benjamin Britten rehearsing for the opening concert at the Queen Elizabeth Hall in March 1967, with the English Chamber Orchestra.

I n 1955, the London County Council took the decision to build a second concert hall on the south bank, independent of the Royal Festival Hall, and an art gallery (for a history of the Hayward, see chapter five). Leslie Martin had already left the London County Council when the first designs for the new arts venues by Norman Engleback were completed in 1957, but he had been involved in their conception. It was immediately apparent that the latest trends in architectural thinking were reflected in the design, with its emphasis on cast concrete and monumental solidity. Brutalism had reached the south bank [see panel on page 88].

For those critical of the Queen Elizabeth Hall's architecture, it is worth noting that the original brief for the project came with fairly stringent clauses. It was not to block the view of St Paul's Cathedral from the Royal Festival Hall's terraces, and it was not to challenge the larger hall's visual domination of the site. However, even before it was built, some had their doubts about its Brutalist design. Hubert Bennett, who took over from Martin as the London County Council's chief architect, was not an initial supporter and wanted to bring the Queen Elizabeth Hall more in line with the Royal Festival Hall. Only the threat of mass-resignation by Engleback and his team – many of whom went on to work for the maverick architectural practice Archigram – kept the design in place. Bennett

did succeed in modifying the exterior in one significant way – pre-cast aggregate panels were used instead of board-cast concrete. (Many of the concrete stairwells, including those inside the Hayward, were board-cast, as was the foyer's ceiling. You can see the wood grain imprinted in the surface and the vertical joins where the planks butted up to each other.)

There was another reason why 40-centimetre thick concrete walls were seen as an asset for the Queen Elizabeth Hall. The London County Council (which became the Greater London Council in 1965) had recently

granted permission for aeroplanes to use the Thames as a test flight path, and there was even talk of a heliport being placed on Waterloo station. Although noise regulations eventually prevented a helicopter service being launched, at the time the hall was conceived it looked as if it might well come into being.

The final design was ready by 1959 although, two years later, it was revisited once more when it was decided that a small recital room included in the plans should be doubled in size. The 370-seat Purcell Room, named after the seventeenth-century English composer Henry Purcell, was added, and the contract to build the two auditoria was finally put out to tender in 1963. The Queen Elizabeth Hall and Purcell Room opened in March 1967, at a cost of £2.7m.

Above: The Brutalist entrance of the Queen Elizabeth Hall and Purcell Room.

The Queen Elizabeth Hall was designed with a single tier of steeply raked seating. (Construction photographs show the extent of this, and reveal why there are no sightline issues in the hall.) Bennett had managed to change the decision to have concrete Helmholtz resonators lining the Queen Elizabeth Hall, and wooden ones were installed instead. The concrete structure of the foyer was in part hidden by crystalline white Macedonian marble which stretched across the floor and half-way up the walls. The ribbon windows and glass entrance doors were made with heavy aluminium frames, their rough surface anodized to turn them brownish-purple.

Right and opposite: The futuristic foyer, shared by the Queen Elizabeth Hall and Purcell Room, in 1967.

One of the key elements of both the Queen Elizabeth Hall and the Purcell Room was that their interiors were seen, or at least hinted at, from outside. Both auditoria stood in their own separate buildings, linked by concrete corridors to a shared foyer. A roof terrace, accessed from an external staircase near the main doors, extended above, and was linked to one of the Hayward's sculpture courts via a walkway. Below, an undercroft (now frequented by skateboarders) led to a street-level entrance for car passengers, which opened on to a staircase leading to the foyer.

Despite the six pairs of doors on Riverside Terrace, the entrance was rather overwhelmed by the hulking concrete that massed all around it. But once inside, all sense of density and bulk disappeared. The foyer was a bright, open space. Tall mushroom pillars supported the roof, where ceiling lighting, hidden behind strange asymmetrical protrusions, illuminated the white marble floor. Scattered around were circular black leather seats supported on translucent bases so that they seemed to float like flying saucers across the floor. There was no café, but interval coffees could be pre-ordered at a trestle table located between the pillars.

Above: The Purcell Room in 1979.

Both the Queen Elizabeth Hall and Purcell Room audiences shared the foyer, and all efforts were made to stagger start times and intervals so as to avoid confusion when audiences were asked to take their seats. The Queen Elizabeth Hall was reached using broad corridors either side of the entrance, and the right-hand corridor extended further to provide access to the smaller Purcell Room which stands perpendicular to the Queen Elizabeth Hall. (The gently raked seating of the Purcell Room is

cantilevered out over the road below and the concrete wall demarcating
the back of the hall faces the entrance to the Hayward.)

Both halls share the backstage area and artists' entrance. At the
time of opening these facilities were seen by some reviewers as almost
luxurious, offering as they did the only carpeted areas in the whole
building. The artists' bar – a squeeze for the orchestras who recently used
the Queen Elizabeth Hall when the Royal Festival Hall was refurbished in
2005-07 – was designed to accommodate chamber groups, and led directly
to the dressing rooms. A grand piano, one of five in the building, sat in the
green room. This must often have been filled with musicians warming
up and practising, as there are no dedicated practice rooms. Some solo
performers would practise in the Purcell Room during the day; others
preferred to use their modest dressing rooms.

A door opposite the main dressing rooms led to the Queen Elizabeth
Hall stage. The larger hall seated 1,106 when it opened, and was designed
for chamber music and contemporary recitals (for access and safety
reasons, it currently seats 917). After the acoustic problems of the
Royal Festival Hall, attention was paid to the absorbency of materials
used in the auditorium (there is no carpet, for example), and Helmholtz
resonators were fitted in the walls from the outset to control low-level
frequencies. A low stage and a single bank of seats offered performers
an intimacy that was lacking in the Royal Festival Hall, and it was more
technologically advanced, with a thirteen-piece stage that could be moved
electrically into different configurations. A chamber organ with one pedal
and two manuals, designed by DA Flentrop in conjunction with Ralph
Downes, could be raised from a sealed organ store below, and one piece
of the platform could be lowered to the piano store underneath, so heavy
instruments could be lifted directly on to the stage. (At the Royal Festival
Hall at the time, pianos had to be rolled into the auditorium then hoisted
on to the stage. On one occasion, as a piano was being removed during an
interval, it rolled over an audience member's leg, breaking it.)

On 1 March 1967, the Queen Elizabeth Hall and Purcell Room were
declared open by Her Majesty Queen Elizabeth II. She was taken on a
tour, shown a model of Southbank Centre and attended a short concert.
Whether the tour overran, or the Queen had been held up by a prior
engagement, broadcaster Richard Baker remembers that the Queen was
late taking her seat in the royal box for the concert. He was providing
live BBC coverage, and fortunately had prepared for such an eventuality.
But he was pleased when she arrived, as he recalls: "I had been reduced
to talking about the aluminium used in the construction of the seats
and the fact that the same material was used for the dust-carts of the

Top and opposite: The Queen
Elizabeth Hall in 1979, with the
stage set for a chamber group
and, top, an organ recital.
Above: HM Queen Elizabeth II
studies the model of Southbank
Centre with Sir Hubert Bennett,
the London County Council's
chief architect, before opening
the Queen Elizabeth Hall on
1 March 1967.

BRUTALISM

The Hayward, Queen Elizabeth Hall and Purcell Room [above] are seen as exemplifying Brutalism, an international architectural movement of the 1960s and 1970s. It is characterised by a heavy-handed use of concrete, and can be traced back to Le Corbusier who, since the 1930s, had been working in new ways with the material.

Le Corbusier manipulated exposed concrete panels to create a stippled effect, and made visible the casting technique by using wooden boards that left their grain imprinted on the rough grey surface. This was known as *breton brut* (raw concrete), and the *brut* could be seen as connecting with the term Brutalism. However, the name is credited to the design critic Reyner Banham, who used it first in 1955 to describe the work of young architects Peter and Alison Smithson.

The Smithsons won a competition to design Hunstanton School in Norfolk while still in their twenties, and used the commission to design a school that reflected their aim to make honest buildings for a Welfare State society. Although controversial when it opened, the skeletal glass and steel structures established the Smithsons' reputation as leading British architects. A year later, Banham dubbed them Brutalists, and the term stuck. Supposedly he had come up with the name in part inspired by Peter's university nickname, Brutus. Architects at the time joked: "Brutalism equals Brutus plus Alison". But the name had a certain harshness to it, a brutality, and although the Smithsons used a variety of materials in their work it came to be associated with the increasingly heavy concrete forms that were built in the 1960s.

All the buildings on the south bank that opened in 1967-68 are predominantly concrete. A mix of boarded concrete and pre-cast concrete panels comprise their blocky exteriors. There are few windows, and those that exist are often hidden away: recessed or giving on to an internal courtyard at the Queen Elizabeth Hall; set in as skylights at the Hayward. Even the doors are mere slits in the original concrete facades.

A core belief of Brutalism was a truth to materials, and the concrete forms of the south bank have an appropriate solidity and density to them. It is easy to see these shapes, thrust together like children's building blocks, as an arbitrary arrangement. But look closer and you can start to "read" them. The architects were honest to the internal structure of the building – from the outside you can see the outline of the foyer, the Queen Elizabeth Hall and the Purcell Room auditoria. You can see they are three separate buildings, and you can make out the corridors that link them, the plant room above, even the ducts ferrying air between them. This exposure of internal structure is in stark contrast to the sleek lines of the 1951 Royal Festival Hall, but follows in the footsteps of the 1950s buildings by the Smithsons. (It was to ultimately lead to the inside-out buildings of Richard Rogers in the 1970s, notably the Pompidou Centre, Paris, and Lloyds of London.)

Other examples of Brutalist architecture include the Smithsons' Robin Hood Gardens housing estate in East London – a failed attempt to improve on earlier housing models – and Basil Spence's now demolished tower blocks in the Gorbals, Glasgow. However, despite the many problems associated with the style, it has recently enjoyed a renaissance. Former council flats in Erno Goldfinger's Trellick Tower (completed in 1972) now exchange hands for substantial sums of money, and the 2,000 flats in the Barbican Estate's three tower blocks, built by Chamberlain, Powell and Bonn in 1969, are seen as highly desirable places to live.

Greater London Council." The first public concert, the following day, was an extended version of the programme heard by the Queen. The English Chamber Orchestra was conducted by Benjamin Britten and Sir Arthur Bliss, and the concert featured a new work for voices by Bliss, commissioned for the occasion, called *River Music 1967.*

On the whole, when the venue opened, critics initially focused not on the acoustics but on the internal and external architecture. HAN Brockman, architectural correspondent of the *Financial Times*, felt there was a lack of integration between the new venues, the Royal Festival Hall and the Shell offices. While he admired the "intimacy" of the Purcell Room, claiming "an interior such as this could hardly be bettered for listening to serious music", he felt that the concrete and pale wood panelling of the Queen Elizabeth Hall meant that it lacked warmth. In conclusion, he berated the fact that the building had been designed by committee: "In the case of highly specialized public buildings of prestige value such as this, the mark of individual inspiration is essential to the creation of consistent character and detailing throughout." Adam Lynford, writing in the *Illustrated London News*, likened the exterior to a "nuclear-bomb shelter". The public were not impressed either, and in October 1967 *Daily Mail* readers voted the Queen Elizabeth Hall "Britain's Ugliest Building".

The most striking feature of the new concert halls and gallery in photographs, as we look back from the twenty-first century, must be the colour of the concrete. We are used to the buildings being a streaked dun colour, stained by decades of rain and weathered by the winds that whipped around the walkways. But when they opened 40 years ago,

Above: Album cover for an Aram Khachaturian concerto recorded in 1967 at Southbank Centre.
Below: A 1968 aerial view reveals that the concrete used for the Hayward, Queen Elizabeth Hall and Purcell Room initially toned with the stone-clad Royal Festival Hall.

Below: An Opera Factory
performance at the Queen
Elizabeth Hall in August 1987.

corners were crisp, elevations well-defined and the concrete was pale grey, a contemporary approximation of the cool Portland stone of the Royal Festival Hall. The colour was described by Brockman in the *Financial Times* as "neutral grey", although he was the first to realize that the complex wouldn't stay this way for long, now it was exposed to the elements.

With the addition of the Queen Elizabeth Hall and Purcell Room, the south bank could now offer a far wider range of music than before. The halls were known collectively as South Bank Concert Halls, and could accommodate every type of performer. Chamber orchestras such as the London Mozart Players continued to play at the Royal Festival Hall as they had a large and loyal following, but other chamber groups chose to play in the more intimate surroundings of the Queen Elizabeth Hall, where there was more connection between performers and audience. Prior to the Queen Elizabeth Hall opening, soloists or groups had to choose between the 3,000-seat auditorium of the Royal Festival Hall, or the 540-seat Wigmore Hall. London could offer no middle-sized venue. John Denison, general manager of the newly affiliated South Bank Concert Halls, told the press that he hoped the new venues would allow audiences to become acquainted with the music of the Middle Ages, Renaissance

and early Baroque, with French and English song, and with the best of modern music. William Mann, music critic for *The Times*, mentioned that the Queen Elizabeth Hall was fitted with "many-channelled stereophonic amplification", making it suitable for "electrically reproduced sounds", and concluded: "There is certainly plenty of use for these two new halls – they duplicate no other. Mr Denison has given the two new halls their most encouraging motto of justification: 'supply creates demand'." However, he warned: "One must add that the demand depends on the known quality of the supply. A preponderance of dud concerts would quickly render the two new halls redundant. It is up to concert-goers, and the general manager, to make sure that South Bank Concert Halls remain dedicated to first-rate musical performance."

Right from the outset, the Queen Elizabeth Hall and Purcell Room have been associated with some legendary concerts and series. Pink Floyd played at the Queen Elizabeth Hall two months after it opened, on 12 May 1967. They were there just after their first album, *The Piper at the Gates of Dawn*, had been released, at a time when they were touring the country gigging at clubs and town halls (after their south bank gig, they made their way up to Hinckley in Leicestershire to play at St George's Ballroom the following night).

The South Bank Summer Music festival, founded in 1968 by Denison, started out as a bid to find something to programme while the Proms were on. (The Royal Festival Hall held a Festival Ballet summer season.) Denison asked 26-year-old Daniel Barenboim to commission a two-week festival of chamber music. Barenboim called in his friends and family – his wife, the cellist Jacqueline du Pré, took part – and it was a huge success. Over the years all manner of international artists directed it, from André Previn to Sir Simon Rattle.

More recently, the Queen Elizabeth Hall has been a central venue for the London Jazz Festival, Dance Umbrella and Southbank Centre's own Meltdown [see chapter seven]. In the late 1980s and 1990s, operatic companies used the newly improved stage to put on productions that even had their own orchestra in a makeshift pit. Both venues regularly host Southbank Centre's associated artists – the Orchestra of the Age of Enlightenment, London Sinfonietta, Takács Quartet, The Sixteen – as well as its artists in residence such as Stan Won't Dance and Saint Etienne.

While musical programming in the Queen Elizabeth Hall and Purcell Room may have a rich and respected history, the same cannot be said for the interior decoration. Just a year after the Queen Elizabeth Hall and Purcell Room opened, their joint foyer was carpeted. The white marble floor was seen as too cold and unwelcoming, and so it was covered over.

Alistair Spalding, during the years that he was responsible for dance [at Southbank Centre], saw Alain Platel's work and fell in love with it. The only problem was that there was no space left in the Queen Elizabeth Hall that season and we had to stop touring that particular production (*Bonjour Madame*) because the new one was coming out soon – and for the first time was commissioned with real money – so it was then or never. Alistair had this excellent idea: there is no space *in* the Queen Elizabeth Hall but there is *above*, and so we performed three times on the roof. The entrance fee was £1 and guess what? It only rained two times out of three!
Lieven Thyrion and Alain Platel, Les Ballets C de la B

Above: An attempt to make the entrance more attractive led to the addition of awnings, flags and whitewashed stairs.

When I was young my overall career wasn't sensational at all, it rather progressed step by step. But then, one day I was performing a Beethoven programme in the Queen Elizabeth Hall. It was quite an unpopular programme. I didn't even like it much myself and the next day I got three offers from record companies. It seemed really rather grotesque, like a slow hardly noticeable rise on a thermometer or a kettle warming water suddenly beginning to boil and to bubble and the steam comes out.
Alfred Brendel, pianist

In 1978 the stark beauty of the original design was further marred, thanks to the arrival of a brown chevron carpet, a platoon of tan leather seats and a regiment of rubber plants. It was only in 1986 that Nicholas Snowman, the incumbent general director (arts) of the newly formed Southbank Centre, suggested the carpet be ripped up and the marble floor revealed. Unfortunately, the floor quickly became all but invisible under a battalion of ornate garden furniture, which seems to have marched on to Southbank Centre one night and set up camp both outside the Royal Festival Hall and inside the Queen Elizabeth Hall. Externally, flagpoles, a frilly awning, a whitewashed set of external stairs and advertising hoardings must have been added with the idea of making the hall look more welcoming, but succeeded only in making the whole place look a bit of a mess.

Nowadays the carpet, awning, garden furniture and pot plants are only memories. In September 2006 the foyer was refurbished, adding two new permanent venues, The Front Room and The Soft Space. The Front Room is a performance space with a stage that can accommodate a grand piano. Anyone walking into the foyer can sit down and listen to performances there, in much the same way as you can listen to foyer jazz at the Royal Festival Hall. A gently curved wall like an undulating sound wave, designed by Michael Vale, provides the minimum of architectural underpinning to demarcate the space. The Queen Elizabeth Hall now provides Southbank Centre with a second free daytime programme, with foyer events scheduled to complement those at the Royal Festival Hall.

Right: The airport-lounge makeover for the Queen Elizabeth Hall foyer in 1978. Opposite: The foyer suffers an infestation of pot plants and garden furniture in 1987.

5
ART FOR ALL

9 March 1996. In a darkened gallery on the top floor of the Hayward, five men sit in five glass boxes. Part of an installation called In the Dark, *they are actors, and they are naked. In front of them, spot-lit on long trestle tables, an assortment of props have been laid out, a cluster for each day. The props for 9 March suggest Sunday school – hymnbooks, sticks of chalk, Bible stories. Alongside, all the day's newspapers are displayed. Behind you, by the door, banks of flip-down cinema seats have been installed and people are sitting down as if to watch a film.*

Except that the film isn't complete. It isn't even a film, but an artwork by Peter Greenaway. He is one of ten artists and filmmakers who have been commissioned to make new work for "Spellbound: Art and Film in Britain". Greenaway has been exhibiting his paintings in galleries for years, but he has never created anything like In The Dark *in Britain before. Better known for his rich and complex films –* The Draughtsman's Contract; Prospero's Books *– Greenaway has cast aside his director's hat today and expects the audience to pick it up.*

The actors cross their legs, stretch, blink, as the seats fill up. Looking out across the gallery from your cinema chair, you have a film in front of you, but it is in component parts. You have to construct it for yourself. Your first question might be, why are there five naked men in glass boxes?

Previous page: Visitors to the Hayward's "Pop Art" show, 1969. Above: Peter Greenaway's installation *In The Dark*, part of "Spellbound" in 1996.

Each day a different "type" of actor – actors who have played Hamlet, or Queens, or are tall, or related, or blind – step into the boxes and look out over the props tables. Your second question might be, why Sunday school props with naked men? The two seem wildly incongruous. Are these defrocked priests, or are we not intended to "read" them together? Stories in the newspapers also catch your eye: Australia's new prime minister, the Iraq disarmament crisis, the Canary Wharf bombing, the "Deep Blue" computer that beat Garry Kasparov at chess. With each story, the actors and props take on new meaning. Are the men soldiers being tortured, or are they potential streakers at a chess match? Loud music thumps away as you try to figure it all out. Are you in fact part of the film? Are the actors the viewers? They stare at you through the darkness with voyeuristic zeal. Who is watching whom?

The Hayward opened to the public on 11 July 1968. It was designed in tandem with the Queen Elizabeth Hall, and much of its exterior is similar – the pre-cast concrete panels made with Cornish aggregate, the blocky construction that expresses each interior volume, the clearly visible service ducts, the aluminium and glass doors. However, it opened more than a year later than its neighbour, and cost considerably less – £750,000.

Unlike the Queen Elizabeth Hall and Purcell Room, which were always affiliated to the Royal Festival Hall, the Hayward was designed in uneasy partnership with the Arts Council of Great Britain. A mid-size gallery had been part of the London County Council's plans for the site from as early as 1955, but in 1960 it was suggested that it be leased to the Arts Council for a peppercorn rent to provide a permanent home for their exhibition programme and growing collection [see panel on page 103].

The London County Council architects working on the gallery – Hubert Bennett, Norman Engleback and team – were asked to make some changes once the Arts Council was on board. The size of the gallery was to be not less than 1,900 square metres, some of which must be in the form of sculpture courts. The proposed lighting for the upper galleries had to be changed – Henry Moore, who sat on the Arts Council's advisory panel on art, thumped the table in disgust when he learnt that the galleries had been designed without natural light – and pyramid-shaped windows were added to the roof.

Between 1960 and 1963 the design was modified many times but, finally, it was agreed that there would be five galleries arranged over two floors around a central services core (stairs, lift and toilets), with three outdoor

The "Outsiders" exhibition at the Hayward – the art of the wayward – an intensity which would stay with me as I made my way out dayward. They say that the unremitting "grey" face of this place refers not to the colour and variety of what occurs roundabout and within, don't they?
**John Hegley,
performance poet**

Above: Installation view of the inaugural Matisse exhibition in 1968. Below: The Hayward's first private view invitation. Previous pages: The Hayward in 1998.

sculpture courts. Because of the Arts Council's collection, the gallery also had substantial storage facilities that occupied the entire ground floor, with a car park below. The entrance to the gallery was therefore at walkway level.

It must have been quite a change for Arts Council staff to suddenly have their own gallery to programme. Since 1947, a year after its inception, the Arts Council of Great Britain had been based at 4 St James's Square, just off Piccadilly. Almost immediately, parts of the building were used to mount exhibitions. The first, held in the front room and inner hall, was dedicated to Old Master drawings; an Alberto Giacometti show was held in the garden in 1955. (A good average attendance for these shows was 100 people a day.) For a period, the Arts Council rented the New Burlington Galleries from the Ministry of Works for their more ambitious shows but, by 1955, these were foregone in favour of holding exhibitions at the V&A and Tate.

The problem with the Arts Council exhibitions held at the V&A and Tate was that a proportion of the museum's permanent collection had to be taken down each time. So the Arts Council began looking around for a permanent venue, just as the London County Council started contemplating renting their planned art gallery to a third party. A deal was struck, and the Arts Council finally took control of the Hayward on

We were walking down Albemarle Street and a guy who was on the exhibition committee at the Hayward crossed the street and said to Mark [Boyle, her husband], "Oh, Mark, I've been meaning to get in touch with you. We thought you might like to do a show at the Hayward" – just like that. And we were absolutely flabber-founded and dumb-gasted! We decided to take all the partitions down on the top floor and it made for a fantastic, open space. There were 174,000 visitors – a huge number for the time. On the last weekend, there was a queue coming down the outside staircase. We were so happy and pleased that so many people wanted to get in. A lot of people came for the Rodin [the other Hayward exhibition in the lower galleries], but I don't care, because lots of them said, "I've paid for the ticket, I'll go and see what's upstairs". It was really a great step for us.

Joan Hills, member of the Boyle Family, artist

20 December 1967, after a naming ceremony that dedicated the building to the former leader of the London County Council, Sir Isaac Hayward.

The Arts Council intended to use the first few months in the building as a "commissioning period", and the first exhibition didn't begin until the following summer. On 9 July 1968, the Queen opened the Hayward and its major Henri Matisse retrospective. There was no great fanfare, just a couple of minutes of speeches and a tour. The show ran for two months, and 118,000 people went to see it.

Many people had, and still have, an aversion to the Hayward's Brutalist exterior, calling it an "enormous nuclear fall-out shelter", a "rough-cast pillbox" or a "forbidding bunker-like structure, which fails to make visitors feel at all welcome". Sir Nikolaus Pevsner, writing about the Hayward in his influential *Buildings of England* series, compared it to Piranesi's *Carceri* (a series of etchings of fantastical prisons which have endless walkways, bleak walls and little natural light). But most contemporary critics agreed that the interior of the Hayward was technologically impressive and very flexible. Four of the five galleries could display heavy sculpture on their tiled floors, and the upper galleries

Left: Installation view of a work by Richard Long in "The New Art" exhibition, 1972.

Right: A view of Anthony Caro's work on one of the Hayward's sculpture courts as part of his 1969 exhibition.
Below: Invitation to the Vincent van Gogh retrospective in 1968.
Opposite, right: Antony Gormley, *Field for the British Isles*, 1993.
Opposite, below: Richard Wilson, *Facelift*, 1991.

Vincent van Gogh
24 October 1968 to
12 January 1969
Daily 10.30–7 Sunday 10–6 Admission 5s

Hayward Gallery
South Bank
The Arts Council

were climate controlled to such a level that, as John Gainsborough observed in *Arts Review*, they had "a ventilation standard higher in some respects than that employed in hospital operating theatres under current Ministry of Health standards." Natural light – filtered to remove damaging ultraviolet – was also a feature, and came from self-cleaning glass pyramids set into the roof. The lower galleries had artificial lighting hidden in ceiling panels and a versatile exhibition system that allowed everything from a Florentine fresco to a skip to be displayed.

The galleries' flexibility was just as well, as the Arts Council was keen to maintain a varied exhibition programme that included contemporary solo shows, modern master retrospectives, group shows of non-European art and photographic exhibitions. In the opening year, two blockbuster exhibitions of work by Matisse and Vincent van Gogh were followed by an ambitious show of new Anthony Caro sculptures and then "Frescoes from Florence". There was an initial plan at the outset to show young British artists' work in between the major shows, to ensure the gallery always had something to offer the casual passer-by. So, after the Matisse show, John Walker and William Turnbull were given an "interval exhibition" for a month while the main galleries were prepared for the van Gogh retrospective. Sadly, only a few interval exhibitions were held over the coming decade and, for the most part, the gallery was "dark" for over a month between shows to allow for the changeover of exhibitions.

From the outset, the Hayward and its programme were the responsibility of the director of art at the Arts Council. In 1970 Gabriel

THE ARTS COUNCIL COLLECTION

The Arts Council Collection is one of the foremost collections of post-war British art and the largest loan collection of British art in the world. It was founded in 1946 along with the Arts Council, and built on the 75 paintings and watercolours acquired by the Council for the Encouragement of Music and the Arts during the Second World War. It now stands at over 7,500 works, and includes sculpture, prints, photographs, drawings, paintings, multiples and digital art.

The original and idealistic intention of the Arts Council was to establish a national collection to encourage a greater understanding of the visual arts. This aim has been honoured throughout the history of the Arts Council Collection, and now one third of the collection remains on public display at any one time thanks to a comprehensive touring exhibition programme maintained by the Hayward. Since the mid-1990s, as the collection and its reputation has grown, there has been an increasing demand for exhibition loans to both national and international museums and galleries, and the collection has

also been made available for long-term loan to publicly funded institutions such as universities and hospitals.

The Arts Council Collection acquires new work each year. The head of the collection invites the collection's senior curator and three external advisors – an artist, a writer and a curator – to sit on the acquisitions committee. Former selectors have included critic David Sylvester, artist Yinka Shonibare, former director of Tate Sir Alan Bowness, and academic Griselda Pollock. Historically, works have been bought at an early stage in each artist's career – to support them both financially and critically – and the collection now boasts key works by Francis Bacon, David Hockney and Bridget Riley, as well as Damien Hirst, Rachel Whiteread and Antony Gormley [above]. Until 1987, the collection and its touring shows were managed by the Arts Council, but following the abolition of the Greater London Council and the Arts Council's decision to cease direct management of the Hayward, the collection – along

with the gallery – became the responsibility of Southbank Centre. Charles Saatchi donated 100 works by young British artists to the collection in 1999, and in 2003 he donated a further 34 sculptures, including work by Marc Quinn, Richard Wilson [below left] and Gary Webb. In the same year, the Arts Council Collection transferred its sculptures to Longside, in the grounds of the Yorkshire Sculpture Park. The collection shares an exhibition programme with the Yorkshire Sculpture Park at Longside, and is home to specialist staff. Prior to its opening, much of the collection was stored on site at the Hayward. In 2005, the two-dimensional works also moved out to a new facility in south London, which allowed works to be accessed more conveniently by potential borrowers and curators.

In 2006, the Arts Council Collection celebrated its sixtieth anniversary with an exhibition at Longside – "60: Sixty Years of Sculpture in the Arts Council Collection" – and a major exhibition at the Hayward: "How to Improve the World". The Hayward exhibition was the first in 25 years to focus on the collection, and 180 works – by Sarah Lucas, Gilbert & George, Mona Hatoum, Susan Hiller, Richard Long, Barbara Hepworth, Lucian Freud and many others – revealed the breadth and diversity of the collection.

In November 2006 the entire collection went online at www.artscouncilcollection.org.uk. A changing selection of works from the collection may also be seen around Southbank Centre.

British Painting '74 Hayward Gallery
Arts Council of Great Britain 26 September to 17 November 1974
Monday to Friday 10 to 8/Saturdays 10 to 6/Sundays 12 to 6
Admission 30p/Children, students and pensioners 15p
10p all day Monday and between 6 to 8 Tuesdays to Fridays

White, director of art when the Hayward opened, was replaced by Robin
Campbell. During these early years, the gallery continued to show a wide
range of exhibitions, but increasingly it focused on contemporary art and
living British artists. It rapidly became an important venue, and was often
at the centre of national and international debate. *The Sun* reviewed its
large "Pop Art" show of 1969 – "The stuff that artists use today are the
materials of everyday" – while the Soviet Ministry of Culture demanded
that certain abstract artworks in "Art in Revolution: Soviet Art and
Design since 1917", 1971, be taken off display. The Hayward held an early
exhibition of video art in 1973, "Identifications" (from which the Arts
Council Collection acquired its first video work, Gilbert & George's
A portrait of the artists as young men), and it staged many important solo
shows by artists including Bridget Riley, Bill Brandt, Frank Stella, Mark
Rothko, Lucian Freud, Diane Arbus, Morris Louis and Antoni Tàpies.

The Arts Council's commitment to supporting young artists was
exemplified by the neon tower that, until recently, lit up the skyline
of the Hayward. Philip Vaughan and Roger Dainton had won an Arts
Council prize for their neon sculpture *Ziggurat* at the 1969 "Young
Contemporaries" exhibition, and they were commissioned to make the
Southbank Centre tower the following year. A model was included in the
1970 Hayward show "Kinetics", and the finished work was plugged in
on 1 February 1972. It featured 108 neon tubes on a geometric armature
that stretched 15 metres into the sky. A weather vane dictated which
arrangement of lights would turn on and off, and the rapidity of each
sequence was dependent on wind speed, measured by an anemometer
at the top of the tower. Yellow and magenta neons spiralled upwards,
while red, green and blue tubes ran along the horizontal struts, and lit up
Southbank Centre's skyline.

Above: Installation view of the
Gilbert & George show in 1987.
Below: Examples of different
light formations possible on
Philip Vaughan and Roger
Dainton's weather-controlled
neon tower, mounted on top of
the Hayward.
Opposite: Poster for the "British
Painting" show of 1974, by Alan
Fletcher.

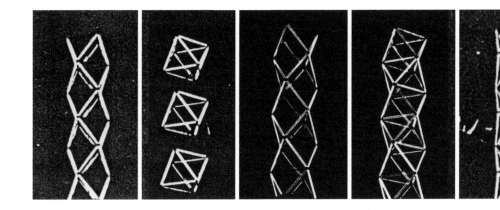

Right: An installation view of the "Kinetics" exhibition in 1970. Opposite: Poster for Lucian Freud's exhibition of paintings and drawings in 1974.

Joanna Drew was appointed director of exhibitions at the Arts Council in 1975. She became director of art in 1978, and remained in charge of the Hayward until her retirement in 1992. As director of exhibitions, she was involved in the inauguration of the 1977 "Hayward Annual", a yearly look at the best contemporary art around. Controversy surrounded the show for its ten-year run. In the first year, critics complained that it was full of male artists – including David Hockney, Allen Jones, Michael Craig-Martin and Eduardo Paolozzi – and, by 1979, disgruntled artists not included in the show were staging protests in front of the gallery.

Despite the Arts Council's commitment to showing contemporary art, it was the retrospective exhibitions of past masters that drew in the crowds in the 1980s. The 1981 Picasso exhibition was seen by 215,000 people; in 1985, the Renoir show attracted 364,000. Rodin, Leonardo da Vinci and Raoul Dufy retrospectives were all hugely successful, both in terms of visitor numbers and revenue. In contrast, the 1980 exhibition "Hungarian Avant-garde: The Eight and the Activists" attracted less than 10,000 people and "Pier and Ocean: Construction in the art of the 1970s" appealed to only 7,000. However, solo shows fared better, and Lucian Freud's paintings were seen by 119,000 people in 1988.

Despite these fluctuations in visitor numbers, the Hayward remained the leading contemporary art venue in London. Until, that is, the Greater London Council threatened the Arts Council with eviction. The chairman of the Arts Council, Sir William Rees-Mogg, issued a statement on 24 September 1984: "The Greater London Council's action in giving us six

LUCIAN FREUD

HAYWARD GALLERY
25 JANUARY - 3 MARCH 1974
ARTS COUNCIL

months' notice to quit the gallery is unconscionable and irresponsible…
The Council's tenancy agreement implicitly recognizes the impracticality
of disrupting a planned exhibition programme at less than eighteen
months' notice." If Rees-Mogg appeared incensed about the Greater
London Council breaking the terms of the agreement, Sir Roy Strong –
chairman of the Arts Council's advisory panel on art as well as director of
the V&A – issued a more heartfelt plea for the Hayward to remain an Arts
Council gallery: "The Greater London Council's action is a major blow
to the visual arts in this country. The Hayward not only provides great
exhibitions for countless Londoners and visitors to the capital; it is the
centre for the Arts Council's travelling exhibitions and its loan collection
of British art. If the Hayward goes it is a loss to the nation."

Politics, politics. Writing in 1992, critic Tim Hilton suggested that Sir
William Rees-Mogg and Sir Roy Strong had in fact been "enemies" of
the Hayward, who were not in favour of its increasingly contemporary
programme. Hilton said Rees-Mogg was the one who initiated talks with
the government about extricating the Arts Council from the gallery.
But whatever went on behind closed doors, Rees-Mogg's victory was
bittersweet. The Hayward remained a gallery, although within three
years it was no longer run by the Arts Council.

In 1986, the Greater London Council – about to be abolished by
Margaret Thatcher – commissioned a report on the future of the
Hayward. It was written by critic Richard Cork, artist and novelist
Balraj Khanna and photographer Shirley Read, an independent panel
who knew that their findings would never be acted upon as the Greater
London Council would no longer exist. So they directed their comments
to the newly formed South Bank Board. They stated that the Hayward
should be integrated with the other venues on site, and that the site itself
should be livened up. The Hayward needed a café, a membership scheme,
artists in residence, a comprehensive education programme. It needed to
feel welcoming and dynamic; it needed a smaller gallery to show the latest

One of those "twenty questions"
articles recently asked me what
had been my favourite project.
I said the Hayward exhibition that
I made in 1993. It got terrible
reviews but was a turning point
for me, an amazing opportunity
that pushed me and the work
to be much more ambitious and
brought together all my disparate
ideas. I still look back to that
exhibition for new solutions. Henry
Meyric Hughes went out on a limb,
inviting me to make a one-person
exhibition in virtually all of the
spaces and I remain very grateful
to him. As I worked with the
spaces, outdoor and in, I began to
understand the building better.
I was allowed to clear some of
the galleries and extend the
exhibition on to little-used
sculpture balconies. The
materials, vistas, spaces and
flow of the gallery made itself
clear. Within the Brutalist concrete
architecture is a very delicate,
sophisticated and grand
showing space.
Julian Opie, artist

contemporary art while the main galleries were closed. Sadly, nobody paid the report much attention when it was published, and only now are many of these ideas being implemented.

Above: Work by Julian Opie on one of the Hayward's sculpture courts during his 1993-94 show. Below: An installation view of "Cities on the Move", 1999.

The South Bank Board took over the administrative running of the Hayward from the Arts Council in 1987, and all those previously employed by the Arts Council to curate exhibitions and look after the collection transferred over, including Joanna Drew, who became the Hayward's first dedicated director. (The Arts Council was no longer involved directly with the exhibitions, and concentrated on its advisory and funding role.) At first, exhibitions continued much as they had done before. Living artists – Bridget Riley, Nam June Paik, Eduardo Chillida, Richard Long, Julian Opie – continued to receive major shows, and blockbusters such as Toulouse-Lautrec in 1991 (266,000 visitors) and Magritte in 1992 (154,000 visitors) periodically helped to swell the coffers. But increasingly the Hayward focused on ambitious contemporary group shows and they came to define the decade.

The 1990s saw the Hayward curate many important themed exhibitions, including "Doubletake" (1992); "Unbound" (1994); "The Epic and the Everyday: contemporary photographic art" (1994); "Spellbound: Art and Film in Britain" (1996); "Material Culture: the Object in British Art of the 1980s and 1990s" (1997), and "Cities on the Move: Urban Chaos and Global Change" (1999). The gallery became a place of debate, a place to see the latest contemporary art and understand the latest theories. The Hayward didn't stop exhibiting individual artists – Anish Kapoor's show in 1998 had the highest daily attendance rate on record for a contemporary

The Hayward is a venerable institution, and part of doing a show there is taking on the history and the building. What I tried to do was to get upstairs and downstairs to be one experience, so I worked with the architect, Claudio Silvestrin. The Hayward is a complicated space, full of awkwardness, and it's that awkwardness that I think makes a show really work, that allows it to sing. Without too much undue immodesty, people are always saying to me how they remember that show, which is a very nice thing. I suppose it came at a point for me where a certain body of work was at its fruition and so it represents a certain time for me. It was also a moment when, even though I'd done a few things here and there, the work was known but not really and properly seen and so a lot of people came to the work who might have heard of it but they hadn't really experienced it before. **Anish Kapoor, artist**

show with 1,500 visitors a day – but it staged solo shows less frequently.

The Hayward's exhibition programme continued despite an ongoing threat of the gallery being demolished. Its lack of office space meant that many of the former Arts Council staff had to be based at the Royal Festival Hall, and the lack of storage space meant that one exhibition had to be fully removed before another could arrive (hence three "dark" months a year). Neither was acceptable, and the South Bank Board was quoted in the *Sunday Times* as saying, in 1993, that the Hayward would probably be torn down "by the millennium", with a new gallery built on the car park facing Jubilee Gardens.

Following the retirement of the influential Joanna Drew, Henry Meyric Hughes was appointed director in 1993. During his three-year tenure, he reinstated the original aim of having young artists present work in the building while the main galleries were closed and, in 1995, the "Turnaround" series was launched. Artists including Gary Hume and Gillian Wearing plastered the exterior with billboard posters, presented films on monitors visible from outside the main entrance and installed artworks on the surrounding walkways. But, despite the success of "Turnaround", there was still no getting away from the fact that – in stark comparison to the other buildings on site – the gallery was effectively closed for three months of the year.

In 1996, Susan Ferleger Brades became the Hayward's new director. Despite English Heritage's refusal to list Southbank Centre's Brutalist structures – the Hayward, Queen Elizabeth Hall and Purcell Room – it seemed as if people were slowly coming round to them, even viewing them sympathetically. In 2003 Roly Keating, then controller of BBC4, went as far as naming the Hayward as his favourite building, saying in the *Guardian*, "I love its drama and unpredictability – its hidden terraces, its spiky rooflights, its quirky one-up-one-down staircases. Together they create a mad modernist *Gormenghast* that somehow brings out the best in the art it celebrates." But if Ferleger Brades liked the Hayward for what

Above: Gary Hume's installation for the Hayward "Turnaround" series, 1998.
Opposite: Anish Kapoor's *At the Edge of the World II*, shown in his 1998 retrospective.

Above: The new entrance to the Hayward, featuring Dan Graham's *Waterloo Sunset* pavilion.

it was, she also campaigned for improvements, and in the same year the gallery closed for ten months for a facelift that added a new glass foyer, café and an elliptical pavilion. (This was the first major element of the Rick Mather masterplan to be completed. It was selected by the South Bank Board and the decision was supported by the Arts Council.)

The glass pavilion was designed by artist Dan Graham, whose earlier structures – including the one at the DIA Foundation in New York – were well known. Ferleger Brades approached Graham directly, and asked him not only to create a pavilion for the Hayward, but also to design the entire extension. He said he couldn't do it without an architect to work with, and was duly introduced to Graham Haworth from Haworth Tompkins. The resulting foyer was a collaboration between the artist and architect, and the mirror-glass pavilion, *Waterloo Sunset*, was placed on an out-of-use terrace above the old director's suite (now the café), with stairs leading up to it from the entrance. The entire project cost £1.8m, and was designed to create spaces within the Hayward that could be accessed all year round.

In some ways, *Waterloo Sunset* – named after the Kinks song and the nearby railway station and bridge – acts as a folly. It doesn't have a clearly defined role, and was designed as a space to simply enter and enjoy. It offers weatherproof views of the Thames, as well as monitors that once ran cartoons and are now earmarked to show the latest video art. It can hold drinks receptions or whole classes of schoolchildren; you can stand in it and outside it, as part of a group or on your own.

In 2004, Ferleger Brades resigned. Several acting directors – Caroline Felton, Martin Caiger-Smith and Susan May – managed the gallery until Ralph Rugoff, former director of the CCA Wattis Institute for Contemporary Arts in San Francisco, was appointed in May 2006. Within two months he had made his presence felt, implementing commissions that led to art cropping up in the most unexpected of places, and to the Hayward embracing its position on the south bank.

Below: Cartoons play on the video screens in *Waterloo Sunset*.

6

OPEN ALL HOURS

Above: Browsers at the Royal
Festival Hall record shop, 1983.
Previous page: Foyer music on
22 June 1987.

*13 March 1983. It is lunchtime, and a woman sits at a table in the bar of
the Royal Festival Hall foyer. A five-piece jazz band is playing, and her
foot taps to the beat of "Summertime". Her children are running up and
down the stairs that lead to the auditorium, and she takes a sip of tea and
flicks through the monthly Southbank Centre concert programme.*

*The woman and her family have come with friends who are going to
see their nephew play with the Young Musicians Symphony Orchestra
that afternoon. Earlier in the week, the friends had suggested meeting in
the Royal Festival Hall café for lunch beforehand. "Isn't it closed in the
day?" she had asked. She had been to see the Festival Ballet there with
her daughter the previous Christmas, and thought the Royal Festival
Hall only opened at night. Her friends had heard that it now opened at
midday, with an "Open Foyer" programme that was going to include
free music and exhibitions. They wanted to see it for themselves. So here
they all were on a Sunday afternoon. The woman looked at an advert
for "Open Foyer" in the March programme. "Open from 12 noon to*

everyone everyday", she read. It listed all the activities you could do in the foyer now – eat, drink, shop, see exhibitions, listen to music. Under "Foyer Music", it listed all the things you might encounter: "Madrigals or modern jazz, raucous mediaeval dance music or less boisterous melodic rock. Broadway melodies, delicate Elizabethan lute songs, classical and romantic trios, jazz standards…" The list went on. She was pleased they had happened upon jazz. "Summertime" had finished, and the band were now playing "Ain't Misbehavin'". Her husband preferred classical music to jazz. He had sauntered off to the foyer record shop some time ago, and now returned to her table holding an LP of Sir William Walton's Symphony No. 1, conducted by Sir Bernard Haitink, and the latest issue of Gramophone.

Their friends joined them shortly afterwards, laughing and gesticulating. "Have you been down to the exhibition on the ballroom floor yet?" they asked. "There are some hilarious sculptures by Gerald Scarfe, the cartoonist. There's Margaret Thatcher as Boudicca, Ronald Reagan with giant Mickey Mouse ears, and Field Marshal Montgomery propped up on scarecrow legs. You should take a look; it's free."

They talked for a while about the exhibition, then stood to go – it was just after three, and the concert began soon. The woman looked up the concert in the monthly programme, and told them they would be treated to a medley of Rossini, Grieg, Strauss and Ravel. "As long as our nephew doesn't break a string, we don't care what he plays," they laughed, and made for the stairs. "Send the children down," said the woman. She had seen a concert for five-to-eleven-year-olds advertised for the following Sunday afternoon that she thought they might like. It was in the Purcell Room, a mix of stories and poems set to music. Their father could take them, she thought, and she could sit in the foyer again – you never know, there might be more jazz on the way.

> In the late 1970s, while the *Sunday Times* diarist, I remember somehow managing to set maestro Carlo Maria Giulini's hair on fire while lighting his cigarette over dinner after a concert.
> **Anthony Holden, journalist and writer**

The "Open Foyer" programme was launched at the Royal Festival Hall by the Greater London Council in March 1983. Prior to this date, only the ground floor café and the box office were open in the day, with the hall opening an hour or so before evening concerts. The opening up of the foyer allowed daytime access to the entire building and, significantly, a wide variety of music could be heard for free.

South Bank Concert Halls already provided a broad range of music to suit most tastes, thanks to the addition of the Queen Elizabeth Hall and Purcell Room in 1967. The Royal Festival Hall was home to London's major orchestras, including the London Philharmonic and Philharmonia,

Above: Spanish soprano Monserrat Caballé in 1968. Opposite: Natalia Makarova dancing with Rudolf Nureyev in October 1970, the year she claimed asylum in Britain.

who played around 30 concerts a year there. Throughout the 1970s, the BBC Symphony Orchestra, London Symphony Orchestra, Royal Philharmonic Society and Royal Philharmonic Orchestra also played there regularly.

The great conductors of the 1950s and 1960s continued to demonstrate their prowess on the Royal Festival Hall's platform, by now with the aid of walking sticks and podium chairs. Otto Klemperer and Sir Adrian Boult conducted some of their final concerts in the hall, the tiniest movements of their batons controlling the orchestras. Pierre Monteux actually collapsed on stage while conducting Beethoven's Fifth Symphony and was carried out. An announcement minutes later said that he apologized for the interruption and hoped he would be back shortly, and sure enough he returned to the stage to finish the concert. Other conductors who were in their prime – Sir Neville Marriner, Carlo Maria Giulini, Pierre Boulez – were regular star attractions, alongside solo artists such as Maria Callas, Montserrat Caballé and Jacqueline du Pré. Caballé remembers her London debut in 1968 at the Royal Festival Hall, where she was performing in Donizetti's opera *Lucrezia Borgia*: "At the end of the first scene in the ensemble finale, I have to sing a very long, soft note, I think it's a B flat. Anyway I held it, and when I stopped singing, from all around the hall I heard a sort of sigh, because the audience had been holding its breath with me. I think I can say that night was a little like the beginning of a love affair." Dame Janet Baker sang in the Royal Festival Hall throughout the 1960s and 1970s, and remembers the excitement of singing when Klemperer or Giulini were on the podium. She also recalls that it was a big auditorium in which to give a solo recital, but that she loved singing there. "You see," she says, "in an opera house you have to get across the orchestra pit, and negotiate the distance imposed by the proscenium arch. On the concert platform it's just yourself and your accompanist, and of course the audience. We always felt that the Festival Hall was the centre of everything that was fine and excellent in music then."

The Royal Festival Hall was also the location for momentous and moving events. The night Du Pré died, 19 October 1987, a fellow cellist was scheduled to play at the Royal Festival Hall. Lynn Harrell walked on to the stage carrying Du Pré's cello. He stated that Du Pré had owned the Elgar Cello Concerto in E minor, and that he would play it in her honour that evening. In 1968, demonstrators opposed to the Soviet occupation of Prague chained themselves to a box during a concert given by the USSR State Orchestra and, in 1970, Natalia Makarova from the Kirov Ballet threw her ballet shoes in her dressing room wastepaper basket and disappeared. She had just finished a six-week residency at the Royal

My most important personal memory dates from 1973, when I was a boy reporter for the still-young *Rolling Stone* magazine. I was attending a Bee Gees concert and saw Elton John in the audience. I followed him into the gents during the interval. He was actually in mid-flow when I introduced myself and asked if he would like to do the cover interview. He would have had every right to make a hostile reply, but instead he very tactfully said, "Helen Walters at DJM takes care of those things. Ring her." Elton probably thought Helen would brush me off, but she thought it a fabulous idea. We did the interview and Elton became a lifelong friend. When the cover story appeared Helen took me to lunch to thank me and brought along her husband, John Walters, who was John Peel's producer. He was starting a rock magazine programme on Radio 1 that autumn and wondered if I would like to do a ten-minute American look at the scene. So it was that I began my BBC career. It happened thanks to the kindness of Elton John and John Walters... and to the men's toilet at the Royal Festival Hall.

Paul Gambaccini, broadcaster

Festival Hall and decided to claim asylum, turning up at a police station saying, "I dance for democracy". Pianist Mikhail Pletnev, making his UK debut at the hall in 1970, was turned out of his dressing room by an over-zealous usher for playing the piano too loudly. Pletnev had been entertaining a couple who had heard him play before the interval, and had gone to see him backstage. Pletnev wasn't on stage in the second half, so decided to play Bach-Busoni's *Chaconne* for them, only to be told by the apoplectic usher that he could be heard in the auditorium and that he had no right to be backstage creating such a racket.

Classical music aside, jazz greats continued to choose the Royal Festival Hall for their concerts. Fats Domino bumped his grand piano across the stage during an encore and Nina Simone broke from her set to discuss domestic violence, prompted by a member of the audience. Frank Sinatra gave a midnight concert accompanied by Count Basie

Right: Backstage at the Royal Festival Hall in 1981.

Left: Richard Hickox and the
City of London Sinfonia on stage
at the Royal Festival Hall in 1977.
Below: 1951 illustration of
musicians at the Royal
Festival Hall.

and his orchestra that ended with "My Way", a rendition that left the
audience silent in awe. Occasionally the hall even saw pop acts take to
the stage. Esther and Abi Ofarim appeared less than two months after
their international hit "Cinderella Rockerfella" in 1968. However, due to
the length of time required to programme orchestras and classical stars
– often three years in advance – pop acts rarely made it to the stage (a
cancellation led to the Ofarims' concert being held there). They did make it
into the audience though, and everyone from Elton John to Tom Petty was
spotted attending Royal Festival Hall concerts in the 1970s.

Despite the auditorium's acoustics, which meant there wasn't a bad seat
in the house, regular concert-goers often had their favourite locations.
For many, the choir seats behind the orchestra were favoured. These
were available for a relatively low price if there were no choirs included in
the programme and the concert was likely to be sold-out. Despite being
backless benches, many chose them for their proximity to the musicians,
who were almost close enough to touch. Others were fortunate to be
allowed into the Ceremonial Box, usually reserved for the Royal family.
However, this honour didn't come without caveats – one had to dress
soberly, not sit in the Queen Mother's chair, and applaud so one's hands
could be seen by the audience. Some schools were allowed to take pupils
to rehearsals in the hall, usually held in the daytime. Again, strict rules
were in place – no talking in the auditorium, and the children had to sit
still, although they soon learned that if the soloist went wrong and the
orchestra stopped and laughed, they were allowed to laugh too.

The Royal Festival Hall continued to hold all manner of events

THE SAISON POETRY LIBRARY

Obviously, for me, a big thing is the Poetry Library. It's amazing given that us Brits, though we might think of ourselves as being appreciators of poetry, are not great at doing things like actually buying it. So for us to have got it together to organize such a resource is fantastic. I'm so neurotic about people seeing what I'm working on that I haven't sat in there and written anything but I have often gone to look things up, particularly when I was working on my anthology of First World War poetry. You can use the internet these days but nothing quite beats the library for those accidental felicities and connections.
Andrew Motion, Poet Laureate

In 1981, Philip Larkin wrote: "The Arts Council Poetry Library is one of the occasional pure flowerings of imagination for which the English are so seldom given credit: the creation of a public library devoted entirely to modern poetry." He had written the foreword to the Poetry Library's 1981 catalogue of books, which contained 30,000 titles. The Saison Poetry Library, incorporating the Arts Council Poetry Collection [above], now holds 100,000 titles, including everything ever published by Larkin (and almost every other major British and Irish poet since 1912, for that matter). It buys two copies of every poetry book published in Britain – one for reference, one for lending – as well as books by other English-speaking poets and poems translated into English.

The Arts Council established the Poetry Library in 1953, declaring it a national archive that would be free to use and open to everyone. TS Eliot and Herbert Read spoke at the opening, and numerous poets, including Ted Hughes and Seamus Heaney, used it frequently. In 1978, the novelist Marghanita Laski suggested a message-board of lost quotations be established, and the library's noticeboard and website continues to list fragments of unattributed poetry sent in by the public for library-goers to identify. (18,000 people contact the library each year looking for information about particular poems.)

The Poetry Library had several homes before moving to level five of the Royal Festival Hall in November 1988. Southbank Centre had recently appointed its first head of literature and talks, Maura Dooley (herself a poet), and she immediately resurrected Poetry International. The biannual festival had been founded by Ted Hughes in 1967 and, in its new incarnation, it featured talks and readings by poets from around the world.

There are now over 25,000 members who regularly use the reference and lending libraries, the listening booths for audiovisual material, the noticeboards listing poetry competitions and the comprehensive racks of magazines. Many published poets from Andrew Motion to Chrissie Gittins use it on a regular basis. Chrissie Gittins wrote a children's poem entitled "Death in the Poetry Library", where two boys inadvertently squash a poet between the moving stacks. Ivor Cutler could often be found browsing between the shelves, as could Roger McGough, who staged a similar "death" with novelist Romesh Gunesekera for a BBC radio programme.

In 2003 the Poetry Library launched www.poetrymagazines.org.uk, a digital archive of the library's collection of British poetry magazines. Its entire book catalogue is now also available online, at www.poetrylibrary.org.uk. However, as Andrew Motion says above, there's nothing quite like the serendipity of browsing in the actual stacks: you might come across poems by Pam Ayres while searching for WH Auden, or reach for Benjamin Zephaniah only to be distracted by Louis Zukofsky.

alongside its concert programme. Everything from the World Congress of Cardiology to the ongoing army reunions were held in the auditorium in the day and, at night, the platform could be transformed to house a cinema screen or theatrical sets. As part of the Queen's Silver Jubilee celebrations in July 1977, Tom Stoppard's ambitious play *Every Good Boy Deserves Favour* was premiered, featuring music by André Previn and the London Symphony Orchestra. Set in a Soviet psychiatric hospital, it featured Ian McKellen and John Wood as "inmates", and Patrick Stewart as the doctor who emerged from the ranks of the orchestra in his dinner jacket and bow tie, holding a violin.

Above: A trade exhibition on the ballroom floor in 1980.

The Royal Festival Hall had held its own Silver Jubilee a year earlier, with a special programme of twelve concerts and an accompanying exhibition. The exhibition explored the 25-year history of the hall, both musically and architecturally, and was held on the ballroom floor. But, as this was some years before the "Open Foyer" programme, the exhibition was only open to concert-goers. The concerts began with a performance by the London Philharmonic Orchestra of Benjamin Britten's *War Requiem*, shortly followed by the official "Anniversary Celebration" in the presence of the Queen and the Queen Mother, which was "an entertainment in sound and vision devised and presented by Antony Hopkins Festival". This cost £2.50 a ticket, including refreshments. However, you could hear the London Symphony Orchestra conducted by André Previn and Sir Adrian Boult or mezzo-soprano Dame Janet Baker for under £1 if you sat in the choir seats, or attend Ralph Downes's organ recital and Sir Clifford Curzon's piano concert for just 75 pence. The finale of the programme was the acclaimed Herbert von Karajan conducting the Berlin Philharmonic Orchestra playing Beethoven's Symphony No. 8 in F, with a hefty top ticket price of £12 (more than double the price of any other concert in the series).

All this celebrating went on as the nearby National Theatre prepared to open its doors – and foyers – to the public. On 25 October 1976, the Queen

Whenever I'd go to the south bank, I'd nip into the Poetry Library for a quick hit of *terza rima*, or a draft of *vers libre* to clear my head. One time, a familiar voice greeted me, as if on stage – "There I see someone I know..." – and Roger McGough then added my name to this little speech he seemed to be rehearsing. He sounded oddly formal, until I spotted his radio producer leaping with a microphone between the bookshelves. They were making a serious programme but we quickly turned it into a skit on the hundreds of unsuspecting poets who come into the library and are trapped and pressed and bound in the book stacks. I shall never forget Roger's yelp of "Help, murder," between the journals as I turned the wheels on the metal carriages and they rolled towards each other. He was caught, like a flattened Indiana Jones, in between. His producer was convinced that, despite the creepily silent trolley mechanism, somehow it would make great impromptu radio that just had to be recorded in this cathedral of art.

Romesh Gunesekera, novelist

Top: Riverside Terrace in front of the Royal Festival Hall in 1984. The giant cake celebrating the 95th birthday of the London County Council can be seen in the background.
Above and opposite: Illustrations by Kenneth Browne from *The Architectural Review* in July 1979, showing proposed changes to Southbank Centre.

opened the theatre, declaring: "It stands as a tribute to all those who dreamt of it". The opening marked its own silver anniversary – the Queen had laid its foundation stone next to the Royal Festival Hall 25 years earlier. Sir Nikolaus Pevsner was quick to compare the National Theatre, designed by Sir Denys Lasdun, to its neighbours the Hayward, Queen Elizabeth Hall and Purcell Room. In his *Buildings of England* series, he wrote: "Historically the two belong together, with their confidence in raw concrete and in the diagonal, the chamfer, the bevel. But walking from the National Theatre to the Hayward area – Denys Lasdun looks positively elegant. Brutalism is a term often used for the style of the sixties and seventies. It applies without reserve to the Hayward group with its overbearing cyclopean forms and its consistent stress on horizontals. The National Theatre instead lets its horizontals be answered by the verticals of its towers."

South Bank Concert Halls and the Hayward realized something had to be done about their approaches and exterior image, and in July 1979 they mounted an exhibition with *The Architectural Review* in the Royal Festival Hall ballroom of plans to rejuvenate the surrounding area. Colin Amery, reviewing the Royal Festival Hall exhibition in the *Financial Times*, pressed them to accept that the south bank of London was not the Costa Brava – "it is a wet, windy, rivery kind of place" – and that they should follow the National Theatre's lead with its "generous provision of strikingly designed foyers that are open day and night."

All this went on against a backdrop of changes at the Greater London Council, which led to South Bank Concert Halls being moved from the Clerks to the Parks department, which became the Recreation and Arts department in 1980. The following year, two appointments went in the south bank's favour – Tony Banks became the chair of the Recreation and Arts department, and Ken Livingstone became leader of the Greater London Council. Until it was abolished by the Conservative Party in 1986, the Greater London Council provided significant funding and support for the halls and gallery. The constant aim of Banks was to make the arts more accessible, and in 1983 he successfully launched the "Open Foyer" programme, which saw the Royal Festival Hall's foyer open from midday (and shortly afterwards from 10.00) until 22.30 seven days a week. Anyone could enter the building, and anyone could sit down and listen to the free concerts that were laid on.

Early opposition to the programme – radical for its day – came from the hall's administrators who were more traditional in their approaches to "access". But the Greater London Council sanctioned a television advertisement promoting the "Open Foyer" scheme, and in 1984 George

Above: Concert-goers queue for tickets at the Royal Festival Hall box office in 1987.
Right: Riverside Terrace with garden furniture, liberally used at Southbank Centre in 1987.

Melly fronted a commercial, which highlighted all the things that could now be done in the hall. The week it aired, over 45,000 people visited the hall, many for the first time. The Royal Festival Hall had finally succeeded in offering democratic access to the arts – everybody had an equal right to be there. And the free events were not limited to the foyer. In the same year as the commercial, and to celebrate the 95th birthday of the London County Council (by now the Greater London Council), a giant pink cake was built in front of the Queen Elizabeth Hall. A 72-hour pianola marathon took place that year inside the cake.

By this time, the Greater London Council's days were numbered. Livingstone, Banks and others campaigned against its abolition (hence the cake, emphasizing its heritage) but on 31 March 1986, at midnight, it ceased to exist. To mark the occasion, Haydn's *Farewell Symphony* was played at the Royal Festival Hall. Officially known as Symphony No. 45 in F sharp minor, the *Farewell Symphony* ends with each musician in the orchestra ceasing to play in turn, snuffing out the candle that lights their music stand, and walking off the platform. A final pair of violinists close the movement, and snuff out the remaining candles. The audience couldn't help but be moved. Until, that is, Ken Livingstone walked on to the dark, empty stage and lit a new candle to a round of applause.

After the Greater London Council was abolished, a board of directors under chairman Sir Ronald Grierson was appointed by the Arts Council – who now owned the freehold – to run South Bank Concert Halls. They were called the South Bank Board, and, in 1988, this charitable trust, under the guiding hand of the new general director (administration) Richard Pulford, took over the management of the Hayward as well, and Southbank Centre was created. A general director (arts) – Nicholas Snowman – was also appointed for the first time. Snowman (who later became chief executive of Southbank Centre in 1992 when the two general director posts were amalgamated), had previously been assistant to Pierre Boulez at the avant-garde music organization IRCAM, based at the Centre Pompidou in Paris, and had co-founded the London Sinfonietta in 1968. The South Bank Board embraced the "Open Foyer" policy, and were keen to build on it. Snowman also wanted the programming across the four buildings to be more coherent, and for cross-disciplinary events to be more frequent. In his first year as artistic director, he adapted the Queen Elizabeth Hall so it could play host to opera and dance, and started to initiate festivals that involved collaborations between Southbank Centre and other partners such as the National Theatre. In an attempt to make the external spaces of Southbank Centre more appealing, the concrete stairwells were painted white, and the Royal Festival Hall café spilled

out on to the walkway. Banners were draped over the concrete and stone facades, and hoardings advertised all the latest Southbank Centre shows.

These changes were all made in the year the South Bank Board commissioned architect Terry Farrell to devise a masterplan for the site. The board understood that, while the halls and gallery were successful in terms of their exhibitions and performances, they urgently needed modifying internally, and the site didn't have a sense of coherence or a strong identity. This wasn't the first time a masterplan had been commissioned. Leaving aside the London County Council plans in the first half of the century, the Greater London Council had, in fact, commissioned architect Cedric Price to envisage a new and improved Southbank Centre in 1984. As part of his masterplan, which recognized a need for "calculated uncertainty and conscious incompleteness", Price proposed a new pedestrian link bridge above the Hungerford bridge, and a large Ferris wheel on the banks of the Thames. Neither was acted upon, and his plan was abandoned when the Greater London Council was abolished.

Farrell's first masterplan for Southbank Centre – there were to be three – suggested that the walkways surrounding the venues should be demolished, and each building should be made accessible from ground level. He also proposed that an overarching fabric roof, designed by engineer Peter Rice, should join the venues together and allow for some activities to take place outdoors. Despite the relatively modest cost of this masterplan (£15m), it wasn't realized. One problem was the listing of the Royal Festival Hall in 1988, the result of a campaign by the Twentieth Century Society and *The Times*.

The Twentieth Century Society, founded in 1979, had long campaigned for the government's criteria for listing buildings to be changed. Before the statutory instrument of April 1987, which implemented a 30-year rule for buildings to be considered for listing, the only buildings that could be listed were those built before 1939. An increasing number of post-war buildings were under threat, and the Twentieth Century Society, chaired by Gavin Stamp, was relieved when it succeeded in having

Right and below: an aerial artist's impression and scale-model of Terry Farrell's Southbank Centre masterplan.

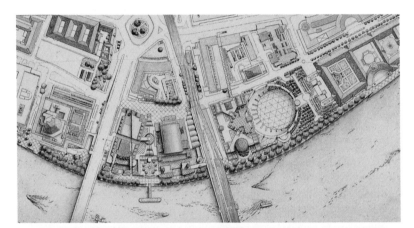

Bracken House, the former home of the *Financial Times*, listed in 1987. The rules for listing were amended shortly afterwards, and the *Sunday Times* ran a readers' poll of post-war buildings that should be listed. The overwhelming favourites were the Royal Festival Hall and Coventry Cathedral. English Heritage produced a list of buildings now eligible for listing and, in March 1988, the Royal Festival Hall became Grade I listed, a listing that included the auditorium's organ. (An ongoing campaign to list the other Southbank Centre buildings has so far been unsuccessful.)

While the listing of the Royal Festival Hall stopped Farrell's first masterplan in its tracks, it didn't stop developments happening inside the building and, in the same year, the Arts Council moved their Poetry Library into a former conference and rehearsal room on level five [see panel on page 122]. Farrell's masterplan, on the other hand, went back to the drawing board. The Conservative government was insistent that any redevelopment of Southbank Centre must be funded privately, and so a second masterplan appeared, this time created in partnership with Stanhope Properties. It was more dramatic than the first, in that it proposed the removal of the concrete outer skins of the Hayward, Queen Elizabeth Hall and Purcell Room. The funding for this ambitious scheme came from the commercial property that was to be built nearby, overlooking Jubilee Gardens. With the property market crash in 1991, any hope for the realization of this plan was lost.

Above: Southbank Centre as seen from the Thames in 1987.

7

TOWARDS THE FUTURE

Above: Participants in the 2006 Peckham Splash playing the Southbank Centre gamelan. Previous page: A member of Rennie Harris's Puremovement performing *Roman Jewels* in May 2002.

6 July 2006. Four hundred and fifty children aged between seven and eighteen have arrived at the Queen Elizabeth Hall and are running around backstage. It's 18.30, and they are going on stage in half an hour. Some are in school uniform, others in colourful costumes. There's a cluster all wearing red T-shirts; there's one dressed as a giant spider. For three months these children have been working together to create "Endangered Species: The Peckham Splash 2006", a night of music, puppetry, plays and singing for a 900-strong audience.

The Peckham Splash 2006 is organized by Southbank Centre and Peckham Education Action Zone. It brings together children from ten different schools in the London borough of Southwark and is typical of Southbank Centre's partnerships with school and community organizations. Eugene Skeef, its artistic director, worked with a team of dancers, puppeteers, animators and musicians to prepare the children for the event, as well as with Southbank Centre's gamelan artists. It's the first time the gamelan – an orchestra of Indonesian percussion instruments – has been used by these children, and it is going to provide all the music for the first half of the evening. After the interval, there's to be a children's gospel choir, a play with giant puppets and African drumming. But, for the moment, all eyes are on the gamelan that is now assembled on stage, the gongs, drums and metallophones waiting for the concert to begin.

The gamelan in the Queen Elizabeth Hall this evening has been designed to be taken on the road to schools and colleges. It is known as the "portable" gamelan – another one is permanently installed in the Royal Festival Hall – even though it takes a couple of people and a van to transport it around. For the last two months it has been installed in Gloucester Primary School, and classes of children from five local schools have all been learning how to play it. Pupils have spent weeks learning traditional Indonesian pieces as well as composing their own rhythms and special effects to accompany the plays and puppet shows that have been devised by their classmates. One play features a tiger who is made to wait around, and the gamelan will become a giant ticking clock, the gongs chiming the hour. One of the wayang puppet shows features heavy rain, and the pupils have devised a way to recreate the noise using the gamelan (and the floor).

Initially all the pupils who saw the gamelan were in awe of it, impressed by its size and different components. Then they all had a good go at striking it, making the gongs sing out. They would leave gamelan workshops with their ears ringing, happy and eager to play it again. Now, two months down the line, the first pupils file on to the stage and take their positions. Earlier in the day, at the dress rehearsal, they entered the auditorium for the first time. It is a big hall, particularly when viewed from the stage. Many had never been in a building like it before and stood open-mouthed, suddenly aware of what they were being asked to do that night.

Undaunted, they now position themselves behind the instruments. In the audience parents sit nervously, waiting for the concert to begin. A look of pride and concentration can be seen on the children's faces as the lights come up, and the first performance of the evening gets underway.

Maybe because I grew up in this place – I was thirteen years old when I first walked on the stage [as a pianist] – I have a lot of affection for it, and I like so many things about the way it looks. If they manage to improve the acoustics, which undoubtedly need to be improved, and modernize the look of it and make it more comfortable backstage… This is really a very, very major handicap. You know, for an artist to give his best onstage, he has to feel comfortable backstage.
Daniel Barenboim, conductor and pianist

As Terry Farrell was drawing up his first masterplan, Southbank Centre acquired its first gamelan. It was a gift from the government of the Republic of Indonesia to the British people to promote an understanding of southeast Asian music in the west. Initially it was going to be given to a university, but the composer Alec Roth, who worked extensively with gamelan, argued that it should be located at the Royal Festival Hall, where public access would be far greater. Not convinced, the Indonesian government agreed to place a gamelan in the hall on loan for a year, to assess how successful it was. One year later, in 1988, "The Venerable Spirit of Perfection" gamelan was gifted to

Above: Performers enjoy making music using Southbank Centre's gamelan.

Southbank Centre. It was the first to be accessible to the public in Britain (now there are over 150 gamelans in the country).

Each important gamelan made in Java receives its own name. *Kyai Lebdhajiwa*, or "The Venerable Spirit of Perfection", is unique, as no two gamelan are tuned exactly alike. It comprises two sets of instruments that reflect two tuning systems, a five-tone scale (*slendro*) and a seven-tone scale (*pelog*). Each set is made up of metallophones in the centre, which play a middle-register skeleton melody (*balungan*), surrounded by a range of gong-chimes, xylophones and zithers. Each instrument within the gamelan has its own name and role, and can be played by a number of musicians. A drummer in the centre controls the performance, which can last for several hours.

"The Venerable Spirit of Perfection" was joined by a smaller gamelan in December 2004, which is used for residencies and touring programmes. Both are regularly used for workshops, performances and creative projects. The eminent Javanese composer Rahayu Supanggah, as an associate artist at Southbank Centre, is involved in the continuing development of gamelan music in Britain, as are the Southbank Centre Gamelan Players (established by Alec Roth in 1987).

Strangely, for such a large and complex instrument, it is not difficult to learn to play. While it may take years to understand its full range of musical nuances, a satisfying sound can be produced by a group of beginners in minutes. Which is just as well, as gamelan performances in the Royal Festival Hall foyer, Purcell Room, Queen Elizabeth Hall and Southbank Centre's terraces are often given by schoolchildren or groups of adults who have only been playing for a matter of weeks (or days), as well as by professional musicians.

Southbank Centre often resonates with the noise of audiences making music for themselves. For nine weeks in 2006, boxes representing every seat in an orchestra were arranged on Riverside Terrace in front of the Royal Festival Hall. *PLAY.orchestra* invited you to do just that – as you

The Voice Box beside the Poetry Library at Southbank Centre looked, in the day, like a rather uninspired office conference room. But at night, the wide open glass walls brought in the colour of the epic sky, the lights from the streets and the rest of London spilled in, and the room's lighting was typically low, yellowy and...

well, warm. In this space poets read to about 40 or 50 listeners, and in this embracing light, something magical could happen. I have seen it happen many times. Once I saw novelist Colin Channer transport a room full of sceptics to a place of belief, a place in which his opening his arms wide and singing "I'll Fly Away" in the Rasta

way, as he read a funeral scene from his novel *Waiting In Vain*, did not seem like sentimentality or even a gimmick of art, but seemed like a holy moment, an instant of art revealing its power to be wholly self-assured and powerful.
Kwame Dawes, poet, actor, critic and musician

sat on each box, your "instrument" joined in the performance. If 59 people joined in, you heard the Philharmonia Orchestra in all their glory; if there was just one person, only a solo violin, cello or flute would play, depending on where they sat. In total, 220,000 people (and the odd animal) took part.

In 2004, percussionist Evelyn Glennie was commissioned to celebrate ten years of the Rhythm Sticks festival and she created *Bang on the Hall*. Music by MJ Cole derived from the local environment – train announcements from Waterloo station for example – was broadcast over the tannoy system, then performers from the London School of Samba were joined by local community group members who started to drum on anything they could find, including the banisters, waste bins and the floor. The finale was an ear-splitting percussive explosion in the ballroom.

Many people who happen upon such unexpected events would say that the spirit of Southbank Centre resides in them. Whether you experienced the veteran choreographer Peggy Spencer headlining a day of ballroom dancing in the foyer, children leaping from room to room in Jeppe Hein's fountain, Andrew Baynes's nine-ton sand sculpture of a horse, Bollywood dancers on open-top buses, an allotment planted on the Royal Festival Hall roof or Patti Smith reading poetry in the ballroom, there is something unforgettable about witnessing something you hadn't expected.

Below: People participate in PLAY.orchestra on Riverside Terrace in 2006.

Dance often springs up around Southbank Centre seemingly spontaneously. CandoCo, a dance company that works with disabled and non-disabled dancers, worked with Newham Sixth Form College to create films of dancers moving around the Royal Festival Hall as it closed its doors to the public in 2005 for major refurbishment work. The films were projected on to the exterior of the hall and accompanied by live music. The Urban Classicism Dance Company worked with pensioners who danced on the roof of the Queen Elizabeth Hall, and choreographers Akram Khan and Javier de Frutos have both worked with groups of older adults, rehearsing in Southbank Centre for sold-out performances. (This happens alongside an international programme that brings dancers from all around the world to perform at the Queen Elizabeth Hall and Purcell Room. Southbank Centre has a long tradition of staging dance that stretches back to the Festival of Britain, when the acclaimed Indian dancer Ram Gopal played to 3,000 people on two occasions in 1951.)

Many of these events take place thanks to a progressive education programme at Southbank Centre, initiated in 1986 when the South Bank Board took over management of the site. The programme has also maintained a close and creative relationship with artists who undertake residencies across the centre, since Opera Factory became the first artists in residence in 1987. Now there is a changing residency programme with dancers, solo musicians, choreographers and artists all working on site at the same time.

The Royal Festival Hall's main orchestras became resident artists in the 1990s, starting with the London Philharmonic Orchestra in 1990, which played its first season in 1992. The Philharmonia Orchestra followed in 1995. One woman, Yvonne Pegler, has seen every concert they have played as resident orchestras. Since the box office was computerized in 1992, her ticket sales have been recorded and now total over £30,000. She always sits in the same seat in the front row of the stalls, and often nips backstage to the artists' bar during the interval to have a whisky with the musicians. If she's not in her seat when the performance is due to start, the orchestras will wait for her. She has attended every single concert at the Royal Festival Hall for over twenty years, and has seen scores of outstanding performances. She was in the audience when young pianist Evgeny Kissin received twelve standing ovations in 1999, and when Sir Neville Marriner conducted the Academy of St Martin in the Fields despite having injured himself in rehearsal by getting carried away with the music and accidentally jamming his baton through his hand.

But not all concerts in the Royal Festival Hall are classical. When it first opened, the programme was 90 per cent classical, but by 2001 that

Above: Sir Neville Marriner conducts the Academy of St Martin in the Fields, 1987. Opposite: Teenagers get caught out by the changing room formations in Jeppe Hein's *Appearing Rooms* fountain in 2006.

figure was nearer 65 per cent. Dame Shirley Bassey continued to perform there every two years throughout the 1980s and 1990s, and fans would queue for days to buy tickets. As she rehearsed, nobody was allowed into the auditorium or backstage, and the building buzzed with excitement. When she walked out on to the stage she commanded her audience's attention, graciously receiving the many gifts she was offered. In 2000 the auditorium even became a dance party with a set by DJ Jeff Mills following his soundtrack accompaniment to the film *Metropolis*. During this period, the Queen Elizabeth Hall continued to host cutting-edge music events, from one of the first London performances by Antony and the Johnsons (who went on to win the 2005 Mercury Music Prize) to a night with hip-hop legend Rennie Harris and his Puremovement dance group.

All three concert halls have quick turnarounds from one type of event to another, but until recently the equipment to facilitate the necessary stage changes was mostly hand-operated. Consequently, bands and orchestras had to rehearse in the halls with them rigged for that evening's event. If it was a ballet, the stage would be deepened; an opera, the first rows of seats would be removed to create an orchestra pit. For an amplified concert, speakers and a mixing desk were installed and for an orchestral performance, the stage would be built up into tiers. Solid chunks of stage would be lifted into position; pianos were wheeled through the auditorium and lifted on to the platform from the stalls. Diplomatic relations between staff, jazz promoters and conductors were repeatedly strained when orchestras refused to practise in a hall that was aurally not the same as the one they would perform in (the speakers and mixing desk needed for jazz altered the acoustics, but they couldn't be removed each time an orchestra rehearsed because the time and manpower needed to do this made it prohibitive).

Throughout the 1990s, some conductors also began to complain about the acoustics generally. Sir John Eliot Gardiner didn't rate the Queen Elizabeth Hall at all, and Sir Simon Rattle famously went on record in 1999 to say the Royal Festival Hall was the "worst major concert hall in Europe", and that, when conducting there, "the will to live slips away in the first half-hour of rehearsal". So, while *Evening Standard* readers voted the Royal Festival Hall their favourite London building, the South Bank Board knew they had to revive the masterplan for Southbank Centre, and find the funds to refurbish the Royal Festival Hall's auditorium before senior conductors refused to perform there.

In 1993, following the collapse of the property market, Terry Farrell – as Southbank Centre's master planner – was back at his drawing board again. Then, in February, another architectural practice, Allies &

Opposite: Dame Shirley Bassey performing at the Royal Festival Hall in May 1996.

Above: Sir Richard Rogers's 1994 vision for Southbank Centre, featuring a glass "wave" and a new Skylon.

Morrison, were appointed as architectural advisors to assist in incremental change to the Royal Festival Hall. Farrell was swift to point out that he was still the master planner, and was now working with the South Bank Board, not Stanhope Properties. "I've always preferred our first scheme, which kept all the buildings," he said. "I prefer to keep buildings rather than demolish them, partly because in some way they represent a collective memory." But, by 1994, Farrell's involvement with Southbank Centre came to an end. And still nothing had been built, demolished or refurbished.

In February 1994, a competition was launched to find a new master planner, as an exhibition at the Architecture Foundation called "Building the South Bank" opened. The focus had shifted from the buildings to the environment they inhabited, as the catalogue stated: "the quality of the public spaces between buildings and the relationship to their urban surroundings does not provide a suitable setting for cultural institutions of such prestige." Details of the selection procedure and a brief followed: "The masterplan will provide a context for the refurbishment of the Royal Festival Hall and the extension and transformation of the Hayward and the Queen Elizabeth Hall, as well as the provision of new performance and educational spaces. Equally important is the need for a creative approach

to the enhancement and utilization of the spaces between and around the buildings." Ten architects would be selected from open submission, and a final shortlist of three would have a further month to develop plans before a decision was taken in September.

Over 100 architectural practices submitted proposals, and eventually Sir Richard Rogers was appointed the new Southbank Centre master planner. Much was expected from the man behind the Centre Pompidou in Paris, and he didn't disappoint. He designed a vast glass "wave" that would roll over the Hayward, Queen Elizabeth Hall and Purcell Room, and ripple along between the Royal Festival Hall and the Thames. It would visually unite the site, Rogers explained, as well as creating a warm outdoor environment – the glass would create a microclimate akin to southern France – for performances, events and alfresco dining. It was a visual nod to the 1851 Crystal Palace that had housed the Great Exhibition. It would be magnificent. And it would be expensive. The final quote for the roof was £68m. With the planned refurbishment of the Royal Festival Hall, costs rose to £171m. However, with the new millennium lottery fund and the Arts Council's initial support for a *grand projet*, the South Bank Board were confident the money could be raised.

Above left: The old pedestrian walkway on the Hungerford railway bridge.
Above right: One of two new Golden Jubilee bridges that flank Hungerford railway bridge.

Unfortunately, the masterplan quickly ran into red tape, and endless meetings ensued as every last detail of the proposal was discussed. Chairman Sir Brian Corby guided the organization through all the lottery applications but, in March 1998, the Arts Council announced it could only give £25m to the project after all, and the South Bank Board were back to square one. (There was sensitivity at the time that too much money was going to London arts organizations, and the scheme also proved too inflexible to be implemented in stages when funding became available.)

However, by the summer a new redevelopment campaign had been launched, this time spearheaded by Chris Smith, Secretary of State for Culture, Media and Sport. By December, new Southbank Centre chairman Elliott Bernerd had announced his plans to reinvigorate the site. "Our vision for the new South Bank," he said, "is to create a free-flowing cultural campus providing world-class arts and entertainment venues in an attractive and welcoming riverside setting." The Royal Festival Hall would stay open for the millennium year, and then restoration work would begin in 2001. And, he added, a new master planner would be announced to flesh out a vision that could be implemented incrementally. The interview process – which included a selection panel of thirteen stakeholders,

MELTDOWN

I read with Patti Smith at her Meltdown festival – now that was special. It was in the foyer of the Royal Festival Hall. They'd transformed the ballroom floor into a stage with bean-bags for the audience. It was a happening. I was transported to the time when I was born, when poetry was at its most popular. Everyone was either a poet or wanted to be a poet or wanted to watch poets. I was MC-ing the event – introducing a group of poets and reading some poems of my own. Before introducing Patti Smith, I asked her if I could read a poem. She spiritedly said yes. I read and looked back towards her – her hands were in the air above her head clapping. It's the best you can do for a great artist, to introduce them through a good reading. "Ladies and Gentlemen, Patti Smith..." Lemn Sissay, poet

Meltdown is Southbank Centre's most celebrated annual festival. Each year it has a different renowned artistic director, who selects a programme of concerts, exhibitions and events that take place over a few weeks in summer. It has included everything from Radiohead to Les Ballets C de la B's *Bonjour Madame*, it crosses every artistic divide and occupies the entire site.

Founded in 1993, Meltdown started as a week-long celebration of "music, dance, film and performance at the cutting edge". Its first artistic director was composer George Benjamin, and his programme included concerts by the London Philharmonic Orchestra and London Sinfonietta alongside Just Merit's machine-art performance *Radical Disruption*. Composers Louis Andriessen and Magnus Lindberg also directed Meltdown in the early years, as did singer-songwriter Elvis Costello [right], who celebrated his classical influences as well as introduced some pop elements into the festival for the first time. Then, in 1997, came musician

and performance artist Laurie Anderson, who brought Lou Reed to the Royal Festival Hall and whose programme included work by artist Jessica Voorsanger, Scottish poet Ivor Cutler and composer Michael Nyman.

John Peel was reluctant to take on the festival for 1998 because the dates clashed with the World Cup. After assurances that screens would be set up for people to watch the football he agreed to do it, and brought

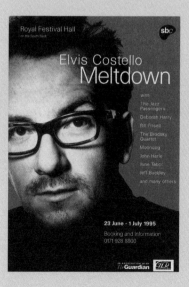

together a riotous mix of bands including The Jesus & Mary Chain, Cornershop and Gorky's Zygotic Mynci. A highlight of his Meltdown was an evening that began with The Delgados, continued with Spiritualized and finished with Sonic Youth.

Since 1999, Meltdown has been directed by Nick Cave, Scott Walker, Robert Wyatt, David Bowie, Lee "Scratch" Perry, Morrissey and Patti Smith. Smith's 2005 Meltdown was memorable for her energy as she fronted concerts and talks, danced with the audience and performed her entire 1975 album *Horses* in front of an ecstatic crowd. Her Meltdown included folk musicians and young bands, actors and poets, art films and artists. It featured several evenings during which some of the world's most acclaimed musicians collaborated to create electric and varied tributes to William S Burroughs, Jimi Hendrix and Bertolt Brecht.

David Bowie's 2002 Meltdown, which celebrated the tenth year of the festival, also included a wide range of artists and performers. In one month, you could hear his Philip Glass and Brian Eno collaboration, the Low and Heroes symphonies performed by the London Sinfonietta, discover the outsider rock'n'roll of Daniel Johnson and hear Finnish punk-accordionist and composer Kimmo Pojhonen. You could also witness a "Sound and Vision" exhibition in the ballroom, hear Asian Dub Foundation's film score for *La Haine* and listen to sets by Mercury Rev.

including Lambeth Council and neighbouring landowners – began again, and Rick Mather was appointed in May 1999.

The initial proposal, laid out by Bernerd, was for the outright demolition of the Hayward, Queen Elizabeth Hall and Purcell Room. But Mather developed a four-option strategy that ranged from refurbishment of the auditoria to building new concert halls and a gallery next to Jubilee Gardens. He quickly grew to see the positive side of the Brutalist buildings: "You wouldn't call these buildings beautiful," he said, "and since they were built I've been standing there thinking how I'd improve them. But they're the most potent period piece of the 1960s. The pendulum of taste is swinging back to the 1960s; just ask anyone under 30."

Pedestrian circulation was seen as an important issue that needed to be addressed, as did disabled access, and the river needed to become part of the site once more. Service lanes and yards were separated from pedestrian thoroughfares and plans were put in place for each building to have a ground level presence. Southbank Centre needed to be brought to life, with cafés, restaurants, shops, rehearsal rooms and studios built in disused undercrofts and railway arches. The one new building he did propose was a new national film centre, which would bring together the British Film Institute, the National Film Theatre and the Museum of the Moving Image. (The British Film Institute's IMAX cinema had just opened in Charlie Chaplin Walk, next to Southbank Centre, in 1999.)

Meanwhile, Southbank Centre's artistic programme continued to develop, with many new festivals and events. "Ballroom Blitz", "Escapade" and "The Great Outdoors" brought thousands to the Royal Festival Hall's foyers and outdoor spaces to dance, sing and have fun. The Rhythm Sticks percussion festival started in 1995, and the London Jazz Festival, International Mime Festival and Dance Umbrella all started to use Southbank Centre as a venue. A major theme of the 1990s was "Towards the Millennium", a series devised by Sir Simon Rattle and Michael Vyner to consider the achievements of the twentieth century. In 1996, for example, an exhibition of Festival of Britain sculpture was

I have a piece of the Hayward on my desk at The Fruitmarket Gallery. It's a core sample taken during the rebuild of the foyer, which was given to me as a leaving present [she was a curator at the Hayward 1998–2003]. It's the best present I could possibly have been given – a big, brutal, beautiful reminder of a building with the same qualities. My memories of the Hayward are all bound up with the building and with the total joy of installing an exhibition in it. I have wallpapered it, clad it in mirrors, filled it with the music of wildly competing sound installations, and put the subtlest and most attention-seeking art in it. It takes it all and makes something extraordinary out of it.
**Fiona Bradley, director,
The Fruitmarket Gallery**

held in the Royal Festival Hall, with concerts, performances and talks all exploring the 1950s. The series finale featured Tasmin Little playing Ligeti's 1992 Violin Concerto, conducted by Rattle. Other major festivals included Meltdown, which began in 1993 [see panel on page 143] and featured concerts and events organized by a practising musician, and the biannual Poetry International, which was revived in 1988.

Poetry International was brought back to life by Maura Dooley, Southbank Centre's first head of literature and talks, in the year the Arts Council's Poetry Library moved in to the Royal Festival Hall. Dooley appointed poets in residence, who included Sinead Morrissey and John Agard. Agard's book, *A Stone's Throw From Embankment*, is full of poems inspired by his year in residence in 1993 [see page 10]. And she also initiated a talks programme that has since seen novelists from Bret Easton Ellis to Hubert Selby Jr speak and sign books.

Hubert Selby Jr appeared at Southbank Centre in 2001, the year his novella *Waiting Period* was published. It was almost 40 years since *Last Exit to Brooklyn*, and he was very frail and ill. The event was a sell-out, and afterwards a long queue formed for the book signing. When everyone had left, he was taken to dinner at the People's Palace, the 200-seat restaurant in the Royal Festival Hall that overlooked the Thames.

Above: The gamelan is performed outdoors at Southbank Centre in summer 2006.

Below: "Escapade"
– a Bollywood-style filmic
extravaganza – engulfed
Southbank Centre in 2002.

The pianist Alfred Brendel was also in the restaurant, and the head of literature and talks asked if Selby would like to meet him. He said yes, so she asked Brendel to come over. Hubert took the pianist's hands in his, and kissed his fingers in honour of his talent.

Many non-fiction writers have also spoken at Southbank Centre. The Dalai Lama has conducted all-day question and answer sessions for 3,000 people, with members of the audience quietly performing T'ai Chi on the terraces outside during the lunch break. Mo Mowlam also spoke in the Royal Festival Hall when her memoirs were published in 2002. She strode on to the platform for a rehearsal with less than an hour to go, and realized she had forgotten her notes. She had left them on the kitchen table and nobody was at home, so she jumped into a taxi, raced to Hackney and returned with five minutes to spare. After a quick glass of whisky in her dressing room with Fergal Keane, she walked on to the stage.

The year before Mo Mowlam's mad dash, the Royal Festival Hall had celebrated its fiftieth anniversary. It still hadn't been refurbished, but a fundraising campaign was launched by Joanna Lumley at a celebratory concert held 50 years to the day after the King had declared the Festival of Britain – and the Royal Festival Hall – open. The concert on Thursday 3

May 2001 was attended by the Prince of Wales, as well as Peter Mandelson – his grandfather, Herbert Morrison, had been the Festival of Britain's chief supporter. The concert featured the Philharmonia Orchestra conducted by Valery Gergiev, with soloists Angela Gheorghiu, Marcello Giordani and Dmitri Hvorostovsky. A new chief executive, Karsten Witt, had brought with him a deep knowledge of contemporary classical music and the concert also included a specially commissioned fanfare by Sir Harrison Birtwistle. The celebrations continued over the weekend, with a Meltdown special that featured stars who had organized the festival to date, including Elvis Costello and Nick Cave. Sir Simon Rattle conducted the Orchestra of the Age of Enlightenment, Ian Bostridge and Melanie Diener sang Benjamin Britten's *War Requiem* and Sir Peter Maxwell Davies conducted the premiere of his *Antarctic Symphony*.

Lord Hollick joined Southbank Centre as chairman in February 2002, and appointed a new chief executive, Michael Lynch, later that year. Lynch moved to London from Australia, where he had run the Sydney Opera House, and he was determined to get the Royal Festival Hall refurbishment underway. Enough money was raised to close the hall temporarily in 2005 and the renovation finally began.

8 SOMETHING OLD, SOMETHING NEW

Previous page: Shops and restaurants spill out onto Riverside Walk, 2005.
Below: The Royal Festival Hall's auditorium during the 2005–07 refurbishment, with the birdcage scaffold in place.

3 October 2006. It is blustery and autumnal as project director Ian Blackburn begins a site tour of the Royal Festival Hall. At the moment, the project to refurbish the hall is on time and on budget, but both depend on Blackburn ensuring tight deadlines continue to be met. A dozen people in high visibility vests, hard hats and protective boots, follow him as he walks through the drizzle to the site entrance, down a gantry and into the temporary access lift that takes workmen up the outside of the building to all levels of the hall. There are tours of the buildings most days – for patrons, dignitaries, architects, journalists, members of the public – and the workforce is used to accommodating clusters of curious visitors.

Today's tour offers the last chance to see the hall's famous undulating ceiling up close. Next week the upper levels of the vast birdcage scaffolding

that, until recently, filled the auditorium will be removed. Work began on the ceiling as soon as the scaffold was assembled a year ago. Acres of asbestos were ripped out and all but one panel of the original "wavy" ceiling removed. The original ceiling should have been made of thick panels of dense plaster designed to reflect low-frequency sound and aid the hall's acoustics, but it ended up being constructed from thin fibrous plaster sheets filled with lighter cement. Acoustically, it never functioned as well as it should have, so a replacement ceiling has been included as part of the refurbishment, and now ten-centimetre-thick curved plaster panels hang nose to tail just above Blackburn's head. It still looks much like the original ceiling, and it still shrouds the necessary plant and equipment that is lodged in the attic space above it (which now draws air up through the hall instead of pumping it downwards).

Workmen in the attic are handing down scaffolding poles through a slim gap in the ceiling panels. Blackburn walks around them and towards the edge of the scaffold. He gestures down to the platform area, where workmen operate under a net canopy. From the top of the birdcage scaffold, the men appear minute and the sheer volume of the auditorium triggers a strong sense of vertigo. Workmen are preparing the platform for the installation of the organ; the boxes on either side of the stage are hidden under protective wrapping. The stalls seating has yet to be reinstated and the auditorium floor is a mass of grey concrete planks demarcating each row. Next week, work begins to strip the hall of the 30 miles of scaffolding and 40 miles of planks that currently fill it. And, in less than six months, the refurbishment of the Royal Festival Hall has to be complete for the inauguration weekend in June.

Above: The Royal Festival Hall shrouded from view in October 2005.

The Royal Festival Hall closed for refurbishment on 4 July 2005. In a little under two years it would reopen again but, in June 2005, the auditorium was full of performers saying goodbye. Pianist Alfred Brendel performed the last classical concert on 22 June and the previous night the Philharmonia Orchestra, under Vladimir Ashkenazy, performed the final movement of Haydn's *Farewell Symphony* as an encore, with each member of the orchestra leaving the stage in turn. Spontaneous parties had broken out all week. After the Philharmonia's final concert the ballroom floor was commandeered for a party, with Ashkenazy duetting with pianist Hélène Grimaud in the bar. Patti Smith had the honour of hosting the hall's last public event as she closed Meltdown on 26 June. Chief Executive Michael Lynch buried a time capsule in the ballroom and then staff danced there at a closing party held

One of my most vivid memories of the Royal Festival Hall is of being part of a crowd nearly taking its ceiling off with the cheering and clapping – at a silent film. It was at the hugely celebratory second showing of Abel Gance's brilliant *Napoléon*, with Sir Carl Davis conducting his own fine score. Near the end the screen splits into a triptych of different images, each tinted a different colour, to make the tricolor, the orchestra played the *Marseillaise*, and something strange and revolutionary swept through the London audience, which stood up and yelled with excitement at the orchestra and the screen. I've seen several of the Royal Festival Hall's silent film events, with Davis conducting, including a screening of Charlie Chaplin's *The Circus* which, as soon as it's on a big screen, accompanied by its full score, can be seen for the masterpiece it is. Just a couple of reasons why the Royal Festival Hall is a pretty special and versatile space.

Ali Smith, novelist

on 30 June. Contractors ISG InteriorExterior and Southbank Centre finally signed the refurbishment contract the following day.

By this time, the Royal Festival Hall was already being disassembled. Because of the demanding deadline for the reopening of the hall, ISG InteriorExterior was on site clearing out certain areas before the hall had closed. Work officially began on 4 July with the removal of the organ, the lowering of the platform canopy and the lengthy process of stripping out all the asbestos from the building. The "net and ball" carpet, in situ since 1951, was taken out, divided up and sold in squares to the public, to make way for a freshly woven replica.

Ian Blackburn, the project director for the refurbishment, was appointed back in 2003, but the plans for the conservation and restoration of the Royal Festival Hall stretch back a decade earlier than that, when Allies & Morrison were appointed house architects in 1993. After the hall became a Grade I listed building in 1988, lengthy planning applications had to be made before any internal or external work could be done, and Allies & Morrison were appointed as advisors. Their early work in the building included restoring former spaces such as the ground floor foyer back to their original use, and creating new ones such as the Hothouse studio and gamelan room. They also suggested that all internal paintwork should be changed from institutional green to white.

As part of the lottery bid for Sir Richard Rogers's "wave" masterplan for Southbank Centre, and to conform to the requirements set by the Heritage Lottery Fund, Allies & Morrison wrote the Royal Festival Hall *Conservation Plan* in 1996. They argued that the original design for the building had great clarity and was full of good ideas, many of which had been lost in subsequent years. They advocated rediscovering these original ideas and restoring them, taking into account current needs. This would include returning former circulation systems, reopening the roof terraces and removing offices that impinged on public areas.

Although the 1997 Rogers bid was unsuccessful, Allies & Morrison continued to work with Southbank Centre to develop plans for a refurbishment of the Royal Festival Hall. It took a further eight years of design and planning to be in a position to close the hall and undertake the restoration. The Arts Council agreed to allow £20m of the £25m allocated to the masterplan to be spent on the refurbishment of the Royal Festival Hall, on the understanding that this would provide the impetus for implementing the rest of the new Rick Mather scheme. Elliott Bernerd, the mastermind behind Mather's masterplan, had to relinquish his chairmanship due to illness, and Lord Hollick was appointed in 2002 to deliver his vision.

During this process, Graham Morrison and Di Haigh – who had joined Allies & Morrison to write the initial *Conservation Plan* – talked to several of the original architects including Sir Leslie Martin and Peter Moro. They warmly supported the campaign to bring back the hall's 1951 circulation plan, and agreed that the transparency of the building, compromised by shops and wooden panelling in the foyer, should be restored. Allies & Morrison were keen to retain the ideas and spirit of the original building, while making it function as a world-class twenty-first century concert hall. Where they could, they looked at restoring original fixtures and fittings, such as the "Mexican hat" lights in the foyer and the cigarillo door handles. They stipulated that Moro's "net and ball" carpet should be rewoven, and the tapestries behind the boxes be cleaned and restored. New additions to the hall were planned, including the latest acoustic technology, lighting for the auditorium and glazed pergolas on

Below: Two illustrations by Allies & Morrison showing the original entry points to the Royal Festival Hall in 1951 (left), and the reorientation following the 1964 extension (right). The original 1951 entrances have now been reinstated.

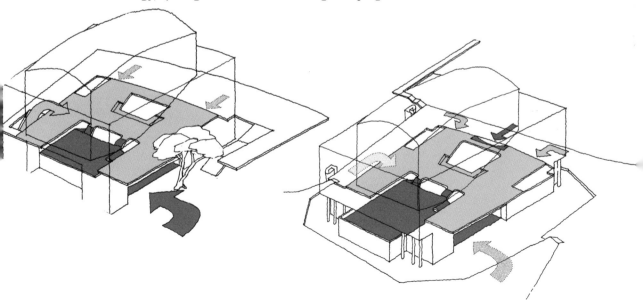

Above: The Front Room by Michael Vale, added to the Queen Elizabeth Hall foyer in 2006.
Opposite: David Batchelor's *Festival Remix*, commissioned by Southbank Centre for Christmas 2006.

the roof terraces. Disabled access was considered and a new glass lift designed. Finally, Allies & Morrison commissioned a colour survey, to dig deep into the surface of the Royal Festival Hall's walls and discover what lay underneath layers of redecorations.

In July 2005 all Southbank Centre staff formerly based in the Royal Festival Hall had to be relocated. Allies & Morrison had argued in the conservation plan that, for the Royal Festival Hall's public spaces to be recreated, the offices that had been added piecemeal throughout the years – halving the floor space of bars and roof terraces – would have to go. But go where? Rick Mather's solution was to relocate them in a new building, and Allies & Morrison designed a slim, four-storey building with two floors of offices that stretches the length of Festival Terrace along the side of the hall. Staff moved in to the new Southbank Centre Building in April 2006 after spending a year off-site in temporary accommodation, and consequently 35 per cent more public space was able to be restored to the Royal Festival Hall public areas.

Throughout 2006, as the hall remained closed, things started changing across the entire site. The Hayward was relit, and the Queen Elizabeth Hall received a foyer makeover that added a new performing space, The Front Room, and opened up the building to free daytime entertainment. The Queen Elizabeth Hall's backstage area had recently received its own modest refurbishment in an attempt to cater for Southbank Centre orchestras whose programmes transferred to the smaller hall for the duration of the closure. Projects including PLAY.orchestra and Trading Places livened up Riverside Terrace.

Following the appointment of artistic director Jude Kelly in September 2005, and a new director for the Hayward, Ralph Rugoff, in May 2006, commissions and installations by artists started to crop up beyond the confines of the gallery. Jeppe Hein's *Appearing Rooms* fountain occupied Riverside Terrace in front of the Royal Festival Hall that summer, the first in a regular programme of temporary fountains that recreate one aspect of the original Festival of Britain – a sense of unexpected fun. A few months later the first annual Christmas lights commission, *Festival Remix* by David Batchelor, was unveiled. Batchelor used coloured plastic bottles to create substantial fairy lights that were strung along Riverside Terrace, and his trademark neons illuminated building pallets, cement mixers and a commercial bin seemingly left out by the builders at the side of the Royal Festival Hall on Festival Terrace.

When Kelly arrived, she was keen to reinvigorate not just Southbank Centre buildings but the entire site. She advocated a return to the spirit of 1951, when the south bank was full of fountains, lights and flags.

Hugh Casson, one of the architects involved in the Festival of Britain, wrote of the 1951 South Bank Exhibition: "By now perhaps it is dusk, the buildings and flags are floodlit, the lights twinkle in the trees, and gas flames leap between the fountains." Blue lights are now planned for the branches of the London plane trees that line the river, and flags have already returned to the site. A changing programme of artists' flags now fly from the original 30-metre Festival of Britain flagpole. The flagpole occupies a corner of Jubilee Gardens, itself earmarked for development by Dutch design group West 8 in consultation with Southbank Centre, local landowners and the neighbouring community. A national film centre is planned nearby that would bring together all the British Film Institute's interests including the National Film Theatre.

On Friday 8 June 2007, almost two years after it closed its doors, the Royal Festival Hall shrugs off its scaffolding and reopens. In celebration, an "Overture Weekend" features 48 hours of free events across the entire Southbank Centre including a gamalan marathon, converging marching bands and a 1,000-strong choir arriving by candlelit boat. The first concert at the hall is the following Monday, 11 June, a coming-together of over 250 musicians from all four resident orchestras – the London Philharmonic Orchestra, Philharmonia Orchestra, London Sinfonietta and the Orchestra of the Age of Enlightenment.

The opening programme offers the first opportunity to hear the Royal Festival Hall's new acoustics, and explore the refurbished building. Even

Above: Yinka Shonibare's flag flies at half-mast on the original Festival of Britain flagpole, in January 2007.
Right: An artist's impression of the redesigned Jubilee Gardens, proposed by West 8.

from the outside, it is clear that the hall has changed. The original entrance has been renovated at ground level, and faces Waterloo bridge. A bank of glass doors lead from Southbank Centre Square (now inset with LEDs that respond to music being played in the hall) into the restored entrance. Since the 1964 extensions were added, this area was home to stores, offices and the Hothouse studio. The walnut cloakroom counters had been ripped out, replaced by a staff dining room. Now, a new cloakroom recreates the dynamic zig-zag of the 1951 design. To replace the original box office on this level, electronic ticket machines have been installed. Tickets in hand, you can follow the original route to the main foyer and watch the building unfold, climbing broad open stairs to the ballroom floor (or taking the lift) and progressing up to the level two foyer and bar. When the orientation of the building was changed in 1964, this key design objective was lost. New entrances on Riverside Terrace allowed instant access to the entire level two foyer and took away any sense of the building slowly opening itself up to each visitor. (Riverside entrances at both ground level and level two remain, and are now signalled by distinctive yellow canopies.)

Above: A computer-generated image of how the Royal Festival Hall auditorium will look in 2011, when the organ is fully reinstated.
Overleaf: An artist's impression of the refurbished Royal Festival Hall seen from the north bank.

Although the book and record shops that used to occupy the foyer have now been relocated to the riverfront retail development, the hall's own bar, café and gift shop still remain. The bar is located where it has always been, overlooking the ballroom but no longer sunken, and the café has returned to its original 1951 position facing Riverside Terrace with tables both inside and out. Seating sympathetic to Robin Day's original designs has been installed throughout. Each quadrant of the hall has its own sign colour, which stretches up across every level of the building.

The original stairs have been restored, and rise above the level two foyer in symmetric pairs. They were originally built by Airscrew and Jicwood, manufacturers of aeroplane propellers during the Second World War, and were then at the forefront of innovative design with their slender treads made from laminated plywood reinforced with steel. Paired flights of stairs climb up to the top of the building where the level six roof terraces have been reopened. The white armatures of the original pergolas have been glazed over, and offer views of St Paul's Cathedral to the east and the Houses of Parliament to the west. These roof terraces once teemed with plants maintained by the London County Council gardeners, and were popular locations to spend the interval. But, in the 1980s, the terrace overlooking Hungerford bridge had been covered in makeshift offices, and its sister terrace closed to the public.

Below: 1951 illustration of the original cloakroom.

Left: 1951 illustration of the
Royal Festival Hall roof terrace.

The rich wood and leather auditorium has always been the beating heart of the Royal Festival Hall. During the hall's closure, the entire interior of the auditorium was taken apart piece by piece, with all the walnut, oak and elm panelling restored, stiffened and remounted so as to improve the acoustics. Larry Kirkegaard, the hall's acoustician, was involved with every aspect of the interior's remodelling as he attempted to rectify the short reverberation time and the subsequent dryness of sound. However, at first glance, the auditorium looks very familiar. Wherever possible, the original materials have been conserved. Even the seats designed by Robin Day are refurbished originals, albeit with extra padding and new fabric covers. But almost everything has been adjusted

When I think of the Festival Hall, I think of the back stairs. There was never time to wait for a lift and the three of us working on literature events were forever running round the building looking for something or one another. One of us might be giving tea to Margaret Atwood or Seamus Heaney, while the other two searched for a lost podium or negotiated with a consulate over a Romanian writer's visa. Front of house, the stairs were shallow and carpeted. The backstairs were sealed by fire doors, unmarked, concrete and steep. They meant business. Running around the building all day meant that I glimpsed and overheard all aspects of the life of the hall: a singer in rehearsal, dancers stretching outside their dressing rooms, a school choir, deliveries of instruments, champagne and flowers; talk of contracts, press releases, a leaky roof. I relished these casual encounters with things I might not otherwise seek out – the perpetual gamelan, the pensioners' tea dances, the craft shop, exhibitions and the endless range of foyer events as well as the chance to hear everyone from Alfred Brendel to Miles Davis. I grew to love the building's complexities - its least accessible corners, its terraces and those back stairs.

Lavinia Greenlaw, writer

to improve acoustics and visitor (and performer) comfort. There's an extra eight centimetres of legroom in each row of the stalls for example, at a loss of 125 seats, and the new sycamore ceiling above the orchestra is now reflective so that it can contribute to the hall's acoustic. The remounting of the panelling and the new plaster ceiling have aided the sound-absorption problems, and a state-of-the-art lighting rig – hidden behind moveable lightweight canopies above the platform – and deployable absorbers ensure that the hall can present rock and pop concerts as well as more traditional recitals.

The organ has been moved further back to make the stage more flexible for dance and operatic performances. The two mechanized stage lifts, added in 1964, have been replaced by eleven new lifts, and a piano store at platform level means musical programmes can be more varied, with instruments easily added to the stage during the interval or between pieces. The original stage was only 45 centimetres above the level of the audience, placing the performers at eye level with the stalls. This was to break down the barriers between those on stage and those in the audience, and while tastes changed and the stage rose accordingly, the platform still intentionally lacks a proscenium arch, aiming to bring the two sides of the hall – performers and audiences – as close together as possible. Reconfiguration of the blast walls, replacement of the original canopy and modifications to the panelling surrounding the platform means that sound now feeds back to performers, something that hasn't happened before.

Beyond the new Australian walnut doors of the auditorium, the level four interval bars have been transformed. Offices had encroached on them until they were less than half their original size, but now they have been returned to how Martin and his team envisaged them. The restaurant has also been remodelled and renamed, and the 240-seat Skylon restaurant, designed by Sir Terence Conran, includes a brasserie and a bar.

Overleaf: A cutaway showing the interior of the refurbished Royal Festival Hall, 2007.

As with many massive cities, it is possible to be completely alone, isolated and filled with the writerly sense of anonymity that makes you want to write poems about rivers, about art, about strangers, about history and about loss. When I come to London, I crave that sensation. And I ritualize my behaviour. I always travel to Southbank Centre. I cross that bridge at dusk, make my way to the large, brightly lit ground floor of the building where people are drinking coffee, buying books, staring at exhibits, enduring dates, breaking up, reading newspapers, killing time from work, or waiting to see a show. I know no one there. I find a seat with a table near the glass sidings that look out to the Thames. It is as much about being close to where fascinating art is being made, about knowing that just upstairs major authors are reading their work and major musicians are making music in this building, as it is about finding a warm place where tea and dessert are served, where the light is rich and copious and where I can feel as if I am a writer whose books are on the shelves of the bookstore. **Kwame Dawes, poet, actor, critic and musician**

SOUTHBANK CENTRE: THE FUTURE

The Royal Festival Hall reopens its doors in June 2007 after a major refurbishment. At the same time, the surrounding terraces, squares and outdoor spaces [below] have received much-needed attention, and the entire Southbank Centre has been reinvigorated. Now you are as likely to see concerts, artworks and events in the open air as in the Royal Festival Hall, Queen Elizabeth Hall, Purcell Room and Hayward.

It is not only the front of house facilities that have been modified. Backstage, the dressing rooms used by choirs and visiting corps de ballet now have en suite facilities so ballerinas no longer have to step into the main corridor after showering before darting back into their dressing rooms between costume changes. (A modesty curtain had to be rigged up at both ends of the corridor when they were in residence previously, which only worked if no member of staff wanted to go to the toilet – staff toilets were located at the end of the corridor.)

Many favoured haunts in the Royal Festival Hall have returned, such as The Saison Poetry Library and the level five balcony terrace. But other areas are new. When Allies & Morrison began researching the Royal Festival Hall conservation plan, they came across an area on the ground floor that turned out to be the original foyer for the proposed second hall. The smaller auditorium was never built, and the foyer was soon divided into stores. Now it has been opened up and offers a dedicated entrance to Spirit Level, a new centre for participation and creativity that has been created on the ground floor in former plant rooms. (It is the first time that there has been dedicated space at Southbank Centre for this kind of activity.) The area houses the gamelan and the Royal Festival Hall Archive, but it also includes colour-coded rooms whose function changes depending on what's happening inside them. They may be places to hear live poetry or performance art; they may be transformed into a radio station or even an Arctic headquarters: climate change explorers Cape Farewell are resident artists at Southbank Centre until 2010.

Left: The Noorderlicht at Kongsvegen Glacier, the base for the 2004 Cape Farewell expedition.

Not everything has been returned in time for the Royal Festival Hall's reopening. While one third of the restored organ is in place – enough for it to be played as an orchestral accompaniment – the remaining pipes won't be in situ for several years. However, the framework for the pipes has been raised so when they do return home they will now all be entirely on show, and new organ doors will allow conductors to control how much of the organ will be on view during concerts. The fully restored organ is scheduled to be completed by 2011.

The opening of the Royal Festival Hall has been seen as an opportunity to reawaken the entire site. Events all over Southbank Centre such as Stan Won't Dance's *Off The Wall*, which includes free-runners and circus acrobats, will take place alongside concerts featuring Pierre Boulez, Judith Weir, Sir Simon Rattle, Angelika Kirschlager and Brian Wilson. A raft of artists including composer Nitin Sawhney, designer Michael Vale, cult band Saint Etienne, flamenco artist Paco Peña, lighting designer Willie Williams and choreographers Maresa von Stockert and Rafael Bonachela have formed alliances with Southbank Centre. In future, the centre aims to be less of a receiving house and to become more directly involved with commissioning new work and initiating projects between choreographers, musicians, visual artists, poets and dancers. New temporary venues are planned to appear in 2008 and beyond, such as the London International Festival of Theatre's "new parliament" and the Udderbelly, a 300-seater venue to be run by teenagers. There are plans for a smaller gallery space to open in the Hayward to show work by young artists, and to restore full access to the roof terrace above the Queen Elizabeth Hall. New rehearsal rooms and artists' studios will appear when undercrofts on site can be cleared, and there is even talk of a hotel near Waterloo bridge. Landscape architects Gross Max are transforming the urban environment of Southbank Centre, including remodelling Southbank Centre Square and Riverside Walk.

Now, in tandem with Tate Modern and nineteen other not-for-profit arts organizations located on or near the south bank, there are ambitious plans for Southbank Centre and affiliates to become London's cultural quarter for the 2012 Olympics. It's hard to imagine that just 60 years ago the south bank was a muddy riverbank with derelict workshops, the odd working wharf, a functioning shot tower and a disused brewery. The south bank has finally succeeded in becoming a cultural destination, and Southbank Centre is at its heart. With its mix of concert halls and galleries, free foyer and terrace performances, restaurants, bars and shops it represents what a twenty-first-century cultural centre can and should be – exciting, inspiring, surprising, breathtaking, unforgettable.

South Bank and Bankside Cultural Quarter

A coalition of not-for-profit arts organizations working together to create a vibrant cultural quarter for London

1 British Film Institute
2 Borough Market
3 Design Museum
4 Globe theatre
5 Imperial War Museum
6 Jerwood Space
7 London Philharmonic Orchestra
8 London Sinfonietta
9 National Theatre
10 Old Vic Theatre
11 Orchestra of the Age of Enlightenment
12 Philharmonia Orchestra
13 Rambert Dance Company
14 Siobhan Davies Dance Company
15 Southbank Centre
16 Southwark Playhouse
17 The Architecture Foundation
18 The Mayor's Thames Festival
19 Tate Modern
20 Unicorn Theatre
21 Young Vic

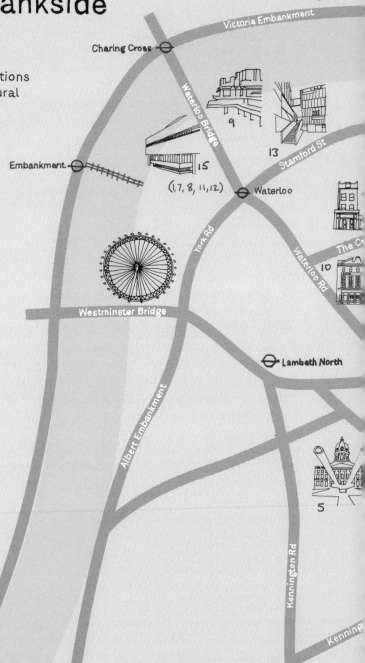

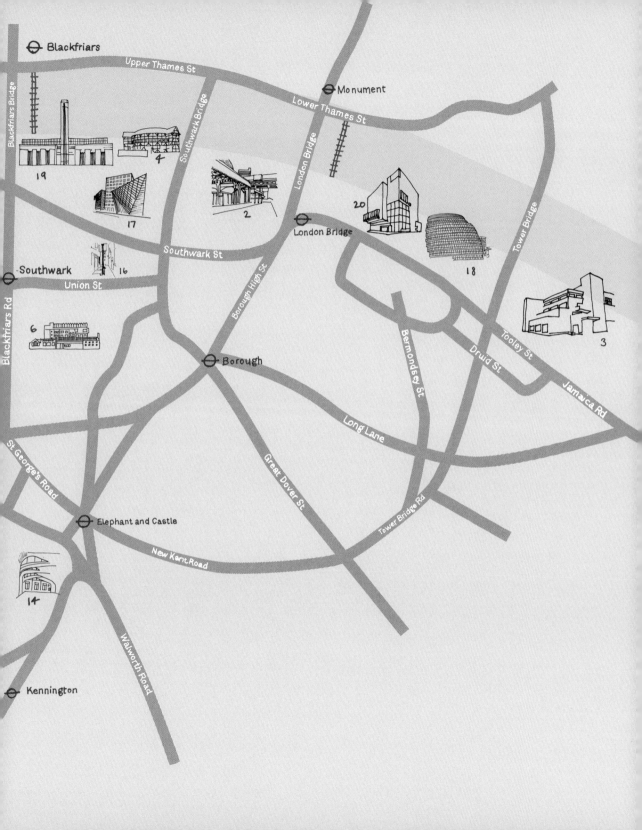

⊖ Blackfriars

Upper Thames St

Blackfriars Bridge

⊖ Monument

Lower Thames St

Southwark Bridge

London Bridge

Tower Bridge

19

4

17

2

20

18

3

⊖ London Bridge

Southwark St

Borough High St

⊖ Southwark

16

Union St

Blackfriars Rd

6

Bermondsey St

Druid St

Tooley St

Jamaica Rd

⊖ Borough

Long Lane

St George's Road

Great Dover St

Tower Bridge Rd

⊖ Elephant and Castle

New Kent Road

14

Walworth Road

⊖ Kennington

The river light that floods the upper floors. The wicker hampers outside dressing rooms on level four each Christmas, out of which would spill – between performances of *The Nutcracker* – a mouse's ears, a sugar plum fairy's tiara or a velvet cape. David Glass and Heathcote Williams celebrating whales in a double bill. Meeting Messiaen. Watching Louise Bennett, "Miss Lou", triumphant in a standing ovation at the Storytelling Festival. The opening of the Poetry Library in 1988, when Seamus Heaney cut the book-shaped cake and rejoiced in the Royal Festival Hall as the newest, latest, address to put fire in the soul of any aspiring poet. Creeping into the dark and empty auditorium to watch Nureyev practice. The full force of Germaine Greer's withering glance at the grumpy man in the second row. Audiences picnicking in the intervals of the annual St Matthew Passion. Hearing Keith Jarrett warming up. Seeing tears in the eyes of Nobel Laureate Czeslaw Milosz, when an elderly Polish steward arrived backstage with the apple cake she had made to welcome him. The regular sight of Ivor Cutler, in bicycle clips, changing his library books. Alfred Brendel. How very long a Javanese wayang can be. The brilliance of Brendan Kennelly's *Medea* in its week's run at the Purcell Room. Billy Bragg coaxing a reluctant Leon Rosselson on stage to sing "The World Turned Upside Down", written by Rosselson and a hit for Bragg, only for a member of the audience to take over when they both forgot the words. The search all over London for the right raw fish for the Inuit throat singers. A whole new chapter in my education.

Maura Dooley, poet

THANKS AND ACKNOWLEDGEMENTS

Many people have made this book possible. Particular thanks go to John Agard, Simon Armitage, Paul Ayres, Maureen Ayres, Daniel Barenboim, Stephen Bayley, Ellie Beedham, George Benjamin, Pierre Boulez, Fiona Bradley, Alfred Brendel, Kenneth Browne, Chuck Close, Sir Terence Conran, Alison Coutinho, Celeste Dandeker, Kwame Dawes, Lucienne Day, Robin Day, Michael Frayn, Paul Gambaccini, Ian Grant, Peter Greenaway, Lavinia Greenlaw, Romesh Gunesekera, Di Haigh, Elain Harwood, John Hegley, Joan Hills, Anthony Holden, Robert Hylton, Shobana Jeyasingh, Mala Jones, Anish Kapoor, Akram Khan, Richard Mallett, Andrew Motion, Lesley Mullins, Charles O'Brien, Julian Opie, Yvonne Pegler, Courtney Pine, Alain Platel, Tero Saarinen, George Simner, Lemn Sissay, Ali Smith, Matthew Sweet, Jean Symons, Lieven Thyrion, Mitsuko Uchida and all Southbank Centre staff.

Throughout the book I have drawn on memories submitted to the "Love the Festival Hall" campaign, specifically those by Michael Ajerman, Janey Antoniou, John Barney, Jeanne Becker, Nancy C Bilderbeck, Simon Black, Helen Braiden, Alice Bree, Rachel Brittle, Brenda Burkill, Ian Burr, LN Butler, June Charman, Peter Clark, Theresa Clark, Revd John Coghlan, John Collis, Cathy Cooper, CJ Connolly, Julia Curl, Rachel Curtis, Maureen Davey, Vicki Davis, Ellen Dewalliter, Richard Drakeford, Jill Edwards, Jo Feeney, Julia Garratt, Geoffrey Goleseir, Ami John Golland, Andrew Grumbridge, Signe Schou

Hansen, John Hawley, I Hornby, Laura Hulse, Philip Hutchinson, Tony Israel, Susan Jeffery, Susie Johns, Martin Jones, Rupert Jones, Tom Keller, Ferhat Khwaja, Cynthia Lacy, Guy De Launey, Rex Lawson, Becca Leathlean, Lucy Lepchani, Sue Levinson, Paul Maguire, Hannah Maier, Sara Masson, Wendy Mathews, Paul McCann, Danny McCarthy, Melody McLaren, Sybil Michelow, Hamid Moham, Vernon Morgan, Judy Murdoch, Caroline Myddelton, Christine Oxland, Dee Palmer, Fred Peskett, Alex Pollard, Neil Roberts, Jane Robinson, Valerie Ryalls, Ian Seadon, E Sharp, Adam Shaw, Richard Sheldon, David Shelton, Liz Sweetland, Guy Taylor, Margaret Taylor, Ken Thompson, Chris Tyrrell, Shaney Vere-Dresser, Elizabeth Anne Webb, David Welsh, Garry Williams and Mark Wilsher. All memories can be read at www.lovethefestivalhall.org.uk.

Southbank Centre would like to thank the 18,000 donors who contributed to the "Transforming the Royal Festival Hall" campaign. Their names run alphabetically throughout this book. (Every effort has been made to check names and titles. The book includes donors up to 1 January 2007.)

TRANSFORMING THE ROYAL FESTIVAL HALL

Southbank Centre is grateful to the
following donors for their support

Anonymous Donors

The 29th May 1961 Charitable Trust

3i Group

American Fund For The Southbank Centre

Arts Council England

Mr Elliott Bernerd

Mr Peter Borender

The City Bridge Trust

Clore Duffield Foundation

The Clothworkers' Foundation

The John Coates Charitable Trust

The John S Cohen Foundation

Sir Ronald and Lady Cohen

Mr and Mrs GL Collins

Columbia Foundation

Sir Brian and Lady Corby

Department for Culture, Media and Sport

Devereux Family Trust

Lloyd and Sarah Dorfman

Dame Vivien Duffield DBE

Dunard Fund

The John Ellerman Foundation

The Fidelity UK Foundation

The Foyle Foundation

The Gatsby Charitable Foundation

The Goldsmiths' Company Charity

Donors to the Lord Goodman Fund

The Hedley Foundation

Heritage Lottery Fund

Hollick Family Trust

The JP Jacobs Charitable Trust

JCB

JPMorgan Chase Foundation

Mr and Mrs Donald Kahn

Gilbert and Lena Kaplan

The Kresge Foundation

The Linbury Trust

The Mercers' Company

The Modiano Charitable Trust

The Monument Trust

Sir Mark and Lady Moody-Stuart

Mr and Mrs Paul Morgan

Mr Martin Myers

The Jack Petchey Foundation

The Roger and Ingrid Pilkington
    Charitable Trust

The David and Elaine Potter Foundation

PRS Foundation

The Rayne Foundation

Richmond Associates UK Limited

Sir John Ritblat and Family

The Rothermere Foundation

The Coral Samuel Charitable Trust

Schroder Foundation

Shell 🐚

Mrs Lois Sieff OBE

Southbank Centre Governors

Charlotte and Dennis Stevenson

The Bernard Sunley Charitable Foundation

Dr Christopher and The Lady Juliet Tadgell

The Tussauds Group

The Weston Family

The Wolfson Foundation

Mr Robin Woodhead

PICTURE CREDITS

Cover Southbank Centre
4–5 Luis Artus
11 Richard Haughton
13 Geoff Crawford
14–15 Royal Festival Hall Archive
16 Hayward Archive (top);
Campbell's Press Studio/Royal
Festival Hall Archive
18–19 Royal Festival Hall Archive
21 Royal Festival Hall Archive
22 Royal Festival Hall Archive (all)
23 Royal Festival Hall Archive
24 Royal Festival Hall Archive (all)
25 Royal Festival Hall Archive
26 Historical Picture Archive/Corbis
27 Getty Images
28–9 Guildhall Library, City of
London
30 Royal Festival Hall Archive
31 Royal Festival Hall Archive
32 Sport and General Press Agency/
Royal Festival Hall Archive (top);
Royal Festival Hall Archive
33 Royal Festival Hall Archive
34 Royal Festival Hall Archive
35 Leslie Martin
36 Royal Festival Hall Archive (all)
37 Royal Festival Hall Archive
38 Royal Festival Hall Archive
39 Royal Festival Hall Archive (all)
41 Abram Games
43 Royal Festival Hall Archive (all)
44 HM Stationery Office/Royal
Festival Hall Archive
45 Royal Festival Hall archive
46–7 Royal Festival Hall archive
48 Jarrold and Sons Ltd/Royal
Festival Hall Archive
49 Royal Festival Hall Archive/Mrs
Holland

50 Royal Festival Hall Archive/Mrs
Holland (top); Royal Festival Hall
Archive
51 Royal Festival Hall Archive (all)
52 Royal Festival Hall Archive/Mrs
Holland
53 V&A Images (top); The Official
Record: Max Parrish/LCC
54 Royal Festival Hall Archive (all)
55 Royal Festival Hall Archive/Erich
Auerbach (top); Royal Festival Hall
Archive/Mrs Holland
56 Getty Images/Hulton Deutsch
Collection
57 Royal Festival Hall Archive/
Maurice Wilson
58 Royal Festival Hall Archive
61 Royal Festival Hall Archive
62 Royal Festival Hall Archive
63 Royal Festival Hall Archive
64 Royal Festival Hall Archive
65 Royal Festival Hall Archive (top
left); Royal Festival Hall Archive/
E Locker (top right); The Official
Record: Max Parrish/LCC (bottom)
66 The Official Record: Max Parrish/
LCC
67 The Official Record: Max Parrish/
LCC (all)
68 Royal Festival Hall Archive (all)
69 Royal Festival Hall Archive(all)
70 Royal Festival Hall Archive
71 Royal Festival Hall Archive (top);
Ralph Downes (bottom)
72 Royal Festival Hall Archive (all)
73 The Official Record: Max Parrish/
LCC
74 Royal Festival Hall Archive (all)
76 Higgs and Hill Ltd/Royal Festival
Hall Archive (top); Royal Festival

Hall Archive
77 Royal Festival Hall Archive
79 Royal Festival Hall Archive
80 Raj Pardesi
82 Royal Festival Hall Archive (all)
83 Royal Festival Hall Archive
84 Fox Photos/Royal Festival Hall
Archive (top); Royal Festival Hall
Archive
85 Royal Festival Hall Archive
86 Royal Festival Hall Archive
87 Royal Festival Hall Archive (top);
Central Press Photos/Royal Festival
Hall Archive
88 Royal Festival Hall Archive
89 Hallmark Records/Royal Festival
Hall Archive (top); Gordon Fraser
Gallery Ltd/David Cockroft
90 Royal Festival Hall Archive
91 Royal Festival Hall Archive
92 Royal Festival Hall Archive
93 Royal Festival Hall Archive
95 Central Press Photos/Hayward
Archive
96 John Riddy/Hayward Archive
98–9 Hayward Archive
100 Todd White/Hayward Archive
(top); Hayward Archive
101 Graham Bishop and Corry
Bevington/Hayward Archive
102 John Webb/Hayward Archive
(top); Hayward Archive
103 Arts Council Collection/
Acquired with support from
The Henry Moore Foundation ©
Antony Gormley (top); Arts Council
Collection/Gift of Charles Saatchi ©
Richard Wilson
104 Hayward Archive
105 Hayward Archive (all)

SELECT BIBLIOGRAPHY

Much of the information that forms the basis for this book was gathered during interviews with past and present staff, performers and visitors. Those who have been consulted are acknowledged on page 174. Documents found in the Royal Festival Hall and Hayward archives, including press releases, meeting minutes and programmes, have not been listed but have been extensively consulted.

Ackroyd, Peter, *London: The Biography*, Chatto & Windus, 2000

Agard, John, *A Stone's Throw From Embankment: The South Bank Collection*, Southbank Centre, 1993

Allies & Morrison, *Conservation Plan: Royal Festival Hall*, Allies & Morrison, 1996

Allies & Morrison, *Urban Context: Appendix to the Conservation Plan*, Allies & Morrison, 2000

Amery, Colin, "A cure for the South Bank", *Financial Times*, 2 July 1979

Arts Council Great Britain Annual Report 1967-68, Arts Council, 1968

Baillieu, Amanda, "South Bank commission for Allies & Morrison", *Building Design*, 12 February 1993

Bainbridge, Charles, Earnshaw, Tania et al, eds, *fifty fifty: Fifty Poems from Fifty Years of the Poetry Library*, Southbank Centre, 2003

Baker, Richard, *Richard Baker's London: a theme with variations*, Jarrold Colour Publications, 1989

Banham, Mary, and Hillier, Bevis, eds, *A Tonic to the Nation: The Festival of Britain 1951*, Thames & Hudson, 1976

Barker, Jonathan, "Introduction", Celebration of Poetry programme, 13-19 June 1988

Bartholomew's Reference Atlas of Greater London, John Bartholomew and Son Ltd, 1940

Bean, TE, "A river with two right banks", published in the Royal Festival Hall programme of reopening concerts, February 1965

Binney, Marcus, "Wrong turning on the South Bank", *The Times*, 4 January 1999

Brockman, HAN, "The Queen Elizabeth Hall: Pebbles on the South Bank Beach", *Financial Times*, 1 March 1967

Brunius, Jacques, and Harvey, Maurice, *Brief City*, 1952, 19-minute film on the Festival of Britain, sponsored by the Central Office of Information and the Observer

Building the South Bank, exhibition catalogue, The Architecture Foundation, 1994

Burstow, Robert, *Symbols for '51*, exhibition catalogue, Southbank Centre, 1996

Cairns, David, "Can the new piper afford a new tune?", *Sunday Times*, 29 December 1985

Cherry, Bridget and Pevsner, Nikolaus, *The Buildings of England: London 2 South*, Penguin, 1983

Constantine, Jill, *Art on Loan: Guidelines for the display and care of the Arts Council Collection*, Southbank Centre, 2004

Cork, Richard, Khanna, Balraj and Read, Shirley, *Art on the South Bank: an independent report*, Greater London Council, 1986

Coutinho, Alison, Royal Festival Hall site diary 2005-06, unpublished

Cox, Ian, *South Bank Exhibition: A guide to the story it tells*, HM Stationery Office, 1951

Curtis, Penelope, ed, *Sculpture in Twentieth-Century Britain*, Henry Moore Institute, 2003

Dant, Adam, *Dant's Anecdotal Guide to the History of the Arts Council Collection*, Southbank Centre, 2006

Downes, Ralph, *Baroque Tricks: adventures with the organ builders*, Positif Press, 1999

Downes, Ralph, *The Organ in the Royal Festival Hall*, booklet published by Southbank Centre, n.d. (Royal Festival Hall Archive)

Eastwick-Field, John, and Stillman, John, "Royal Festival Hall: II", *The Architects' Journal*, 26 April, 1951

Evans, David, unpublished research document on the construction of the Hayward, Queen Elizabeth Hall and Purcell Room, 2005 (Royal Festival Hall Archive)

Finch, Paul, "Concrete Boots?", *Art Monthly*, October 1993

Forty, Adrian, "The Royal Festival Hall: A Democratic Space?", in Borden, Iain et al, eds, *The Unknown City: Contesting Architecture and Social Space*, MIT, 2001

Frater, Sarah, "The Brutal Face of Love: Stan Won't Dance", *Evening Standard*, 1 December 2006

Frayn, Michael, "Festival", in French, Philip and Sissons, Michael, eds, *The Age of Austerity 1945-1951*, Penguin, 1964

Gainsborough, John, "London's new public gallery: preview", *Arts Review*, November 1967

Garlake, Margaret, *New Art New World: British Art in Postwar Society*, Yale University Press, 1998

Geographia Visitors' Guide to the Festival of Britain, Geographia Ltd, 1951

Glancey, Jonathan, "Drowning, not waving", *Guardian*, 12 March 1998

Glendinning, Miles, "The Royal Festival Hall: A Postscript", *Architectural History*, No. 48, 2005

Gollancz, Victor, "What the Festival Hall has meant to me", published in the Royal Festival Hall programme of reopening concerts, February 1965

Grant, Ian, "Thirty Years of Great Music", published in the LSO Concert Programme for 3 May 1981

Harwood, Elain and Powers, Alan, eds, *Twentieth Century Architecture 5: Festival of Britain*, The Twentieth Century Society, 2001

Harwood, Elain, "Buildings for Entertainment and the Arts in post-war England 1945-80", unpublished PhD (ongoing)

Hill, Selima, ed, *Paradise for Sale: Poems from the Arts Council Collection at the Poetry Library*, Southbank Centre, 1998

Hilton, Tim, "Hung, drawn but not yet slaughtered: Joanna Drew", *Guardian*, 27 August 1992

Hoge, Warren, "London's Art Bunker Awaits the Kiss of Life", *International Herald Tribune*, 5-6 June 1999

ITN archive news footage of the Festival of Britain, 1951

Jackson, Lesley, *Robin and Lucienne Day: Pioneers of contemporary design*, Mitchell Beazley, 2001

Keating, Roly, "Wonders and blunders", *Guardian*, 18 August 2003

Larkin, Philip, "Introduction", in *The Poetry Library of The Arts Council of Great Britain Short-Title Catalogue*, Arts Council of Great Britain, 1981

Levin, Bernard, *Enthusiasms*, Jonathan Cape, 1983

Lewis, Jon E, ed, *Eye Witness: The Twentieth Century*, Robinson, 1994

Lister, David, "Revamp for 'diabolical' Festival Hall", *Independent*, 21 July 1999

Lynford, Adam, "Radical design for London's new concert hall", *Illustrated London News*, 4 March 1967

Mann, William, "Two new concert halls: supply creates demand", *The Times*, 1 March 1967

Marmot, Alexi Ferster and Wells, Julian, "Life to the South Bank", *The Architectural Review*, July 1979

Marwick, Arthur, *British Society Since 1945*, Penguin, 1982

McKean, John, *Architecture in Detail: Royal Festival Hall*, Phaidon, 2001

Moore, Rowan, "Artists in Glass Houses", *Evening Standard*, 14 October 2003

Mullins, Charlotte, "Reflections on an artist with an eye for the stars", *Financial Times*, 13 October 2003

Mullins, Charlotte, "Peter Greenaway", *The Times*, 5 March 1996

Niesewand, Nonie, "It's a jungle down here", *Independent*, 10 May 1999

O'Connor, Patrick, "That night was the beginning of a love affair", *Daily Telegraph*, 30 April 2004

Pearman, Hugh, "Southern Comfort", *Sunday Times*, 21 February 1993

Peskett, Fred, ed, *Festival Times*, May 2001, No. 40, newsletter published by the Festival of Britain Society

Porter, Roy, *London: A Social History*, Penguin, 1994

Renier, Hannah, *Lambeth Past*, Historical Publications, 2006

Royal Festival Hall 1951-2001: Past, Present, Future, anniversary magazine published by Southbank Centre, 2001

Russell, Gordon, *Design in the Festival*, Council of Industrial Design, 1951

Sewell, Brian, "Send for the Dynamite", *Evening Standard*, 26 February 2002

South Bank Arts Centre, Greater London Council, n.d (technical brochure, Royal Festival Hall Archive)

Stamp, Gavin and Powers, Alan, "The Twentieth Century Society: History", and "The Twentieth Century Society: Casework Reports. The Royal Festival Hall gets a 1950s make-over", www.c20society.org.uk

Stanford's Pictorial Map of London, Edward Stanford, 1950

Stungo, Naomi, "South Bank Postwar Buildings: overabused, overused, overviewed", *RIBA Journal*, August 1993

Symons, Jean, *Royal Festival Hall: Concert Hall Notebook*, Southbank Centre, 2000

"The Architectural Review special issue: Royal Festival Hall", *The Architectural Review*, June 1951, No. 654

The Association of Consulting Engineers: Selected Designs, Princes Press, 1951

"The most expensive lampposts in the world", *Daily Mail*, 2 December 1965

Thomas, Mark Hartland, *The Souvenir Book of Crystal Designs: the fascinating story in colour of the Festival Pattern Group*, Council of Industrial Design, 1951

Waterloo Sunset at the Hayward Gallery, Southbank Centre, 2003

Whitfield, Peter, *London: A Life in Maps*, The British Library, 2006

Whitford, Frank, "Concrete changes sought", *Sunday Times*, 21 February 1993

Williams-Ellis, Clough, *Royal Festival Hall: The Official Record*, Max Parrish in association with London County Council, 1951

Witts, Richard, "The art you own but cannot see: the Arts Council collection revealed", *New Statesman*, 3 April 1998

Woodham, Jonathan M, *Twentieth-Century Design*, Oxford University Press, 1997

Young, Robin, "Plans for South Bank complex would raze site", *The Times*, 9 December 1998

INDEX

Charlotte Mullins is a writer and broadcaster.
A former editor of *Art Review* and *V&A Magazine*,
her recent books include *Painting People*, Thames
& Hudson (2006), and *Rachel Whiteread*, Tate
Publishing (2004). She writes on art for the *Telegraph*,
Financial Times and specialist titles, and is a regular
contributor to BBC arts programmes.

MR DOUGAL MR J MACEWEN MR HENRY MACEY MS ALISON MACFADYEN MR A MACFARLANE MS ANN MACFARLANE MBE MR J MACFARLANE MR DAVID MACFARLANE DR IAIN MACFARLANE MR K MACFARLANE MR A MACGILL MR AND MRS J MACGILL MR M MACGILL MRS P MACGREGOR MRS S MACGREGOR
MS O MACHACEK MR J MACHEN MS J MACHIN MRS A MACINTYRE MS J MACK MRS TESSA MACK MR C MACKAY MRS PAMELA MACKAY MR R MACKAN MRS S T MACKAY MR G MACKEN MR J MACKENNEY MS P MACKENSIE MS ELIZABETH MACKENZIE MR M MACKENZIE MR P MACKENZIE MR
MRS MACKIE MS CHRISTINE MACKIE MRS S MACKIE MRS J MACKINNON MR N MACKINTOSH MS G MACKLIN MRS ROSEMARY MACKLIN MR ANDREW MACKRILL MR MALCOLM MACLAREN MS G MACLELLAN MR A MACLENNAN MS A MACLENNAN SHAN MACLENNAN MRS S MACLEOD MR M
MAHON MR IAN MACMILLAN MRS EVELYN MACNAMARA MRS ANNE MACNEARY SARAH MACNEE MR DUNCAN MACPHEE MS E MACPHERSON MS M MACPHERSON MRS E MACQUEEN DR A MACRAE MRS J MACRAE MR S MACRAE MISS F MACTAGGART MISS F MACTAGGART MISS A MADANAT MR ANDREW
MRS J MAGEE MR JULIAN MADDEN MR ADAM MADDISON MR C MADDOCK MR E MADDOX MRS S MADGWICK MR W MADILL MR H MAEHLER MS D MAFFRE MR H MAGASItHER MRS J MAGAZINER DR J MAGBADELO BELINDA MAGEE MS CATRIONA MAGEE MR P MAGEE MR
MRS MAGEE MR P MAGGIONI MISS M MAGILL MS M MAGIHHIS MS JOSEPHINE MAGNER MRS M MAGON MS M MAGORIAN MR C MAGUIRE DR RICHARD MAGUIRE MR DAVENDRA MAHARAJ MR K MAHBOUBIAN MRS M MAHDAUI MR S MAHDI MRS C MAHER MS E MAHMOUD MR PETER MAHNKE
SSAK MAHOMED MRS MAUREEN MAHON MS C MAHONEY MS J MAHONY MRS R MAHONY MRS D MAHOOD MR P MAHRER MS A MAHTANI MS CONCETTA MAIDA L MAIDA MRS B MAIDMENT MR D MAIER MS H MAIER MR AND MRS DONALD MAIN MR GRAHAM MAIN MRS S MAINI MRS D
MAINWARING MISS FEDERICA MAIORANO MR D MAITLAND MISS M MAJEED MS H MAJEETHIA MRS M MAJOR MR MICHAEL MAKARIOU MRS K MAKEPEACE MRS OLGA MAKHARINSKY MRS B MAKIN MRS S MAKIN MS U MAKINS MR T MAKISHIMA MS K MALACHI MR G MALBY MRS HILARY
MALCOLM MRS VAL MARYVN MALCOLM MR PRAVIN MALDE MR & MRS D MALE MR M MALE NIKA MALEK MRS U MALEWSKI MR A MALIK MS A MALING MRS J MALING MR RUSSELL S MALIPHANT MR AND MRS MALKIN MS R MALLARD MS SEANA MALLAEN MR GEOFF
ALL MR I MRS S MANKIH MS C MANTELOW MS M MANLEY MRS S MANLEY MR T MANLEY MR W MANLEY MR C MANN MRS C MANN MS ELIZABETH MANN MISS GILLIAN MANN MRS H MANN MS HELEN MANN MR J MANN MRS P MANN MRS U MANN MS L MANNERS MR C MANNING MRS
MANNING MR GORDON MANNING MS JENNIFER MANNING MRS L MANNING MS L MANNING MRS MIRANH MANNING MS SHEILA MANNING MS D MANNINGTON MRS K MANHOOCH MR VATCHE MANOUKIAN MR A MANSELL MISS C MANSELL MRS E MANSERGH PROFESSOR
L L MANSFIELD CBE MR D MANSFIELD MR J MANSFIELD MRS S MANSFIELD MS SHEILA MANSFIELD MRS T MANSFIELD MRS TANA MANSFIELD-STEER MS J MANSON MS JUNE MANSOOR MR A MANTALARIS MS J MANTELL MRS S MANTHOS MRS J MANTON MR G MANUELL
MANWARING MS G MANZI MR TERENCE MANZI MS PAM MAPLE MR P MAPLE MRS C MAQUEDA MR U MARAJ MRS L T MARCANO MRS J MARCH MR C L MARCH MR BRIAN MARCHANT MR DAVID MARCHANT MR F MARCHANT MR J MARCHANT MRS ANN MARCUS MR B MARCUS MR CLIVE MARCUS
MS G MARCUS MRS K MARCUS MS M MARCUS-KANNER MISS R MARDEN MR R MARGARA MR H MARGERISON MRS J MARGREE STELLA AND ALEXANDER MARGULIES CHARITABLE TRUST MR D MARIANO MR P MARIGOLD MISS L MARINER MS R MARIHOU MRS URENI MARK
AN MARKEY MISS J MARKHAM MR J MARKHAM MR T MARKHAM DR LAURA MARKOWE MR B MARKS MR B MARKS MR E S MARKS MS F MARKS MR PETER MARKS MRS W MARKS DR A MARKUS MS C MARKWICK MS P WOOD AND MR J MARLAND MS E MARLES MRS L MARLES
MS MARLEY MR A MARLOW MR D MARLOW MISS E MARLOW MRS F MARLOW MR J MARLOW MR R MARLOW MS A MARMO-BISSELL DR A MARMOT MRS A MARHAM MS R MARHEN MRS M MAROHEY MR A MARQUEZ MRS CRISTINA MARQUEZ-LEAMAN MS T MARQUIS MS J MARRAY
MERRAN MARR MS C MARRERO MR M MARRIAGE MR D MARRIOTT MRS H MARRIS MR DAHIEL MARRUZZO MRS H MARS A MARSH MR BENEDICT MARSH E W J MARSH MRS J MARSH MISS K MARSH MRS M MARSH MRS M MARSH MRS ANN MARSHALL MR ANTHONY
SHALL MS B MARSHALL MRS D MARSHALL MR D MARSHALL MS HELEN MARSHALL MR J MARSHALL MRS J MARSHALL MRS J R MARSHALL MS JENNY MARSHALL MR M MARSHALL MRS M MARSHALL DR N MARSHALL MR R MARSHALL MISS T MARSHALL MR &
SIR PETER & GARY MARSHALL MRS R MARSHALL MR ROGER MARSHALL MRS SUSAN MARSHALL MR T MARSHALL MRS U MARSHALL MR W MARSHALL MR GRAHAM MARSHMAN MISS J MARSHMAN MR S MARSHMAN MRS A MARSOHI MR J MARSTON MRS P
STON MS U MARSTON MR MARCO MARTA MR A MARTELL MR J MARTEN MR RODNEY MARTEN MR A MARTIN MRS A MARTIN MS ANN MARTIN MRS BARBARA MARTIN MR B MARTIN MRS C MARTIN MR CHARLES MARTIN MS CLARE MARTIN MR DAVID MARTIN DR
DH MISS H MARTIN MS F MARTIN MR GUY MARTIN MR J MARTIN MRS J MARTIN MS J MARTIN MR JEAN MARTIN DR JOAN MARTIN MRS M MARTIN MRS M MARTIN MR N MARTIN MR PETER MARTIN MISS R MARTIN MR S
RTIN MRS S MARTIN MR STEUEN MARTIN MR T MARTIN MRS LOURDES MARTINEZ MR B MARTINI MR KRUNOSLAV MARTIHOVIC MR PAUL MARTLAND MR B MARTYN MARUSAN EUROPE LTD. MS S MARUYAMA MR P MARVELL MR A MARYHIAK DR & MRS A MARYON DAVIS MRS A
EC-MARSER MRS D MASHIEA MS A MASKELL MISS G MASKELL MRS A MASON MRS AMANDA MASON MR C MASON MRS D MASON MR E MASON MR F MASON MR G MASON MS MASON MS HELEN MASON MRS J MASON MR JOSH MASON MRS K MASON MRS M MASON MRS M MASON MR
F MASON P MASON MS VALERIE MASON MR B MASSEY MR DAVID MASSEY MR G MASSEY MS F MASSIE MS CHANTAL MASSIGES SARA MASSON MS SHEENA MASSON MR S MASSOHE MRS BRENDA MASTERS F MASTERS MR A MASTERS C MASTERSON MR L MASTROPIRRO MR PETER
JIC MS CHRISTINE MATHESON MRS D MATHESON DR JOHN MATHEWS MR G MATHIAS MRS S MATHIAS MR WILLIAM MATHIESON MRS J MATHUR MISS B MATHURIN MRS K MATOS MR H & Y S MATSUDA MR K MATSUO MS M MATSUOKA MRS R MATTER MR A MATTHEWS MRS A MATTHEWS
TTHEWS MR C H MATTHEWS MS CLARISSA MATTHEWS MR D MATTHEWS MR J MATTHEWS MRS JEAN MATTHEWS MRS C MATTHEWS MS K MATTHEWS MS M MATTHEWS MISS P MATTHEWS MR PAUL MATTHEWS MR R MATTHEWS MS W MATTHEWS MRS L
ICK MS L MATTIN MR A MATUSICCA'S MRS ELISABETH MAUGHAM MR GRAEME MAUGHAN MRS S MAUGHAN MRS K MAULE MISS RENEE MAULIK MRS M MAURICE MR H MAURICE MS M MAUROGEORGE MISS J MAW MRS L MAW MR A MAWBY MR M BASHIR MAWAHI MR J MAWAS MRS RACHEL
UGHLIN MR J MCLAUGHLIN MRS MARIA MCLAUGHLIN MR G MCLEAN MRS M MCLEAN MR MICHAEL MCLEAVEY MRS THELMA MCLELLAN MS AHH MCLEOD MR IAIN MCLEOD MR J MCLEOD MR L MCLEOD MRS MURIEL MCLEOD MS OLIVIA MCLEOD MS K MCLEOD ADAIR
J MCLEOD-HATCH MS TERESA MCLIHTOCK MR R MCLHTOSH MR K MCLOONE MS CATHERINE MCLOUGHLIN MISS CAROLINE MCMAHON MR D MCMAHON MISS G MCMAHON MRS J MCMAHON PATRICIA M MCMANUS MRS T P MCMANUS MR HUGH MCMASTER MRS A MCMEEHAN ROBERTS MISS
M MCHISH MR H MCHUGH MR MICHAEL MCPARTLAND MISS E F MCPEAKE MR J MCPHAIL MISS M MCPHILLIPS MS NAD'A MCQUEEN MRS L MCQUILLAN MISS C MCQUILLIN MR GARRY MCQUISTIN MR SCOTT MCREA MRS NAES
MERT PROFESSOR PETER MCRORIE MR D MCSHANE MR G MCSHAME MISS FIONA MCSORLEY MRS S MCSWEENEY MS G MCUEIGH MRS J MCUICAR MRS M MCWILLIAM MRS B MEAD MR BARRY MEAD MR BRIAN MEAD MR ROBERT MEAD MS S MEAD MR BRIAN MEADE MR CHRIS MEADE MRS
ADE MR PHILIP MEADEN MR J MEADER MRS A MEADOWS MR MAX MEADOWS MR P MEADOWS MRS S MEADOWS MR M MEADS MR COLIN MEAGER MR W MEALINGS MISS ESTEFANIA MEANA MRS J MEAHOCK DR M MEARS MISS SALLY MEARS MRS R MEDCALF MR D MEDD MRS J MEDDEMMEN MR
MEDDICK MR NICHOLAS MEDHURST MRS B MEDICOTT MR M MEDLAND MR D MEDLEND MS J MEDLEY MRS B MEDLICOTT MR H MEDORA MRS H MEDORA MR C MEDUEI MR R MEEK MRS MARY MEEKF MR P MEESON MRS F MEGHJI MS J MEGHJI MRS U MEGHREBLIAN MR R MEGROFF MR F
ICH MRS MELANIE MEHTA MS N MEHTA MS RAXA MEHTA MS S MEHTA MR E MEIER MISS J MEIJSSEN MR U MEISEL MS MEISELS MR T MEISSNER MR J MELBOURN CBE MR R MELBOURNE MR D T MELDRUM MR J MELDRUM R GREG MELGAARD MR
LLARD DR S MELLER MR T MELLOM MR J MELLOR MS JUDITH MELLOR MRS JUDITH MELLOR MRS D MELLOWS MR C MELLUISH LADY JENNIFER MELMOTH MR P MELVILLE MR R MELVILLE MRS S MELVILLE MR & MRS PETER MELVIN MRS A MEMMOTT MRS J MEHACHEMSOH MR C
ESCHE MRS E MENCE MRS S MENCE MR R MENDEL MS A E MENDHAM MIS HONOUR J H E MEHDL MRS MENDL-SCHRAMA MRS F MENDLESON MRS H MENDOZA MR S MENDOZA MRS R MENEZES MS S MENIH MS ANNA MEHMUIR MR P MENOH MS H MENSAH MS F MEHTE MS LIZ MENZIES
MENZIES MR MALCOLM MENZIES MR J MEPHAM MR A MEPSTED MS B MERCER MS EUELYH MERCER MS MICHELLE MERCER MR K MEREDITH MR P MEREDITH MS PATRICIA MERLIN MRS O MERLINI MR D MERMELSTEIN MISS J MERMOUD MRS J MERRALLS MRS A MERRICK MISS SARAH
RICK MR PETER MERRICK MRS P MERRIFIELD MR DAVID MERRILL MS J MERRIMAN MR M MERRINGTON MR R MERRINGTON MRS M MERRIOTT DR J MERRISON MR A MERRITT DR ANDREW MERRITT MS M MERRITT MRS S MERRITT MR S MERSER MRS S MERSER MRS S MERSER MRS
MEYER MR M MEYER MRS S MEYER MRS J MEYHELL MR C MEYHELL-SMITH DR GILLIAN MEZEY MR Z MEZQUITA MRS HELEN MICHAEL MRS K MICHAELIS MRS RAE MICHAELIS MR A MICHAELS MR U MICHAELS MRS CAROL MICHAELSON MRS G MICHAELSON MRS S MCKEHHA MR D
ALSKI MS M MICHALSKI MRS J MICHELIN MS L MICHELSON MRS E MICKLEM MRS J MIDDA MS L MIDDLEBROOK MS J MIDDLEDITCH MR ROGER MIDDLEDITCH MRS B MIDDLEMISS MR A MIDDLETON MS B MIDDLETON MISS C MIDDLETON MRS G MIDDLETON MR A MRS N MIDDLETON
ROBERT MIDDLETON MRS S MIDDLETON MR LAURENCE MIDDLEWEEK MS G MIDGLEY MS L MIGLIORINI MS I MIGRINA MS J MIGUII MR P MIKKIDES MR M MIKLOS MRS J MILBANK MRS C MILBORNE MRS I MILBRADT MR D MILDON MR K MILEMAN MR AND MRS P MILES MR A MILES MS A
LER MRS A MILLER MS A MILLER MR A MILLER MR ANTHONY R MILLER MRS B MILLER MS C MILLER MR CLIVE MILLER MRS E MILLER MS I MILLER MRS J MILLER MR JAMES MILLER MR JONATHAN MILLER MR K MILLER MS L MILLER LADY MILLER MR M C MILLER
MP MILLER MR PAUL MILLER MR R MILLER MS R MILLER MR RUSSELL MILLER MRS S MILLER MR S MILLER MS SARAH MILLER MS Y MILLER MS L MILLERS MR A MILLET MRS C MILLETT MRS B MILLIGAH MISS I MILLIGAH MR T MILLIGAN MR P MILLINER MR R MILLINGTON
HG MILLION MRS ERIKA MILLS MRS P MILLHER MISS BEVERLY MILLS MRS D MILLS MR G MILLS MR H MILLS MR J MILLS MRS J MILLS MS MICHAEL MILLS MRS NINA MILLS MRS P MILLS MRS S MILLS MR S MILLS MS MS V MILLS MS
STED MRS E MILMAN MR ANDREW MILNE MR J MILNE MR J MILHER MR C MILTON FIONA MILTON MR S MILTON-THOMPSON MRS STELLA MINDEL MISS SARAH MINDHAM MR J MINDIN MR G MINGAY DR JOHN MINGAY MR P MINIHAN MRS L MINHETTE MISS E MINOGUE MRS R MINOT DR
HSHULL MRS MICHELLE MINSKY MRS P MINTON MR W MINZINGA MR M MINZY MS G MIQUELES MR SERGE4 MIRONENKO MS K MIRZA MRS S MIRZA THE LORD MISHCON QC DL AHD LADY MISHCON MR K MISRI MR J MISSO MS A MISTRI MR D MISTRY MR S MISTRY MRS LESLEY
ME4HELL MS M MITCHELL MRS A MITCHELL MR ALEXANDER MITCHELL MS CATHERINE MITCHELL MR D MITCHELL SIR DEREK MITCHELL MISS E MITCHELL MS HELEN MITCHELL MR J MITCHELL MRS J MITCHELL MISS JOANNA MITCHELL MR JOHN MITCHELL MRS M
HELL MS M MITCHELL MR T MITCHELL MR MITCHELL MR MAX MITCHELL MICHAEL MITCHELL MR S MITCHELL MRS VANESSA MITCHELL MR NEIL MITCHENALL MISS B MITCHENER MR KEHICHI MITOMI MR A
MS MITRA MR P MIX MR OSAMU MIYAHARA MR JAMES MOCHNACZ MISS M MOCHTA MRS A MOCKERIDGE MR K MODABERI MRS G A MODEL MRS POUPAK MODJABI MR S MOEINI MR M MOERI MRS MOERMAN MRS CARINA MOFFAT MISS K MOGER MR T MOGFORD MRS D MOGGACH MR
GHADASSI MS A MOGHAL MRS C MOHAMED MRS REITA MOHAMED MR U MOHAMMADI MR AMIN MOHEBBI MISS GOLI MOHTADI MRS R MOHYLINCKY INGHAM MS C MOIR MR F MOIR MS A MOJSAK MS F MOK DR Q MOK MR AND MRS MOLANA-ALLEN MRS HELEN MOLE MRS J MOLE MS M
AND DR A MOLLEMAN MRS A MOLLER MRS PAMELA MALONEY MISS SINEAD MOLOHEY MRS R MOLONY MR J MOL4HEUX DR NICOLETTA MOMIGLIANO-LONSDALE MS VALERIE MONAGHAN MR H MONCK MS H MONEY MR PETER MONEY DR C MONFRIES MR R MONGRU MR A
MR D MONK MRS J MONK DR MARTIN MONK MS ESTHER MONROE MRS M MONROE MR I MONTAGU MRS A MONTAKHAB MS TESSA MONTERO MS CATALINA MONTESIHOS-BROOKER MR K MONTGOMERY MRS H MONUMENT MRS U MOODIE MRS M MOOD4 MR
D MOON MR S MOORE MRS SARAH MOOH MISS J MOOR MR A MOORCROFT MS A MOORE MR B MOORE MRS C F D MOORE MS CATHERINE MOORE MR E MOORE MRS E MOORE MR E MOORE DR FIONA MOORE DR G MOORE MRS J MOORE MS J MOORE MRS L MOORE
R MOORE MRS M MOORE MR P MOORE MR R MOORE MR RICHARD MOORE MR S MOORE MR T MOORE MR PETER MOORE4 MR J MOORHOUSE MISS A MOOS MS P MORA-FONTAINE MISS ANNA MORAITIS MS F MORAH MR U MORAN MRS RANJAH MORARJI MR MIKE MORFEY
MORGAN MRS A MORGAN MISS J MORGAN MRS CLARE MORGAN MR MORGAN MR DAVID MORGAN MRS E MORGAN MS E MORGAN MRS H MORGAN MS H R MORGAN MR J MORGAN MRS J MORGAN MS JANE MORGAN MRS L MORGAN MRS LUCY MORGAN MS LUCY MORGAN MR
LLA MORGAN MRS PATRICIA MORGAN MR PETER MORGAN MR RICHARD MORGAN DR RONALD MORGAN MR RONALD MORGAN MS SUSAN MORGAN MRS U MORGAN MONSIEUR PATRICK MORGEIR MR I MORI MRS MARTIN MORIARTY MS J MORING MS R MORITZ MS S MORIYAMA MISS MARGARET
AHD MR P MORLEY MS M MORLING MRS M MOROHI MS S MORPHEW MRS I MORRELL MRS J MORRELL MISS M MORRELL MR A MORRIS MRS ANDREW MORRIS ANDY J MORRIS MR AUBREY MORRIS MS C MORRIS MRS C MORRIS DEBBIE MORRIS MRS
RRIS MR G MORRIS MRS J MORRIS MR J MORRIS DR JENNIFER MORRIS MRS JUTTA MORRIS MR K MORRIS MRS KYLIE MORRIS MISS M C MORRIS MR M MORRIS MR MIKE MORRIS MR HORMAH MORRIS MR P MORRIS MR R MORRIS MRS
RRIS MRS RUTH MORRIS MS S MORRIS MISS SARAH MORRIS DR SHEILA MORRIS MR TIM MORRIS MS C MORRISH MR A MORRISON MRS ANGELA MORRISON MS B MORRISON MR C MORRISON MS CATHERINE MORRISON GAYLE MORRISON JOHN MORRISON MS K MORRISON KENNETH
RISON MISS L MORRISON MR U MORRISON MRS MARGARET MORRISON MARY MORRISON MR MS W & MORRISON MRS P MORROD MR S MORROW MR A MORSE MR G MORSE MS S MORSE MRS J MORTEH MS KATE MORTIMER KATHLEEN MORTIMER MS P
MOSS MR A MORTON MRS J MORTON DR JOANNE MORTON MRS E MORTON MRS M MORTON MR M MORTON MRS PAT MORTON LADY G MORTON MR W MORTON MR J MOSCROP DR F MOSDEEN LORD MOSER OF REGENTS PARK KCB, CBE, FBA MR P MOSHIR-FATEMI MR ANDREW MOSLEY MR
MOSS MR B MOSS MRS BETTY MOSS MR H MOSS DR I MOSS MRS L MOSS MS P MOSS MRS M MOSS MR MIKE MOSS MR MONTY MOSS MR N MOSS MR S MOSS MRS NICOLA MOSS MR F MOSS SYLUIA MOSSS MOSS MR W MOSS MISS SUSAN MOSSMAN MR P MOST4M MR MOUSSA MOTALLEBZADEH MR D
DR MOTHAR MS A MOTIUALA DR A MOTT MR JOHN MOTT MRS MARY MOTTURE MR E MOUKARZEL MR T MOULD MS ANDREA MOULDING MS GILLIAN MOULDING MR GERALD MOULT MR B MOULTON MR P MOULTON MRS P MOULTON MRS M MOUNT MR B MOUNTFORD MR P MOUNTFORD DR P
RA-COSTA MS C MOUTELL MS F MOUTOU MRS B MOWBRAY MR U MOWER MISS K MOWLE MR B MOXHAM MRS J MOXHAM MR PETER MOXHAM MR G MOXON MR A MOXON MS L MOXON MRS SALLY MOYH MR GEOFFREY MOYHE MRS S MOYHIHAH MR IQBAL MUBARIK MR E MUBUANGA MS E MUCKLE MRS C
MULCAHY MR I MULCAHY MISS M MULCAHY MR S MULCAHY FREDERICK MULDER MR A MULFORD MRS PAULIHE MULLAN4 MR G MULLAN MR H MULLAN MR B MULLAHE4 MR P MULLER MR PETER MULLER MR P MULLETT MR STANLE4 MULLE4 MR R MULLIGAN MRS H MULLIHER MR A
M MULLO4 MR M MULOCK MRS M MULLANN4 MR G MUMMER4 MISS K MUMMERY MR T MUMTAZ MR K MUNCER MRS B MUNDA4 MR C MUNDA4 MR J MUNDA4 MRS P MUNDA4 MS B MUNDE MS ALICE MUNDURU MRS S MUND4 MR A MUNN MR J MUNNS MR DONALD MUHRO MRS U
RS WEND4 MUNRO MR MARTIN MUNROE MRS N P MUNT MRS P MUNTON MS ANNE MURCOTT MRS HELLA MURDEN MR J MURDOCH MISS JEAH MURDOCH MR K MURDOCH MS SUE MURDOCH MRS U MURDOCH MR ROY MURPHANIS MRS D MURPHAE MR U MURPHE MR U MURO MR A MURPH4 MR
LAH MURPH4 MS AHHA MURPH4 MISS B MURPH4 MR BRIAN MURPH4 MR C MURPH4 MRS C MURPH4 MS D MURPH4 MISS E MURPH4 MRS E MURPH4 MRS ELIZABETH MURPH4 MS ELIZABETH MURPH4 MR F MURPH4 MRS GISELA MURPH4 MRS J MURPH4 MR K MURPH4 MRS J MURPH4 MR L MURPH4
RPH4 MS M MURPH4 MR P MURPH4 MISS P MURPH4 MRS PATRICIA MURPH4 MR S MURPH4 MRS S MURPH4 MS W MURPH4 MR ALAN MURRAH MRS B MURRAH MR G MURRAH MRS I MURRAH MR J MURRAH MS J MURRAH MR L MURRA4
LOUISA MURRA4 MRS M MURRA4 MS MARGARET MURRA4 MRS P MURRA4 MR PETER MURRA4 MS S MURRAH MR T MURRA4 MRS L MURRA4 SMITH MR ALLAN MURRA4-JONES MR J MURRELL MS H MUSGRAVE MR A MUSKER MISS H MUSSELL MRS M A MUSSET MISS G MUSSETT MR G
SETT MRS J MUST MR FORBESS MUTCH MS A MUTHAHA MR I MUZZLE MR ALAN M4ERS MRS I M4ERS MRS J M4ERS MS J M4ERS MR MS KATHLEEN M4ERS MRS L M4ERS MRS N M4ERS MR P M4ERS MR CHRISTOPHER M4GIND MR J M4KILL MR S M4LES MR CHRISTOPHER
MH MR A HACAMULI MRS I HACHTIGAL MS S HACKASHA MRS L HADAL MR JE4ATHARAH HADARAJAH MRS A HADAU DR R HAFTALIN MS D HAGAN MRS J HAGAHUMA MR WILLY HAGEL MR R HAHED MRS H HAIDU MS I HAIR MRS J HAIR MISS L HAIR MRS LELA HAIR MRS J HAIRH MRS P
LM MR PAUL HAISSH MS M HAISH MRS H HAITO MS M HAJAHD MRS Y HAKAI-CORBEH MRS S HAKAMURA-THOMAS MRS T HALLE MR K HAH UAZADEH MR H HANCE DR UASAHTA HANDURI MR HADEESH HARASINGHE MRS L HAQIOUIHG MS B HARIEF PROFESSOR CHRISTOPHER HAPIER MRS R
HATH MR N HARDECCHIA MRS G HARDELL MRS G HAREUSKI MS JUDITH HASAT4R MRS Z HASAT4R MS PAULA HASCIMENTO MRS M HASER MR C HASH MRS E HASH MRS J HASH MR J HASH MS K HASH MR M HASH MRS HIHA HASH MR P HASH MR M HASH MR P HASH MR ROBERT HASH MR P HASSKAU MRS A HATAS
HATH MR B HATHAN MR E HATHAN MR MICHAEL HATHAN MR O HATHAN MR S A HATHAN MR B HATHWANJ MISS M HAUGHTON MISS C HAUMAHH MRS R A HAUHAROHAUMAR DR S HAUARRO-PARRA MS ANNE HAYLOR MR D HAYLOR MRS
LOR MR J HA4LOR MS RUTH HA4LOR MR G HAZARAIH MS ARMINE HAZARI MRS LUISA HEADS MRS AMANDA HEAL MR & MRS G HEAL MS LINDA HEAL MR M HEAL MR MARK HEAL MR E HEAL MR F HEALE MRS D HEALE MR F HEALE MS CAITH HEAL BRIDGET L HEATE MRS C HEATE MS
ATHE4 DR J HEBHRAZAHI PAULINE HEE MR IAN HEEDLEMAN MR L HEEDLEMAN MS L HEIDICH MR B HEIGHBOUR MS J HEIGHBOUR MS D HEIL MRS A HEIL-GALLAGHER MS HEIRA MR G HEISH MR VICTOR HEJO MR R HEKOO MR GIDEON HELLEN
ME S A HELSON MS CATH4 HELSON MS CECILIA HELSON JAHE HELSON DR M HELSON MS H U HELSON MR TIMOTH4 HELSON MRS HELSON-KIRUAH MRS CAROL HEMET MS S HEMTOU MR FELIPE HER4 MR H HESBIT MRS L HESBIT MISS K HESTER
S HETTLETON MR J HETTLETON MISS UERA HEUBAUER MR KLAUS HEUBERG MR HEUBERT MRS M HEURUER MS L HEUARD-O'BRIEN MR E HEUE MS J HEUETT MRS UIUIEHHE HEUILL MRS B HEUILLE MR B HEUILLE MR J HEUILLE MRS J HEUILLE
HEUILLE MS S HEUILLE T H HEUILLE-LEE MRS E HERUKLA MR B HER MR CHRIS HER MR A HERALL MR RICHARD HEUBERR4 MRS S HEUBER4 MR TIM HEUBETT MRS B HEUBUR4 MR K HEUBUR4 MRS U HEUMAH MR DAN HEUMAH MR B HEUMAH DR J HEUMAH
JHOUSE MRS C HEWING MRS DEIRDRE HEWING MS M HEUIHGTOH MS HILAR4 HEWISS MR A HERS DAVID HEUKIRK MR K HEWLAH MR PETER HEUILANDS MR H HEUILING MISS A HEUGARA MR DAVID HEUMAH MISS E HEUMAH MR B HEUMAH DR J HEUMAH
J HEUMAH DR AND MRS H HEWMAH MS S HEWMAN MS T HEWMAH MR U HEWMAH MR & MRS H HEWMAN-HORUELL MR B HEUMAN-TA4LOR MR T HEWMAH-TA4LOR MR M HEWMAH MR S HEWMAH MR AUGUSTUS HEWMAHT MR AUGUSTUS HEWMAHT MS A HEUMAH MR K HEWSTEAD MRS INGRID HEWSTEAD MR
TOH MR G HEWTON MR J HEWTON MRS M HEWTOH D HEUTON MR R HEUTOH MRS S HEUTON MRS HILAR4 HER MR MICHAEL HG MR S HIBBS MR J HIBLETT MRS H HIBLETT MR MICHAEL HIBLOCK MRS ANGELA HICHOLAS MR M HICHOLAS MRS R HICHOLAS MR U HICHOLAS
NICHOLL MRS C HICHOLLS MRS E HICHOLLS MS H HICHOLLS MRS G HICHOLS MR J HICHOLS MR O HICHOLSH MR C HICHOLSOH MR U HICHOLSOH MR ROSS HICHOLSOH MRS S HICKLESS MR B HICKELL MR G HICKELL MR CLIUE HICKOLLS MR J HICKSON
HICKSOH MR C HICOL MRS E HICOL MR JOHH HICOLL MRS M HICOLL MR J HIELSEN MR KEH HIEMAH MRS J HIGHTIHGALE MR J HIGHTINGALE MR E HIHTIHGALE MS H HIKHAM MS J HIMBLETTE MR J HIMMO MRS M HIMMO MRS R HISSAM MRS A HIUEH MRS U
HS HELEH HIXON MR U HIXSOH MRS S HICATAZO DR A HOAD MRS J HOAKES MRS A HOBLE MR AHH HOBLE MR H HOBLE MR H HOBLE MR F HOBLE MS P HOBLE MS B HOBLE-JONES MR CHRISTOPH HOEBEL MR B HOLAH MRS S HOOH MRS M HOOHAH MRS S
DEEH MR H HOPS MR F HORALL MR K HORBER HORBUR4 MRS H HORDLIHGER MR JOHH HORKETT MRS G HORLAND E S HORMAH MR G HORMAH MS H HORMAH MRS JUDITH HORMAH MR H HORMAH LAD4 HORMAH MISS S HORMAH MRS R HORMAH MR M HORO
HOROHHA MR CRAIG HORRIS MR D HORRIS MR J HORRIS MR MALCOLM HORRIS MR R HORRIS MR U HORRIS MRS J HORTH MR B HORTH MR H HORTH MRS MELISSA HORTH MR R HORTH MR S HORTH MR ROGER HORTHCOTT MR MICHAEL HORTHERH MS U HORTHE4 MRS
RTHFIELD MISS UALERIE HORTHORPE MRS S HORTHOUER MR A HORTOH MR BRIAH HORTOH MRS J HORTOH MISS M HORTOH DR ROBERT HORTOH MRS RUTH HORTOH-COLLIHS MS BARBARA HORUELL MS E HORUID MR F HOTTAGE MR E HOTTAGE MRS E HO4 MRS R HUECHTERH MR ANDREW
HUTTIHG MR I K HUAGUE MR DAUID HH MR A OAKLE4 MR ALLAH OAKLE4 MRS D OAKLE4 MS DENNIS OAKLE4 MS G OAKLE4 MR K OAKLE4 MISS PATRICIA OAKLE4 MR PAUL OAKLE4 MRS T OAKLE4 MS C OAKSHETT MRS DAPHHE OATES MR DOHALD OATES MR M OATES MRS S OATES
OATES MRS M OATE4 MRS DIANA OATIS MRS A OBER MRS ESTER OBERBECK MRS H A OBERORIES MRS H OBERSE4KERA MR A O'BRIEH MS AHHA O'BRIEH C O'BRIEH MAR4 O'BRIEH DECLAH O'BRIEH MRS G O'BRIEH MRS ELIZABETH O'BRIEH MR H O'BRIEH MRS J O'BRIEH MR RICHARD O'BRIEH
O'BRIEH MRS S O'BRIEH MS DIANE O'BRIEH-DARCH MR J O'CALLAGHAH MRS LIHDSE4 OCKWELL MRS J O'COHHELL JAMES O'COHHOR MR AHMAHA O'BRIEH ms J O'BRIEH MS AHHA O'BRIEH MR B O'CAROLL MR O HOBLE O'CONNOR MR R O'CONNOR MR U O'CONHOR
P ODIH MR LEIGH ODLIH MS EILEEH O'DOHERT4 MR C O'DOHHELL MR J O'DOHHELL MRS P O'DOHHELL MRS D O'DOHOGHUE MR A O'DOHOUAH MRS A ODUSAHYA MS AHHEGRET O'DU4ER MS T O'FARRELL DR L O'FLAHERT4 MISS E OGBOMO MS J
OHH MS LESLE4 OGDEH MS P OGG MR JULIAH OGILUIE MS J PHILLIPPA OGILUIE MS S OGILUIE THE RT HOH SIR AHGUS OGILU4 KCUO MRS L OGILU4 MR CHRISTOPHER OGLE MR B OGLESB4 MRS AHHETTE O'GORMAH MR E O'GORMAH MS H O'GORMAH MR JAMES
AD4 MR P O'GRAD4 MR MICHAEL OGUHHAIKE MR G OGUHRO MR UICTOR OGURO MRS M OHAHA MR M O'HAHLOH MRS B O'HARA MR JOHH O'HARA MR M O'HARA MR REBECCA OHL MR B OHLSSOH MS A OHHUTEK MR H OHORA MR S OISHI MRS K OKAMOTO MRS M OKAMOTO-MCGRAHH MRS
BERAHT OKE MR H OKE MRS H O'KEEFFE MRS S OKELL MRS B O'KELL4 MR F O'KELL4 MR F OKEHE MR 4 OKUMA MRS C OKUHO MRS OKWUOSA MR R OLARD MRS A OLDAKER MR E OLDEIDE MR A OLDHAM MRS D OLDS MRS U O'LEAR4 MRS E OLGILUIE-SMITH MS J OLIFF MRS A OLIUER MRS C

OLIVER MR C OLIVER MR D OLIVER MR J OLIVER MS J OLIVER RT REVEREND JOHN OLIVER MS KATE OLIVER MR L OLIVER MR M OLIVER MS MARIAN OLIVER MISS S OLIVER MR S OLIVER T C OLIVER MRS J OLIVIER MRS M OLIVIER MRS S OLIVIER MRS C OLIVO MRS K OLLEY MR
OLNEY MS S OLNEY MR A OLSSON RONALD OLUFUNWA MR J O'MAHONY MS S O'MALLEY MS C O'MALLEY-COLLINS MRS I O'MARA MR IYAD OMARI MR C O'MEARA MR P O'MULLANE D G O'NEILL MRS E O'NEILL MR H O'NEILL MISS J O'NEILL MRS K O'NEILL MISS M O'NEILL DR T O'NE
MS C ONISHI MR S ONISHI MR SHOJI ONISHI MR KENICHI ONO MISS Y ONO DR C ONOF MRS E ONSLOW MRS H ONYSKIW Z OODLEBERGER MISS C OPPENHEIM MRS P OPPERMAN MRS V OPPLER MR WILLIAM ORAM MRS E ORANGE MRS Y ORDER MRS M ORDMAN MS J O'REGAN MS C OREI
DR A O'REILLY MRS G ORGAN MS M ORMEL MS N ORMEROD DR J ORMROD MR C ORR MS I ORR MRS J ORR MR JOHN ORRIN MRS A ORSMAN MR R ORSON MR FRANK ORTHBANDT MR S OSADA MR M OSBORN MS I OSBORNE MR J OSBORNE MRS J OSBORNE MR M OSBORNE MS M OSBORNE M
OSBORNE MR S OSBORNE MR C OSEI MR B O'SHAUGHNESSY MR D O'SHEA MS JANET O'SHEA DR MARIA O'SHEA MR D OSMAN MR P OSMOND MR R OSMOND MS J OSSETIN MR A O'SULLIVAN MR B O'SULLIVAN MRS EILEEN O'SULLIVAN MRS J O'SULLIVAN MRS S O'SULLIVAN MISS M OSW
MR MATTHEW OSWALD MS S OTAKI MRS O OTTAWAY MR P OTTAWAY MRS S A OTTEN MS M OTTERWELL MR S OTUDEKO MRS K OUADAH MR D OUGHTON MISS F OUHLA MR RICHARD OUTHWAITE MRS K OVENDEN MR N OVENS MR ARTHUR OVER MRS J OVER MS MARY OVERELL MS B OVESEN M
OVTCHINNIKOVA MRS A OWEN MS ALICE OWEN MISS C OWEN MISS CATHERINE OWEN MRS GRACE OWEN MRS H OWEN MRS J OWEN MR JOHN OWEN MRS L OWEN MS M OWEN MISS P OWEN MS P OWEN MR RONALD T OWEN MR S OWEN MR T OWEN MS URSULA OWEN OBE DR WENDY OWEN
PATRICIA OWENS MISS A OXENHAM MRS S OXENHAM MR F OXLEY MRS L OXMAN-OSBORN MRS P OYARZABAL MRS A OYEDIRAN MRS Z OZBEK MS N OZMERT MR K PABARY MS HARRIET PACAUD MR M PACE MISS G PACHTER MS V PACK MR A PACKER MR J PACKER MISS M PACKER M
PAULINE PACKER MS V PACKER MR STANLEY PACKHAM MR C PACKINGTON MR BARRY PACKMAN MRS PEGGY PADDOCK DR RUTH PADEL MR A PADFIELD MRS B PADFIELD J PADFIELD MRS T PADFIELD MRS M PADGETT MISS K PADGHAM MRS S PADGHAM DR ANA PADILLA NEIL PADOA
C PADOIN MRS S PADOVAN MR P PAGANOTTO MR ALISTAIR PAGDEN MRS B PAGE MR C PAGE MRS CATHERINE PAGE MR D PAGE MISS DIANA PAGE MS F PAGE MR G PAGE MR J PAGE MISS K PAGE MR R PAGE S E PAGE S PAGE MS SALLY PAGE MR T PAGE MISS E PAGE MR MANFRED PA
MS A PAGET MR D PAIBA MRS S PAIK-MAIER MR MARK PAILING MRS DOROTHY PAIN MR G PAIN MRS J PAIN MR PHILIP PAIN MRS B PAINE HELEN PAINE MISS A PAINTER MR A W PAINTER MRS E PAINTER MRS P PAINTING MR DAVID PAISEY MRS M PAISNER MRS H PAKEMAN MR S
MR MARIANO PALAO MR NICK PALEOCRASSSAS MS SOFIA PALEOLOGO MRS R PALETHORPE DR & MRS C PALIN MRS DEIRDRE PALK MRS JEAN PALLANT MR S PALLET MRS W PALLETT L PALLIKAROPOULOS MR F PALLISTER MR A PALMER MRS A PALMER MR ANTHONY PALMER MR C PAL
MRS C PALMER MS CATHERINE PALMER MR D PALMER MRS E PALMER MR GRAHAM PALMER MRS I PALMER MRS J PALMER MRS JOAN PALMER MR JOHN PALMER MR M PALMER MR N PALMER MRS N PALMER MRS P PALMER MS P PALMER MISS Z PALMER MR ALEXANDER PALMIER MR
PAMENTER PAN TRADE SERVICES LTD MR HAMID PANAHINEJAD MS P PANAYIOTOU MISS E PANAYOTOPOULOU MR STUART PANES MR D PANGU MRS N PANIGUIAN MISS MARGARET PANKHURST MR R PANKHURST DR S PANKHURST MS S PANKHURST MRS Y PANNETIER MR N PANTOS M
PANYARACHUN MS J PAPA MR MARIOS PAPADAKIS MISS KLIO PAPADOPOULOU MISS E PAPAIL MR S PAPAPETROS MS SOPHIE PAPASAVVA MISS J PAPWORTH MISS SYLVIE PAQUET DR V PARAMANATHAN MR JANAHAN PARAMESVARAN MRS E PARASKEVA MRS A PARDO JIENA PARDO-ZAM
MR R PARFECT MS CLARE PARFITT MR AND MRS D PARHAM MRS V PARHAM MR S PARIHAR MRS J PARISH MISS L PARISH MISS SANDRA PARISH MRS C PARK MR DOUGLAS M PARK MS M PARK MR R PARKASH MRS B PARKE MRS ANNA PARKER MR B PARKER MR C PARKER MS C PARKER
D PARKER MR DOMINIC PARKER MRS E PARKER MRS F PARKER MR G PARKER MR G R PARKER MR J PARKER MS K PARKER MR M PARKER MR MICHAEL PARKER MR MICHEAL PARKER MRS PIMOLPUN PARKER MR R PARKER MR S PARKER MR STEVEN PARKER V PARKER MRS VERONICA PAR
MR W PARKER MR S PARKHURST MR A PARKIN MR B PARKIN MRS J PARKIN MR JAMES PARKIN MRS K PARKIN MR RICHARD PARKIN MR A PARKINS MISS B PARKINSON MR D PARKINSON MISS J PARKINSON MISS M PARKINSON MR P PARKINSON MR I PARKS MS M PARKS MR D PARLE M
S PARMENTER MRS R PARMESSUR MR W PARR MRS M PARROCK MR ANDY PARROTT MRS D PARROTT DR A PARRY DR HEATHER PARRY MR J PARRY MS LINDA PARRY MRS M PARRY MR R PARRY MR R PARRY JONES MR AND MRS M PARRY-WINGFIELD MR J PARS MR C PARSLEY MS K PAR
MR A PARSONS MR E PARSONS MR G PARSONS MRS J PARSONS MISS K PARSONS MRS M PARSONS MRS M J PARSONS DR MICHAEL PARSONS MRS N PARSONS MRS R PARSONS MR R PARSONS PROFESSOR ROGER PARSONS MR S PARSONS MR I PARSONSON MISS C PARTRIDGE MR
PARTRIDGE MRS HEATHER PARTRIDGE MS P PARTRIDGE MR STEVE PARTRIDGE MR N PARTRIDGE-KING MISS M PARVEZ MS M PASCUAL ZAPF MR D PASHLEY MR W PASHLEY MR VUK PASIC MR E PASK MS J PASKE MRS SUSAN PASKINS MR H PASSER MRS L PASSER MRS J PASSES M
PASSEY MRS E A PASSEY MS H PASSEY MISS I PASSMORE MR P PASSMORE MRS L PASTRONE DR G PASVOL MS ANGELA PATCH MISS A PATEL MR C PATEL MR H PATEL MR J PATEL MR K PATEL MISS M PATEL MR M PATEL DR P PATEL MR R PATEL DR R PATEL MS R PATEL MISS S PA
MISS V PATEL MRS V PATEL MR M PATENALL MS CHRISTINA PATERIS MR A PATERSON MRS E PATERSON MRS H PATERSON MRS J PATERSON MS L PATERSON MRS M PATERSON M PATERSON MR AND MRS W CARR MR S PATIENCE MR D PATON MRS E PATON MR R PATON MRS J A PATRICK
K PATRICK MR RAYMOND PATSTON MR B PATTENDEN MRS C PATTENDEN MR B PATTERSON MR I PATTERSON MRS CATHERINE PATTINSON MR TREVOR PATTINSON MR W PATTINSON MS CHARLOTTE PATTISON MR J PATTISON MS V PATZIG MS S PAU ANN PAUL MR G PAUL MR NEVILLE PAUL
M PAULCHOUDHURY MS BERNICE PAULIN MRS L PAULL MR G PAULLEY MR C PAULY MRS C PAVITT MR AND MRS J PAVITT MRS M PAVLIDIS MR ANTHONY PAVLOVICH MRS GLYNIS PAXTON MR J PAXTON MR M PAXTON MISS C PAYNE MR E PAYNE MRS ELEANOR PAYNE MISS HELEN PA
MR J PAYNE MRS J PAYNE MR JOHN PAYNE MRS LEONORE PAYNE MR M PAYNE MRS R PAYNE MR R PAYNE MR V PAYNE MR TOBIN PAYNE-COOK MR W PEACE MR D PEACH MR J PEACOCK MRS KATHLEEN PEACOCK MISS S PEACOCK MS JUDY PEACOCKE MR G PEAD MISS S PEADON D
PEAKIN MRS C PEAPER MRS B PEARCE MR D PEARCE MS GILL PEARCE MS H PEARCE J PEARCE MRS J PEARCE MRS JULIA PEARCE MRS K PEARCE MISS LINDA PEARCE MR R PEARCE MR SIMON PEARCE MR DAVID PEARL MS M PEARL MR D PEARS MRS A PEARSE MR DAVID PEARSON
G PEARSON MRS J J PEARSON MR J PEARSON MRS J PEARSON MISS J PEARSON MRS M PEARSON MR N PEARSON MR R PEARSON MR ROBERT PEARSON MR W PEARSON MRS B PEASE MISS R.D.B PEASE MRS M PEASLAND MR RICK PEAT MRS M A PEATTIE MRS A PEAY MISS A PECK M
PECK MR N PECK MR R PECK MRS V PECK MISS S PECKITT MR P PECKOVER MS J PEDDAR MS GILLIAN PEDERSEN MR P PEDERSEN MRS ALISON PEDLEY DR BARBARA PEDLEY MRS I PEEK MS J PEEK MRS B PEEL MRS C PEEL MR JOHN PEEL MS P PEEL MS S PEEL MRS JENNIFER P
MISS S PEERMAN MISS SUZY PEERMAN MR J PEGLER AND DR S DAVIDSON MR P PEGLER MRS B PEGRUM MR AND MRS J PEIRCE MR M PIERSON MR R PEIRSON MISS LOIS PELECANOS MS A PELEG MR DAVID PELHAM MS A PELIKAN MR R PELLATT MR JOSE PELLICER GALLARDO M
PELOPIEAS MRS S PELTIER MRS C PEMBERTON MR G PEMBERTON MISS R PEMBERTON MRS M PENDER MR J PENDLETON MR D PENDRILL MR T PENDRILL MR D PENFOLD MRS M PENFOLD MRS ARLETTE PENGILLY MS E PENGILLY MRS J PENN MR R PENN MR THOMAS PENNANT MRS B PEN
MR M PENNIE MRS W PENNINGTON MRS M PENNOCK MR D PENNY MR GILES PENNY MRS SHIELA PENNY MRS C PENNYCOCK MR DAVID PENROSE MR T PENROSE MISS R PENTY THE PEOPLE'S PALACE MS J PEPERA MRS D PEPPER MR K PEPPER MS G PERCEVAL-MAXWELL MRS D PERCIC
P PERCIVAL MISS J PERCIVALL MR A PERCY MS T PERCY HONORABLE SIMON PERCY WINDSOR-CLIVE MRS J PERCY-DAVIS MR JOHN PERCY-DAVIS MR M PEREIRA PROFESSOR L PERERA MR SIDNEY PERERA MR T PERERA MR & MRS I PEREZ MR H PERILLY MS A PERINPARAJA MR
PERKINS MR D PERKINS DR J PERKINS MRS M PERKINS MR NICK PERKINS MR R PERKINS MRS SONIA PERKINS MR J PERLOFF MRS R PERREN MR J PERRET MISS J PERRETT MISS P PERRIMAN MRS R PERROTT MR A PERRY MRS B PERRY MS C PERRY MS CATHERINE PERRY MR D PE
MR G PERRY MRS I PERRY MISS J PERRY MRS J PERRY MR L PERRY M PERRY MRS P PERRY MR P S PERRY MR R PERRY MRS WENDY PERRY MRS L PERRY-MCALPINE MS INGRID PERSAUD MS L PERSAUD MISS SILVANA PERSICHINI MS SOPHIE PERSSON MISS M PERVEEN MR OLIVI
PESCE MS J PESTEL K F PESTELL MRS MIRANDA PESTELL MRS L PESTRIDGE MS A PETARD MRS M PETCH MRS H PETCHEY MR B J PETER MRS H PETER MR M PETER MS GLYNIS PETERKIN MS ALISON PETERS MR C PETERS MR D PETERS MS EMMA PETERS MR MARTIN PETERS MS MIA PET
MR R PETERS MRS S PETERS MS SAROJINI PETERS DR TIM PETERS MRS SYLVIE PETERSEN MR ALAN PETERSON MR DAVID PETHER MRS J PETHERBRIDGE MS M PETHERBRIDGE MR D PETHERICK MRS J PETO MRS M PETRIE MS F PETROVIC MR R PETROVIC MS L PETTIBONE MRS I PETTI
MRS BRENDA PETTIT P PETTITT MR TONY PETTITT MRS K PEYTON MR M PEZARRO MS M PHANTIS MR S PHEASANT MRS A PHELOUNG MR DENNIS PHELPS MR MATTHEW PHELPS MRS B PHILIP MRS E PHILIP MS J PHILIP MR E PHILIPP MR MICHAEL PHILIPS MISS C PHILLIP MRS R PHIL
MRS S PHILLIP MISS A PHILLIPS MR A PHILLIPS MISS CAROL PHILLIPS MR D PHILLIPS MRS D PHILLIPS MS D PHILLIPS MRS ELIZABETH PHILLIPS MRS G PHILLIPS MRS GILLIAN PHILLIPS MR H PHILLIPS MR J PHILLIPS MS J PHILLIPS PROFESSOR J PHILLIPS MR JA
PHILLIPS MS JANET PHILLIPS MRS JOAN PHILLIPS MRS L PHILLIPS MR M PHILLIPS MRS M PHILLIPS MS P PHILLIPS MR P PHILLIPS MRS PAMELA PHILLIPS MS PAULINE PHILLIPS MR RAYMOND PHILLIPS ROSS PHILLIPS MRS V PHILLIPS MR WILLIAM PHILLIPS MS E PHILLIP
MS R PHILLIPSON MRS T PHILLIPSON MR R PHILLPOT MS S PHILP MR J PHILPOTT MR B PHIPPS MRS S PHONGSATHORN MR JOHN PHYSICK MS JOSEPHINE PIA MRS I PICK MR ANTHONY PICKARD MS JULIE PICKARD MR T PICKARD MRS EDITH PICKERDEN MR B PICKERING MRS L PICKER
MRS M PICKERING MRS K PICKETT MR S PICKFORD MS K PICKLES MR DAVID PICKTHALL MR D PICKUP GEOFFERY PICKUP MRS S PICOT MR ALLAN PIELAGE MR CEDRIC PIERCE MS J PIERCE MRS R PIERCE MS S PIERCE MRS A PIERCE-JONES MRS MARGARET PIERI MRS J PIERREPO
MR R PIGGOTT MS T PIGLIA MISS H PIHLAKAS MR A PIKE MR I PIKE MS J PIKE MR J PIKE MISS JUNE PIKE MS M PIKE MR R PIKE MR T PIKE MR TIMOTHY J PIKE MR PETER PILCH MR R PILCHER MS M PILKINGTON MRS P PILKINGTON MR WILLIAM PILKINGTON BAVANI PILLAY MR
PILLER MR J PINCHES MR F PINDER MISS J PINDER MRS PAULINE PINDER MS R PINES MS S PINHEIRO MR C PINK MR D PINK MR R PINKETT MR J PINKEY MR A PINKNEY MR G PINKNEY MR A PINN MR NEVILLE PINNINGTON MS P PINSKER MS S PIPE MRS CAROL PIPER MRS DIANE PI
MRS K PIPER DR T PIPER MR A PIRSON MR GIOVANNI PISANI MR R PISANI MISS C PISHIRIS MR COLIN PITCHFORD MISS SUSAN PITE MRS C PITKIN MR AND MRS C PITMAN DR DEBORAH PITT MR N PITT MR N PITTMAN MRS V PITTMAN MRS R PITT-PAYNE FCA MRS D PITTS MS G PITTS
J PITTS MR RICHARD PITTS MS W PITTS MR NICHOLAS PIZEY MISS E PIZZONI MR B PLACE MR M PLACKETT MR GRAHAM PLAIN R PLAIN MR W PLAIN MS CHRISTINE PLAMPIN MR DAVID PLANK B PLANSKOY MR JAMES PLANT MR N PLANT MISS J PLASKETT MISS M PLASTOW MR JOS
PLATNAUER MR ADRIAN PLATT MR H PLATT DR H PLATT MR M PLATT MR P PLATT MR P PLATTEN MR A PLATTS MRS C PLATTS MS J PLATTS MR P PLAUT MRS NATASHA PLAYER MRS J PLAYFAIR MS J PLAYFORD MRS J PLAYLE MISS J PLEACE MR D PLEASANTS MR ANDREW PLEDGE
EVANGELOS PLITHAS MR DAVID PLUMERIDGE MRS F PLUMMER MRS D PLUMRIDGE MRS B POCKLINGTON MS CAROLINE POCKLINGTON MISS H PODD MS T PODGER MRS M PODHORSKA MRS C PODRO MISS J POGMORE MS P POHL MS R POIGNANT MRS RUTH POISSON MRS N POKROY MS K
POLAND MR S POLANYK MS SARA POLDAAS MR DAVID POLE MR M POLE MR C POLE-CAREW MS M POLETTI MRS E POLFREMAN MR TIMOTHY POLGLASE MRS H POLGLAZE MISS CATERINA POLIDORO MRS L POLISENSKY MS C POLL MR P POLLACK MR I POLLAK MR J POLLARD MISS M POLL
MRS E POLLECOFF MR ROY POLLINGTON MR A POLLOCK MR S POLLOCK MRS A POLLOK MRS KIM POLLOK MS E POLONSKY MR A POLYCHRONIADIS MR J POMFRET MRS P PONCE MS CLAIR POND MR GEORGE PONDER MS P PONS DR J PONTE MS M PONTE MS CONSTANTINE PONTICOS MIS
PONTIFEX MR T PONTIUS MR A POOK MISS M POOK MR MARK POOK MRS C POOLE MR C POOLE D POOLE DAMON POOLE MRS E POOLE MS E POOLE MRS J POOLE MR P POOLE MR S POOLE MISS P POON MR A POPE MR M POPE MRS R POPE MR S POPE MISS T POPE MS V POPE MS BILY
POPOVA MR H POPPER MR K POPPERWELL MR NEIL POPPMACHER MR G PORFIDO MRS J PORGES MR E G PORKISS MRS HIROKO PORTAINER MR C PORTER MR DONALD PORTER MR E PORTER MR G PORTER MR J PORTER DR JANET PORTER KAY PORTER MR M PORTER MRS M PORTER M POR
MRS P PORTER MRS PATRICIA PORTER MR ROBERT PORTER MRS SILVIA PORTER MS B PORTES MR J PORTESS MISS M PORTINARI MR RICHARD PORTNOY MR A POST DR J POST MS JULIA POSTE MR A POSTINS MS J POSTON MR F POTGIETER MS O POTPARIC MR ANDREW POTTER MS
POTTER MR C POTTER J POTTER MS SARAH POTTER MRS M POTTHURST MR SIDNEY POTTIER MISS G K POTTINGER MR G POTTINGER MR R POTTRUFF MR C POTTS MRS PAMELA POTTS MR ROBIN POTTS MS EDITH POULSEN MR R POULTEN MRS A POULTER MR JOHN POULTER MISS S POUL
MRS D POUNTNEY MISS E POUNTNEY R POURESHAGH DR S POURIA MS C POW MRS J POWDERHAM MRS A POWDRELL MR A POWELL MR C POWELL MRS C POWELL MR E POWELL MR F POWELL MRS G POWELL MR GEOFFREY POWELL MR I POWELL MS J POWELL MISS J POWELL MR J POW
DR JANE POWELL MRS N POWELL MR NICK POWELL MISS OLIVIA POWELL MRS P POWELL MISS PAMELA POWELL MISS R POWELL MRS R POWELL MR B POWER J E POWER MR JAMES POWER MS M POWER MR RICHARD POWER MRS V POWER MR A POWLEY MR SEAN POWLEY MRS J
POWLS MR D POWLSON MISS B POWRIE MR J POYNTON MRS G POYNTZ MS A POYSER MR J POYSER MISS MARIA POZZI MS C PRADIER DR D PRAGER MR U PRAGER MS R PRASHAD DR P PRASHNER MR C PRATT MR & MRS A PRATT MRS F PRATT MRS J PRATT MR JOHN PRATT MRS M PR
PRATT MR T PRATT MISS R PREBBLE MS J PREECE DR G PRELEVIC MS A PREMRU MS M PRENTICE MR P PRENTICE MISS R PRENTICE MS T PRENTIS MR C PRESCOD MR A PRESCOTT MR DAVID PRESCOTT MR R PRESCOTT DR G PRESCOTT NUDING MS F PRESS MR PETER PRESS MS C PRESS
MRS K PRESSER-VELDER MRS FEE PRESTON MR & MRS M PRESTON MR L PRESTON MRS M J PRESTON MRS M PRESTON MS M PRESTON MS RACHAEL PRESTON MISS VALERIE PRESTON MS JANET PRESTWOOD MRS M PRETTY DR M PREUSS MR I PREVOST MISS F PREWETT MR A PREZZAVE
MR AND MRS ANNE PRICE MRS C PRICE MR C PRICE MR COLIN PRICE MR DANIEL PRICE MR DENNIS PRICE MRS H PRICE MR J PRICE MRS J PRICE MR JONATHON PRICE MR K PRICE MRS K PRICE MRS KATE PRICE MS M PRICE MR MICHAEL PRICE MR N PRICE MRS P J PRICE PRICE
MYERS MR R PRICE MR S PRICE MRS S PRICE MS SUZANNA P PRICE MRS WENDY PRICE MS P PRICE-TOMES MR COLIN PRICKETT MISS JUDITH PRICKETT DR NB PRIDE MR ROBERT PRIEBE MR P PRIEM MR J PRIEST MS CAROLINE PRIESTLEY MS SUSANNE PRIESTLEY MR S PRIEST
MR A PRILL MR STEVE PRIME MISS FLAVIA PRINA MR C PRINCE MISS C PRINCE MR DAVE PRINCE MS H PRINCE MRS M PRINCE MR R PRINCE DR CAROL PRINGLE MISS EMILY PRINGLE MRS M PRINGLE MR COLLIN PRIOR MRS J PRIOR MS K PRIOR MR M PRIOR MR H PRITCHARD
HELEN PRITCHARD MRS N PRITCHARD MR RICHARD PRITCHARD MS SANDRA PRITCHARD MR J PROBERT MS LAURA PROBERT MR R PROBETT MRS I PROGIN MR M PROLA MR A PROSSER MR D PROTHERO MRS B PROTO MISS O PROTTI MR D PROUDFOOT MR G PROVIDENCE MISS G PROWE M
PROWTING MR M PRUE MR A PRUSS MR JONATHAN PRYCE MR GRAHAM PUGH MISS M PUGH MRS R PUGH MRS S PUGH MRS K PUGSLEY MS J PULFER MR A PULFORD MRS L PULLEN MRS P PULLEN MR R PULLEN MR G PULLENGER MRS E PULLINGER MS N PULLINGER MRS NATASH
PULLINGER MR P PULZER MS SARAH PUMFREY MRS L PUNCHARD MR E PUNTER MR STEPHEN PURCELL MR T PURCELL MR JOHN PURCHASE MR M PURCHASE MS ELIZABETH PURDAM MRS E PURDUE MR AND MRS JOHN PURDY MR N PURI MISS JOY E PURITZ MR H PURKISS MR S.D. PURMA
MR CHRIS PURNELL MRS R PUROHIT MRS S PURPLE MS JANET PURR MR T PURSLOW DR PETER PURTON MS V PUSCH MR D PUSEY MR JULIAN PUTTERGILL MRS ANNE PUTTICK MR DUSAN PUVACIC MS K PUYSER MR C PYBUS MR C PYE MR M PYKE MR P PYLE MRS CUEDDA PYLNIKOW M
B PYM MS RACHEL PYPER MISS M QUADAKKERS MS M QUADAKKERS MISS E QUAIFE MRS C QUAINTRELL MISS N QUANE MS G QUARTLY-WATSON MRS FIONA QUAYLE MS F QUERCIA MRS MARY QUEREE MRS A QUIGLEY MR PETER QUIGLEY MR D QUINLAN M J QUINLAN MS A QUINN MS J
QUINN MRS M QUINN MR P QUINN MISS S QUINN MR STEPHEN QUINN MS T QUINN MS F QUINT MS MAGGIE SAMS QUINTRELL MS JANET QUIPP MR LANCE QUIRICO MR A QUIRK MRS MARGARET QUOW MRS CHRISTINE RAAFAT MR C RABBITE MS M RABOUHANS MISS H RACE MR GRAHAM RAC
MS S RACHMAN MRS J RACKHAM MRS I RADCLIFFE MR MICHAEL RADCLIFFE MRS C RADCLYFFE MISS V RADEMACHER MS A RADFORD MR MALCOM RADFORD MR G RADIC MR S G RADICH MR D J RADIN MRS R RADLEY MRS R RADZIWILL MR A RAE MR G RAE MRS G RAE MRS C RAEB
MRS JULIA RAEBURN DR J RAFFLE MR JOSEPH RAFFOUL MR RAFFOUL MR V RAGOONANAN MR A RAGUNATHAN MR AMIR RAHEJA MR N RAHIM MR M RAHMAN MISS X RAHMAN DR P RAI MRS J RAINA MRS A RAINE MRS S RAINE MRS R RAINER-TODD MR PAUL RAINS MRS H RAJA MIS
RAJEEBALLI MRS L RAKHRA MR BRIAN RALPH MR G RALSTON MRS S RAM MR M RAMADAN MRS M RAMAGE MS I RAMASWAMY MS S RAMJI MS L RAMPTON MR GRAHAM RAMSAY MRS H RAMSAY MRS J RAMSAY MRS JANE RAMSAY MS H RAMSDEN MS SARA RAMSDEN MR G R RAMSELL MR
RAMSEY MR JEROME RAMSEY MISS J RAMSHAW MS BARBARA RAMSOCHIT MR K RANCE MR M RANCE MR C RANDALL MRS EDITH E RANDALL MRS J RANDALL MR M RANDALL MS M RANDALL MARTIN RANDALL TRAVEL LTD MR T RANDALL MR R RANDHAWA MRS M RANDLE MISS W RANDLE
JAIRAJ RANGASAMI MR JAMES RANGER MS CHRISTINA RANGER-REIF MS P RANK MS ELEANOR RANSOM MR J RANSOM MRS A RANSOME MR ENRICO RANZONI MR R RAO MR RAVOORUK RAO MR CHRISTOPHER RAPHAEL MRS E RAPHAEL MS J RAPHAEL MR M RAPOSO MRS S RASHBROOK M
J RATA MISS H RATCLIFF MR SIMON RATCLIFF MR PATRICK RATCLIFFE MS RUTH RATCLIFFE MRS B RATHBONE MR DAVID RATHBORNE MR A RATNAGE MR L RATNAPALAN MR P RATHESAR MRS J RATTENBURY DR K RATTRAY MRS A RAU DAWES MR A M RAUSCH MRS I RAUSCHER MR BA
RAVAL MR H RAVAL MISS R RAVAL MR ANTHONY RAVEN MS H RAVEN MR A RAWAL MRS F RAWLES MR JOHN RAWLINGS MS M RAWLINSON M RAWLINSON THE RT HON THE LORD RAWLINSON OF EWELL QC DOUGLAS RAWLISON MR C RAWNSLEY MR PETER RAWSON MRS H RAY MRS J RAY
P RAY MS JANE RAYBOULD MR P RAY-JONES MR WILLIAM RAYMAKERS MS P RAYMENT MRS J RAYMOND MR R RAYMOND-COX MR B RAYNER MR C RAYNER MS E RAYNER MISS M RAYNES MR K RAYSON MR J RAZ MRS S REA MRS A READ MRS H READ MS KATHLEEN READ MR M READ M
READ MS J READE MR BRIAN READER MRS J READER MR M READER MR J READING MR BRIAN READMAN MR M REAKES MRS R REARDON MRS B REASON MR NICK REAVILL MS P REA-WOODHOUSE MR DAVID REAY GAIL REBUCK MR D RECKLESS MRS J RECKNELL-TURNER MS C RECORDON
R REDDAWAY MR RICHARD REDDAWAY MR J REDDEN MRS L REDDIN MR G REDDISH MISS ARUNA REDDY MS D REDDY MRS C REDFEARN MS J REDFERN MRS S REDFERN MRS A REDFURN MR W REDING MR G REDMAN-BROWN DR MICHAEL REDMAYNE MR G REDSHAW MS H REDSHAW M
REDSHAW MISS S REDSHAW MISS S REDWAY MS P REDWOOD MR C REECE MRS M REECE MR P REECE MR A REED MRS A REED ALAN REED MR B REED MR C REED MR D REED MRS D REED MR IAIN REED MRS J REED MISS K REED KATHY REED MR T REED MS PAMELA REEDER MS L REE
MRS ANNE REES MRS E M REES MR H REES J H REES MR J REES MRS J REES MISS K REES MRS MARGARET REES MR MATTHEW REES MR R REES MISS EIRIAN REES JONES MR DAVID REESON MR J REES-WILLIAMS MRS E REEVE MR G REEVE MR J REEVE MR M REEVE DR BARNABY REE
MR E REEVES MRS J REEVES MRS T REEVES MRS D REGAN MR G REGAN MR R REGAN MRS ROSEMARY REGAN MR W REGAN MR CHARLES REGNIER MR PRAVIN REHEJA MR E REICH MR S REICHENSTEIN MRS ANNE REICHMAN MR ALISTAIR REID MISS C REID MS C REID MR D REID MS D R
MR E REID MR EDMUND REID GRAHAM REID MRS H REID MR I REID MR J REID MRS J REID MRS K REID MRS M REID MRS P REID MR S REID MR J REID MR BERNARD REILLY MS MARGARET REILLY MR NICK REILLY MS M REINHART MR NORBERT REIS MRS C REISER MS M REISHALI-F
MISS B REISSNER MS E REISSNER MR T REISZ MS ANGELA REITH P RELF MISS V RELLSTAB MR B RELPH MISS J REMMETT MS J REMNANT MR DENNIS RENALS MR G RENDLE MR B A RENDTORFF MR J RENNIE MR P RENNIE MRS C RENNIE-NASH MS ANN RENSHAW MRS V RENSHAW M
RENTON MR CAROL RENTOUL MRS M RENTOUL MR F RENYARD MR S RESTALL MR R RESTORICK MRS ELEANOR RETALLACK MR C REUBEN MR J REUBEN MR NORMAN REUTER MRS J REYMER MR A REYNEKE MRS A REYNOLDS MR B REYNOLDS MISS C REYNOLDS MS D REYNOLDS MIS
REYNOLDS MR GERARD REYNOLDS MRS GILLIAN REYNOLDS MR H REYNOLDS MR I REYNOLDS MISS IRIS REYNOLDS MR J REYNOLDS MRS J REYNOLDS MR KEITH REYNOLDS MR L REYNOLDS MISS M REYNOLDS MISS MARGARET REYNOLDS MISS N REYNOLDS MR RICHARD REYNOLDS
S REYNOLDS MR SIMON REYNOLDS MRS SUSAN REYNOLDS MR CHANGIZ REZVANI MRS I RHEA MR B RHODES MR D RHODES MR J RHODES MR JOHN RHODES MISS M RHODES MR P RHODES MR PAUL RHODES DR JOSEPH RHYMER MRS E RHYS PRYCE MS MIRANDA RHYS WILLIAMS MS A RI
MR DINIZ RIBEIRO MISS J RICE MS J RICE MR A RICHARDS MR ANTHONY RICHARDS MS B J RICHARDS MR C RICHARDS MR D RICHARDS MR DANIEL RICHARDS MR DAVID RICHARDS MS F RICHARDS MS G RICHARDS MISS H RICHARDS MRS H RICHARDS MR HUGH RICHARDS MR J
RICHARDS MR KEITH RICHARDS MRS L RICHARDS MRS M RICHARDS MRS MARGARET RICHARDS MR N RICHARDS MR PETER RICHARDS R RICHARDS MS SAMANTHA RICHARDS MRS V RICHARDS MRS WENDY RICHARDS MR A RICHARDSON MR B RICHARDSON MRS CAROL RICHARDSON MS COL
RICHARDSON MR D RICHARDSON MS E RICHARDSON MR E RICHARDSON MR G RICHARDSON MR H RICHARDSON MR I RICHARDSON MRS I RICHARDSON MR JAMES RICHARDSON MRS JANIE RICHARDSON MR L RICHARDSON MR M RICHARDSON MRS M RICHARDSON MS M RICHARDSON MR
RICHARDSON MRS PAMELA RICHARDSON MR P RICHARDSON MR R RICHARDSON MRS S RICHARDSON MISS SHEILA RICHARDSON MR STEVEN RICHARDSON MR T RICHARDSON MR A RICHENDOLLER PROFESSOR ALAN RICHENS MR D RICHES MISS E RICHES MR J RICHES MRS J RICHLEY M
HELEN RICHMAN MR D RICHMOND MRS R B RICHMOND MS C RICHNELL MR J RICHTER JNR MRS L RICK MR PAUL RICKARD MR R RICKARD MRS C RICKETTS MR D RICKETTS DR T RICKETTS MR TIM RICKETTS MR T RICKSON MR M RICKWOOD MR J RIDDICK MISS VIVIAN RIDDLE MS ALI
RIDEM MRS C RIDER G RIDER MS V RIDGEMAN MR A RIDGEON MS L RIDGERS-WAITE MISS J RIDGEWAY MR S RIDGLEY MR S RIDGWELL MISS D RIDLEY MR M RIDLEY PROFESSOR MARK RIDLEY MS E RIDOUT MRS J RIDOUT MISS A RIDSDALE MRS E RIECKENBERG MR CHARLES RIFK
MISS A RIGBY ANNE RIGBY MS S RIGBY MISS SANDRA RIGBY MR VICTOR RIGBY MRS P RIGGALL MISS SOPHIE RIGNY MRS A RILEY DR C RILEY MR E RILEY MS H RILEY MRS HELEN RILEY MR J RILEY MR D RIMES MRS B RING MRS E RINGHAM MR J RINGHAM MR T RIORDAN MR E RIP
MR D RIPPENGAL MR JOHN RIPPIN MR JEFFREY RISBRIDGER MRS L RISBY RISDON MR M RISINGER MISS J RISK MRS A RITCHIE MR A RITCHIE MR N RITCHIE MISS NICOLA RITCHIE MR P RITSON MRS P RITTE MRS LYDIA RITZER THE RIVERS CHARITABLE TRUST MRS B RIVIERE
BRYN ROACH MS D M ROACH MRS J ROACHE MRS M ROAF MR & MRS K ROBATHAN MR A ROBB MR G ROBB MR J ROBB MONICA ROBB MISS JANE E ROBBIE MS ANNE ROBBINS MRS D ROBBINS MISS E ROBBINS MR M ROBBINS MISS P ROBBINS MRS R ROBBINS MISS K ROBBINS-HALLAM
J ROBERTON DR A ROBERTS MR A ROBERTS MR B ROBERTS MRS B ROBERTS MS B ROBERTS MR C ROBERTS MR CRAIG ROBERTS MR D ROBERTS MRS D ROBERTS MS E ROBERTS MR E ROBERTS MRS G ROBERTS MISS GILLIAN ROBERTS MS I ROBERTS MR J ROBERTS MRS J ROBERTS MRS J
ROBERTS MR JOHN ROBERTS MR L ROBERTS MR M ROBERTS MRS M ROBERTS MR N ROBERTS NICK ROBERTS MR P ROBERTS MRS P ROBERTS MR R ROBERTS DR S ROBERTS MS V ROBERTS MR A ROBERTSON MRS B ROBERTSON MISS C ROBERTSON MS E ROBERTSON MR G ROBERTSON M
ROBERTSON MS J ROBERTSON MS JACKI ROBERTSON MR MARC ROBERTSON MRS M ROBERTSON MRS N ROBERTSON DR P ROBERTSON MS P ROBERTSON MISS R ROBERTSON MRS A ROBERTSON-EMPEY MRS F ROBEY MRS J ROBILLIARD MR J ROBINETTE MRS P ROBINOW MR R ROBINS MR
ROBINSON MR ANDREW ROBINSON MISS B ROBINSON MR BRIAN ROBINSON MR C ROBINSON MS C ROBINSON DR D ROBINSON MR DAVID ROBINSON MRS ELAINE ROBINSON MS G ROBINSON MR GEORGE ROBINSON MRS H ROBINSON MRS J ROBINSON MR J ROBINSON MR K C ROBINSON
L ROBINSON MRS M ROBINSON LADY M ROBINSON MISS M ROBINSON MS M ROBINSON MISS MARCIA ROBINSON MR N ROBINSON MR P ROBINSON MS P ROBINSON MISS S ROBINSON MRS S ROBINSON MS S ROBINSON MRS SADIE ROBINSON MR STEVE ROBINSON MS T ROBINSON M
ROBINSON MRS WINIFRED ROBINSON MR BRUCE ROBJENT MRS A ROBSON MR C N F ROBSON MISS E ROBSON MR J ROBSON MISS JENNIFER ROBSON MR M ROBSON MRS SALLY ROBSON MR J ROBURN MR A ROCHE MR K ROCHE MS J ROCHESTER MR J ROCHFORD MRS J ROCK MR P ROCK
JAMES ROCKHILL MISS W ROCKHILL MRS P ROCKLIFF MR BIZHAN RODD MR PHILIP RODDEN MRS B RODEN MR T RODEN DR J RODERIC-EVANS MR P RODERICK JONES MISS SALLY RODGER MRS F RODGERS DR M RODGERS MR I RODIC MRS M RODIN MR C RODMELL MS S RODNEY M
RODOPOULOS MS A RODRIGUES MRS M RODRIGUES MR WILLIAM RODRIGUES MS A RODRIGUEZ MISS F H RODWELL MRS E ROE EVELYN ROE MR G ROE DR I ROE MRS M ROE MR S ROE MR STEPHEN ROE MRS T ROE DR YVONNEKE ROE MR MATTHIAS ROEBEL MS WENDY ROEBUCK MR FLOR
ROECKL MR S ROFF MS A ROFFEY MR J B ROFFEY MS K ROFFEY MR M ROFFEY MR JOHN ROGAN MS SOPHIE ROGER MS A ROGERS MR A ROGERS MRS A ROGERS MR ALAN ROGERS MRS BARBARA ROGERS MRS C ROGERS MS D ROGERS MRS D ROGERS MR E ROGERS MRS J ROGERS MR
ROGERS MR RAYMOND ROGERS MR ROBERT ROGERS LADY ROGERS MR S ROGERS MR STEPHEN ROGERS MS SUSAN ROGERS DR VALERIE ROGERS MRS A ROGERSON MS HELEN ROGERSON MR T ROGERSON MR TIMOTHY ROGERSON MR K ROHEE MS MARTINA ROHR MRS JOANNE ROHRER MR
ROITT MRS G ROLFE MISS T ROLFE MRS J ROLINSON MR S ROLLASON MR R ROLLINS MR M ROLLS MR L ROLPH MISS T ROLPH MS JANET ROMANO MRS J ROMIJN MISS J ROMNEY MRS NORMA ROMNEY MISS N RONDEL MR R RONEY MR P RONS MR PEARCE ROOD MR & MRS R ROOK MR
ROOK MRS G ROOKE MS M ROOKER MR N ROOME MR M ROONEY MRS H ROOSE MRS B ROOTES MRS AMARYLLIS ROPER MISS K ROPER MR T ROPER MRS J ROQUES MR P ROSALBA ROSALYN & NICHOLAS SPRINGER CHARITABLE TRUST MR F ROSAM MRS M ROSARIO MISS E ROSCOE MR
ROSCOE MR CHARLES ROSCORLA MR A ROSE MISS ALISON ROSE MR C ROSE MS C ROSE MR H ROSE MRS I ROSE J & R ROSE MR & MRS J ROSE MRS J ROSE MS J ROSE MRS JOSEPHINE ROSE MR K ROSE MRS L ROSE MS L ROSE MR M ROSE MR P ROSE MRS P ROSE MR PETER ROSE MR
ROSE MRS M ROSEBERG MR AND MRS J ROSEFIELD MRS L ROSELAAR MR A ROSEN MRS JEANNIE ROSEN MRS JOYCE ROSEN MRS P ROSEN MRS SYLVIA ROSEN MR D ROSENBAUM THE NATHAN ROSENBAUM CHARITABLE TRUST MRS S ROSENBERG MR R ROSENBERGER MR L ROSENBLATT M
MARTA ROSENDE MS RUTH ROSENFELDER MRS L ROSENHEAD MR J ROSENHEIM MS HILARY ROSENTHAL MR J ROSENTHAL MRS L ROSENTHAL MR P ROSENTHAL MS S ROSENTHAL MR M ROSEVEARE MR R ROSING MS CLARE ROSKILL MR R ROSNER MRS B ROSOUX CARON ROSOVSKI MR
ROSS MR A ROSS MS A ROSS MISS ANNE ROSS MR C ROSS MS D ROSS MRS FIONA ROSS MISS J ROSS MRS J ROSS MR R ROSS MR RICHARD ROSS MS SUSAN ROSS MS R ROSSELSON DR A ROSSER MR PAUL ROSSI MRS I ROSSIN MRS D ROSSITER MRS A ROSS-KOKOSZKA MR C ROSS-PAR
MR A ROSSWICK MRS E ROSTAING MR OLIVER ROSTEN MR G ROSTRON MR GUY ROSTRON MISS L ROSTRON MR D ROTH MR J ROTH MS JENNER ROTH MISS P ROTH MR P ROTH MRS R ROTHENBERG MR AND MRS J ROTHERY MS G M ROTHWELL MRS H ROTTER MR G ROUBICEK MR JAMES RO
MISS R ROUGHLEY MR F ROUGIER MR D ROUND MRS P ROUND MRS C ROURKE MRS D ROUSSEV MR A ROUTH MS L ROUTT MISS M ROUVIER-ANGELI MR I ROW MR M ROWBERRY MRS S ROWCLIFFE MR B ROWE MR C ROWE MRS J ROWE MRS K ROWE MS M ROWE MR N ROWE MR R ROWE MR
ROWELL MRS C ROWLAND MRS JULIETTE ROWLAND MR M ROWLAND MR R ROWLAND MRS E ROWLANDS MRS I ROWLANDS MRS E ROWLANDS-REES DR V ROWLATT MR B ROWLES MS S ROWLES MS V A ROWLEY MR GEOFFREY ROWNEY MISS J ROWSE MS J ROWSON MR J ROWSWELL MR N
ROXBURGH MRS G ROY MRS H ROY MR J ROY MRS M ROY MR MARTIN ROYALTON-KISCH MS JULIET ROY-CHODHURY MR A K ROYCHOWDHURY MR BRIAN ROYLANCE MISS A F ROYO MS I ROZHDOV MR MARTIN RUBACH MR M RUBENSTEIN MR ALEXANDER RUCK KEENE MR C RUDD MR I R

Z RUDDER MISS P RUDDY MR H RUDEL MARY RUDGE MISS S RUDOFSKY MS M RUEDA MS J RUFF MR J RUFF MR M RUFFLE MR A RUIA MS C RUIZ DR D RUMBALL MR D RUMBELOW MR BRIAN RUMBLE MRS J RUMBLE MR P RUMBLE MRS NADIA RUMBLES MR R RUMBOLL MR DAVID Y MRS L RUMSEY MR C RUNECKLES MR S RUNGASAMY MS S RUNGE MR G RUNNICLES MS S RUPPIN MR R RUSBRIDGE MRS URSULA RUSE MR DAVID RUSH MR SALMAN RUSHDIE MR D RUSHMERE MR A RUSHTON MR IAN RUSHTON MR E RUSOVS MS CHRISTINE RUSS MR A RUSSE MR A LL MRS C RUSSELL MR COLIN RUSSELL MR E RUSSELL MR H J RUSSELL MS H RUSSELL MS HILARY RUSSELL MS J RUSSELL MRS JANIS RUSSELL MR K RUSSELL MRS LEONORA RUSSELL MR N RUSSELL MRS P RUSSELL MRS PAMELA RUSSELL MR R RUSSELL MS R RUSSELL ROBERT LL MS V RUSSELL MRS VIRGINIA RUSSELL MR E RUSSELL-WALLING DR A RUSSO MISS E RUSSO MRS S RUST MR C E RUST-D'EYE MS J RUSTIN MS M RUTH MR L RUTHENBERG MISS A E RUTHERFORD MRS E RUTHERFORD MRS V RUTLAND MRS S RUTSTEIN DR P RUTTER D RUXTON MRS ON MR J RYALL MR DAVID RYAN MS JULIE RYAN MR M RYAN MS M RYAN MR P RYAN MR S RYAN MR W RYAN MR GEOFFREY RYDER MRS V RYE MS R RYLAND MRS J RYLE LT COL J RYMER JONES MS A RYNKIEWICZ MR M RYVES MRS A SAAD MS H SAALER DR M SAARY MR A SABBADINI SABBAGH MRS S SABHARWAL MISS F SABI L SABIELAK MRS M SABINE-BACON MR SANJIV SACHDEV MR M SACHS MR W SACKS MRS MAHIN SADEGH MISS K SHERLOCK MR H SAEED MR ANGUS SAER MR N SAFATY MR SAFFADI MR H SAFFERY MR T SAFFERY MS F SAFIRI MRS B R MR D SAGAR MS H SAGAR MR D SAGE MRS J SAGE MS M SAGOO MS M SAH MR A SAHRAOUI MR A SAINER ALAN & BABETTE SAINSBURY CHARITABLE FUND MR G SAINSBURY MR LOUIS SAINT JUSTE MR H SAKAI MR H SAKALIS MR B H SAKER MS K SAKER MISS E SAKO MRS F SALAMA SALAMON MISS H SALAMONOWICZ MS MELISSA SALAS MS R SALBASHIAN MS S SALBASHIAN MRS B SALBY MRS ALIX SALEEB MRS JANE SALEEM MR N SALEH MR BARRY SALES MR C SALES MR J SALES MR ROBIN SALES MRS MIRNA SALGADINHO MS I SALGADO MISS B SALIBA P SALINAS MISS J SALINSON THE MARQUESS AND MARCHIONESS OF SALISBURY MRS CATHERINE SALISBURY-MEISELS MR D SALLISS DR A SALM MISS C SALMON MR CHRIS SALMON DR E SALMON MS HEATHER SALMON MRS J SALMON MRS L SALMON MS R SALMON MISS R SALMON SALMON MISS S SALMOND MR J SALMONS MR G SALTER MR JEREMY SALTER MISS M SALTER MR M SALTER MR M S P SALTER MR ROBERT SALTER MRS MARIA SALVADOR MRS K SALWAY MR K SALWAY MRS CELIA SALWEY MRS M SALZEDO MRS F SAMARAJIWA DR L SAMARASINGHE SAMGHANI Y R SAMI MR K SAMII MRS JUDY SAMMAN MRS J SAMMARCO MISS A SAMPSON MRS D SAMPSON MRS J SAMPSON MRS JILL SAMPSON MR TOM SAMPSON MRS P SAMSON MR D SAMUEL MR G SAMUEL MRS V SAMUEL MRS BARBARA SAMUELS MR D SAMWAYS MISS J SANCTO SAND MRS H SAND MR GEORGE SANDARS MRS M SANDELL MRS S SANDELL MRS R SANDELSON MRS J SANDER MR J SANDERS MR N SANDERS MR PETER SANDERS MISS S SANDERS MR T J SANDERS MR T SANDERS MRS VENETIA SANDERS MR C SANDERSON MRS C SANDERSON MS H NDERSON MR J SANDERSON MR JAMES SANDERSON MS M SANDERSON MRS S SANDERSON MR PAUL SANDFORD MS B SANDHOUSE MS C SANDISON MRS JENNIFER SANDLAND MRS M SANDLE MRS D SANDLER MRS MARY SANDLING MR R SANDS MR AND MRS SANDWELL MS ELAINE RD MISS T SANGSTER MRS V SANGSTER MR M SANSOME MRS M SANT MISS L SANTILLI MS S SANTOS MRS FAITH SAPHORGHAN MR ALI SARBANOGLU MRS H SAREK MR T SARGEANT MR M SARGENT MRS P SARGENT MR S SARGENT MRS WENDY SARGENT MRS C SARGON DR P SARKAR SARNER MISS LESLEY SARTON MR M SARTORI MRS H SASAKI MRS J SASSON MS EDWINA SASSOON MR ANAND SATHE MR H SATO MS C SAUNDERS MR D SAUNDERS MRS D SAUNDERS MR DAVID SAUNDERS MRS G SAUNDERS MR K SAUNDERS MS K SAUNDERS MR M SAUNDERS MRS ERS MS M SAUNDERS MS P SAUNDERS MRS P SAUNDERS MR R A SAUNDERS MRS S SAUNDERS MR M SAUNDERSON MRS GILLIAN SAUTTER DR E SAUVE MISS A SAVAGE MR B SAVAGE MS ELIZABETH SAVAGE MR K SAVAGE MR M A SAVAGE MR M SAVAGE MRS P SAVAGE MR R SAVAGE OSEMARY SAVAGE MRS E SAVIDGE DAVID SAVILL MR J SAVILL MS L SAVILLE MR AND MRS E SAVITT MS T SAVVOPOULOS MS C SAWARD MR TIMOTHY SAWARD M SAWBRIDGE MRS S SAWTELL MR ALBERT SAWYER MRS B SAWYER MRS FIONA SAWYER MR J SAWYER MRS J SAWYER SAWYER MRS VIVIEN SAXBY MR A SAXTON MS E SAXTON DR R SAY MRS S SAY S SAY MRS KATHERINE M SAYCE MRS A SAYER MISS E SAYER MR ERIC SAYER MRS S SAYER MS HELEN SAYERS MR JOHN SAYERS MRS S SAYERS MR J P SAYLES MR ROBERTO SBRACCIA DR J SCADDING SCALLON MR M SCANLON MRS M SCANLON MRS JOYCE SCARFE MISS Z SCARROW DR J SCHACHTER MR J SCHAEFER MS Y SCHAEFER MR M SCHAICH U SCHARF MS C SCHEER GILL SCHEUER MR DONATO SCHIAVO MR J SCHICK MS KATHY SCHICKER MR ANDRAS SCHIFF MR JULIAN D MR R SCHILLER MRS J SCHIMMELMANN MRS S SCHINDLER MR ANDREJ SCHIPKA MR M SCHIRM MRS P SCHLEGER MR R SCHLESINGER MR & MRS HENRIK SCHLIEMANN MRS JOANA SCHLIEMANN MR CARL SCHMACK ASTRID SCHMETTERLING MRS A SCHMIDT MRS ELIZABETH SCHMIDT SCHMIDT MR F SCHMITT MRS M SCHMOOL MRS B SCHNEIDELER MRS MYRA SCHNEIDER MS JACKIE SCHNELL MRS H SCHNOZELER MRS J SCHOELKOPF MRS E SCHOFIELD MR A SCHOLEY MR MARCO SCHONBORN MRS GILLIAN SCHONZELER MRS A SCHORR MS ANDREE SCHOUTEN MS E SCHRADER MR R SCHRAM MR P SCHRANK MISS M SCHRODER MRS CHARLOTTE SCHROEDER MR FRANK SCHUBERT MRS A SCHUETZ MRS I SCHULENBURG MR B SCHULER MR MICHAEL SCHULZ MISS CARA SCHULZE MR R SCHUMACHER MS A SCHUMAN MRS M SCHUMANN MRS M ICHT MS D SCHWAB DOUGLAS SCHWALBE MR AND MRS SCHWALBE DR F SCHWEITZER MS N SCHWEIZER MRS SHIRLEY SCHWIMMER MRS PATRICIA SCLANO MISS IRENE SCLARE MR C SCLAVOUNIS MS ASTRID SCMETTERLING MS I SCODELLARO MR E SCOFIELD MR R SCOINS MRS A REVEREND SCOTT MR ALLAN SCOTT MR ANDREW SCOTT MR B SCOTT MRS C SCOTT MS CAROLE SCOTT MR D SCOTT MRS DIANA SCOTT MR H SCOTT MRS H SCOTT MRS I SCOTT MISS J SCOTT MS J SCOTT DR JAMES SCOTT MR K SCOTT MS L SCOTT MR L SCOTT MRS M SCOTT DR MARY SCOTT MARY SCOTT MR P SCOTT MR PETER SCOTT MR PHILIP SCOTT MR PHILLIP SCOTT LORD R SCOTT MR S SCOTT MRS S SCOTT MR SAMUEL SCOTT MR STEWART SCOTT MR T SCOTT MRS V SCOTT LADY G SCOTT-HOPKINS MRS DIANA SCOTT-MCCARTHY MR A SCOTT-RUSSELL MS F SCOTT-RT MRS J SCRINE MS T SCRIVENER MRS I SCRIVENER-BECZE MISS ALEXANDRA SCROPE MR W SCRUTTON MR C SCUDDER MR L SCUDDER MR JOHN SCULLY MR V SCWEIZER MR P SEABOURNE MR T SEABORNE MISS S SEAGROVE MISS GLENYS SEAL MS H SEAL MR R SEAL MR G SEALEY UL SEALEY MRS C SEALY MRS K SEAR MRS RUTH SEAR MRS J SEARLE MS K SEARLE MISS P SEARLE MRS R SEARLE MS JENI SEARS MR R SEATON MS AMANDA SEBESTYEN MRS D SECLEVE-GANDERTON MRS P SECRETT MR J SEDDON MR M SEDLER MS P SEEBOHM MS K SEED MR R R ALWYN SEEDS DR H SEELEY MISS D SEEMAN MRS J SEEMUNGAL MR H SEENAN MRS J SEEZ MRS B SEGAL MR J SEGAL PROFESSOR SUSAN SEGAL-HORN DR JOGINDER SEHMI MR S SEKARAN MR MUNEHISA SEKIMOTO MRS T SELBY-LOWNDES SELECT SERVICE PARTNER MR BRIAN MR JOHN SELF MRS E SELIG TAMARA SELIG MR J SELKIRK MR ADRIAN SELLARS MR P SELLARS MR D SELLENS MR F SELLICK MRS V SELLINS DR D SELLMAN MISS KATHERINE SELLS MR TERENCE SELMAN MRS A SELO MRS M SELTMAN MS S SELVARAJAH MICHAEL SELWAY MR YN MR N SEMIT MISS K SEMLER MR H SEN MS INDIRA SEN MS LESLEY SENDALL MR S SENGUPTA MR V SENGUPTA MS DEBBIE SENIOR MISS P SENIOR MRS MIHOKO SEO MRS S SERFATY MR GRAHAM SERJEANT MS R SEROUSSI MR YURI SEROV MRS TATIANA SEROVA MR G SERPIS RIA SERRANO-BERICAT MR ALEXANDER SERVICE MRS SUZANNE SETTELMEYER MRS J SETTER MRS C SETTLE MS CHRISTINE SEVA MR K SEVERN D SEVILLE MR D SEVILLE MRS J SEVITT MRS C SEWELL MISS J SEWELL MRS R V SEWELL SARAH SEWELL MRS MAUREEN SEXTON MR AN MRS S SEYEDI MRS B SEYMOUR MS C SEYMOUR MRS J SEYMOUR MR MICHAEL SEYMOUR MR A SEZER MR L SEZER MRS S SHABABI DR JOHN SHACKLETON MS K SHACKLETON MR L SHADBOLT MRS P SHADLOCK MR M SHAER MRS DOREEN SHAFRAN MR A SHAH MR C SHAH MR AND AVID SHAH MS DINA SHAH MR HETAN SHAH MISS I SHAH MR J SHAH MR N SHAH MRS N SHAH MS N SHAH MISS P SHAH MR P SHAH MS S SHAH MRS B SHAHID MRS S SHAHIN MRS G SHAKESPEARE MRS MARGARET SHALE MRS JANE SHALOM MR B SHANAHAN MR E SHANES ARUN ARDASS MRS R SHANKSTER MRS S SHANNON MS JO SHAPCOTT MRS ALIZA SHAPIRO MS E SHAPIRO MRS J SHAPIRO MRS M SHAPLAND A J SHAPTON MRS E SHARDLOW MR PAUL SHARMA IAN SHARMAN T SHARMAN MR A SHARP MR E SHARP MS E SHARP MS J SHARP JOHN SHARP MS RP MR R SHARP MR ROB SHARP MR T SHARP MR CHRISTOPHER SHARPE MR D SHARPE MISS E SHARPE DR EVELYN SHARPE MR H SHARPE MRS J SHARPE MS J SHARPE MR M SHARPE MR P SHARPE MRS P SHARPE MR RICHARD SHARPE MR K SHARPLES MRS J SHARRATT MRS Y OCKS MR W SHARRON MR IAN SHAVE MR I SHAVE MR DAVID SHAVREEN MR A M SHAW MR A SHAW DR ANGELA SHAW MRS B SHAW MISS C SHAW MS CAROLE SHAW MR CHRISTOPHER SHAW MISS D SHAW MR D SHAW MRS E SHAW MRS G SHAW MR HENRY SHAW MRS I SHAW DR J SHAW HAW MS J SHAW MR K SHAW MR L M SHAW MS L SHAW MISS M SHAW MR M SHAW MR P SHAW MRS P SHAW MR R SHAW MRS R SHAW MR S SHAW MRS S SHAW MR T SHAW MRS V SHAW MR B SHAW-CALVERLEY MISS C SHEA MR H SHEAR MRS M SHEARD MR ANDREW SHEARER MRS HAZEL SHEARING HEARLOCK MR J SHEARMAN MRS PAMELA SHEARMAN MS M SHEARWOOD MR MATTHEW SHEATH MRS P SHEATH MS A SHEEHAN MR PAUL SHEEHAN MR BRENDAN SHEEHY MISS E SHEEN MR PETER SHEERIN MISS ANITA SHELDON MR MARK SHELDON MR ROBIN SHELDON MR I SHELLEY HELTON MISS C SHELTON MRS L SHEMILT MRS B SHEN MISS DASHA SHENKMAN DR B SHENOLIKAR MR A SHENTON MR DAVID SHEPHARD MR KENNETH SHEPHARD MR M SHEPHARD MISS A SHEPHERD MR A SHEPHERD MR ANTHONY SHEPHERD MR B SHEPHERD MR SHEPHERD MS J ERD DR JOHN SHEPHERD MR JONATHON SHEPHERD MR K SHEPHERD MR N SHEPHERD MRS NICOLE SHEPHERD MRS P SHEPHERD MR G SHEPPARD MRS G SHEPPARD MRS GWENDOLINE SHEPPARD DR JILL SHEPPARD MR K SHEPPARD MR R SHEPPARD MRS S SHEPPARD MISS S SHEPPARD HEPPEY MRS L SHER MR OLIVER SHERGOLD MRS C SHERIDAN MRS P SHERIDAN MRS V SHERIDAN MR D SHERLOCK MS S SHERMAN MR A SHERPA MR A SHERRIFF MR E SHERRIN MISS S SHERRY MR A SHERWOOD MRS SHIRLEY SHERWOOD MRS WENDY SHERWOOD MRS K SHEWELL DR HBANY MR C SHIATIS MR N SHIBATA MR Y SHIBATA MRS H SHIEKH MS J SHIELDS MS M SHIELDS MRS SUSAN SHIELDS MR A SHIELLS MRS C SHIELS MR DAVID SHIFF MS CLAUDIA SHILLINGFORD MR P SHILLINGFORD MRS J SHILLITO MS A SHIMMEN DR G SHIN MR A SHINDER SHINE MR J SHINGLES MR A SHIOZAKI MR N SHIPMAN MR A SHIPP MS J SHIPSIDE MS LYNNE SHIPTON MRS D SHIRES MRS S SHIRGAONKAR MS C SHIRLEY MR I SHIRLEY MR K SHIWA MRS S SHIZWE MR M SHOESMITH MRS S SHOOK MISS JACKIE SHOREY MR DENIS SHORROCK SHORT MR P SHORT MS PATRICIA SHORT MRS SYBIL SHORT MR T SHORTALL MS ANN F SHORTER MS S SHREEF MRS VIVIENNE SHREIR MR P SHRIVASTAVA MRS N SHROFF DR AND MRS D SHUEY R A SHUKMAN MS KATE SHUREY MISS A SHUTTLE MR ARMADEEP SIAN MS V SIBLEY MR HORPE MRS ANTOINETTE SICE ANNE SIDDELL MRS RITA SIDDERS MR ALLAN SIDDICK A SIDELL MR M SIDFORD MR K SIDOR MR A SIDWELL THE HON DANIELA SIEFF MR J SIEGERT DR G C SIEGRUHN M SIEMASZKO MRS JUDITH SIENKIEWICZ MRS P SIEQUIEN MRS B SIERATZKI DINA SIEVERS MR NORMAN SIEVERS MR N SIGANPORIA MRS P SIHRA MR Q SILAS MR G SILK MR J SILK DR K SILLITOE MIKE SILLITOE MR DAVID SILVER MRS SANDRA SILVER MS TONI SILVER MR ANDREW SILVERMAN DR C SILVERMAN MRS R SILVERMAN MRS D SILVERSTEIN SILVESTRE MISS LUCIA SILVESTRINI MR GIUSEPPE SILVI MR P SILVIE MS B SIM MRS M SIME MR REGINALD SIMEONE CBE AND MRS JOSEPHINE SIMEONE MRS CAROL SIMIOU MR M SIMM MRS J SIMMINS MRS M SIMMONDS MR T SIMMONDS MISS A SIMMONS EMMA SIMMONS MRS MONS MR M SIMMONS MR R SIMMONS MISS V SIMMONS MRS W SIMMONS MRS B SIMMS MS M SIMOES-BROWN MRS A SIMON MRS KATHLEEN SIMON MS M SIMOND MRS JULIA SIMONNE MRS ALISON SIMONS MRS KATHLEEN SIMONS MR B SIMPER MRS J SIMPKINS MR A SIMPSON MRS PSON MR B SIMPSON MR C SIMPSON MRS C SIMPSON MS E SIMPSON MRS F SIMPSON MS F SIMPSON MR G SIMPSON MR GORDON SIMPSON MRS H SIMPSON MS H SIMPSON MR IAN SIMPSON MRS JEAN SIMPSON MRS J SIMPSON MS K SIMPSON MR L SIMPSON MS MAXINE SIMPSON ORMA SIMPSON MR P SIMPSON MR R SIMPSON MRS S SIMPSON MR DAVID SIMS MRS J SIMS MS L SIMS MRS P SIMS MISS SANDRA SIMS MR ROBERT SIMSON MS G SINCLAIR MRS G SINCLAIR MRS J SINCLAIR MISS JOAN SINCLAIR MR K SINCLAIR MRS L SINCLAIR DR M SINCLAIR SINCLAIR MR S SINCLAIR MISS SANDRA SINCLAIR MRS V SINCLAIR MR ANDREW SINDALL MR A SINDEN MS ROSIE SINDEN-EVANS MRS M SINFIELD MR MICHAEL SINFIELD MR DOUGLAS SINGER MS J SINGER MR JULIAN SINGER MR J SINGER-WASHINGTON MRS E SINGH MR G MISS D SINGLETON MISS MICHELLE SINGLETON MR M SINHA MRS J SINKER MRS SUSAN SINNATT MRS ANNE SINSTADT MR B SIRA MR A SISSON MR ANDREW SISSON MRS N SISSON MR D SITWELL MR D SIU MR A SIVASUBRAMANIAM MRS A SIWEK MISS S SKATES MRS V SKEET MRS T MRS S SKELT MR DAVID SKELTON MR J SKETCHLEY MISS S SKIDMORE MRS SUSAN SKIDMORE MR R SKILLING B C SKINNER MS ELIZABETH SKINNER MR J SKINNER MR JOHN SKINNER MS L SKINNER MR P SKIPP DR MAGDELENA SKIPPER MR R I SKIPWORTH MR JOHN SKITT DR R DR SKOGSTED MS P SKREBOWSKI MISS PAULINE SKUCE MR D SLACK MRS A SLADE MISS J SLADE MS J SLADE MR M SLADE MR P SLADE MR PETER SLADE MR A SLATER MR C SLATER MRS D SLATER DR F SLATER MR I SLATER MRS MARGARET SLATER MS MARY A SLATER MR S R MISS H SLATTNE SLAUGHTER AND MAY MRS J SLAVIK DR P SLAYEN MR C SLEED MRS S SLEEP MR R SLEIGHT MRS S SLIJEPCEVIC MR ALAN SLINGSBY MR E SLOCOMBE MS V SLOCOMBE MR J SLOGGEM MR C SLY MRS VIRGINIE SMAGUE MR T SMAIL MR D SMALL MRS H SMALL MALL MRS SUSAN SMALL MR J SMALLEY MR M SMALLEY MRS INGEBORG SMALLWOOD MR JEREMY SMALLWOOD MR T SMALLWOOD MRS ANITA SMART MR C SMART MR D SMART DR LESLEY SMART MRS D SMEDLEY MR & MRS M SMEE MRS J SMELLIE MR M G SMERDON MR L SMETS I SMIDT MISS J C SMILEY MR E SMIT MR A SMITH MRS A SMITH MS A SMITH MR ANDREW SMITH MR B SMITH MRS B SMITH MISS BRENDA SMITH MR BRIAN SMITH MR C SMITH MS C SMITH MR D SMITH MS D SMITH MR DAVID SMITH MISS DEBORAH SMITH MR DEREK SMITH MRS E MR FRANK SMITH DR G SMITH MR G SMITH MRS GEORGINA SMITH MR GRAEME SMITH MR H SMITH MRS I SMITH MR IAN SMITH MR J A SMITH MR J SMITH J SMITH MRS J SMITH MR JAMES SMITH MRS JANE SMITH MISS JEAN SMITH MR JEFFERY SMITH MISS JENNIFER SMITH MRS MITH MS JOAN SMITH MR JOHN SMITH JOHN SMITH MR JONATHAN SMITH MS JUDITH SMITH MRS JUNE SMITH MS KAREN SMITH MRS KATIE SMITH MS KELLY SMITH MR KEVIN SMITH MR L SMITH MISS L SMITH MR & MRS L SMITH MRS L SMITH MR M SMITH MR M J SMITH MRS M MS M SMITH MRS MARGARET SMITH MRS MARJORIE SMITH MR MIKE SMITH MRS N SMITH MS N SMITH MR P SMITH PROFESSOR P SMITH MR PAUL SMITH MR PETER SMITH MR R C SMITH MISS R SMITH MR R SMITH MRS R SMITH MR RICHARD SMITH MR ROBIN SMITH OSALIND SMITH MRS S SMITH MR S SMITH MRS SALLY SMITH MISS SARAH SMITH MRS SHEILA SMITH MS S SMITH MR STEPHEN SMITH DR STEPHEN SMITH MR STUART SMITH MRS SUSAN SMITH MR T SMITH MR THOMAS SMITH MRS V SMITH MR W SMITH MS J SMITH-BODDEN MRS G ERMAN MISS JANICE SMITHERS MISS R SMITHERS MR C SMITH-GILLARD MRS S SMITH-PRYOR MISS G SMITHSON MR ANDREW SMITH-WEST MRS J SMOKER MR H SMOLINS MS C SMYTH CANON RONALD SMYTHE MR J SMYTHSON MISS J SNAPES MRS I SNEDDON MRS D SHELL MR G MR MALCOLM SHELL MR A SNELLING MRS F SNELLING MRS E SNELSON MRS V SNODIN MISS A SNOW MR JON SNOW MR R SNOW MRS S SNOWBALL MRS B SOAL MR DAVID SOANS MRS H SOCZYWKO MISS M SOESAN MRS NONI SOFOCLEOUS MRS B V SOHNGEN MRS P SOLARES-UHERS OLE MISS J SOLLEN MRS SOLOMAN MRS D SOLOMON MR H SOLOMON MS S SOLOMON MRS J SOLOMONS MRS J SOMANI MRS J SOMERFIELD MR J SOMERSET MISS S SOMERVILLE MR J SOMINKA MR MATTHEW SOMMERS MRS E SOMOGYI MR L SONAIKE MR R SONENFELD MRS M NBERG MRS V SONNENVIRTH MR B SONZOGNI MR E SOOKDIN MRS S SOPER MR T SOPER MISS PENNY SOPHOCLEOUS MR J SOUGHTON MRS M SOUHAMI MR R J SOUPER MR S SOURMY MRS V SOUSLOVA P F SOUSTER MISS FIONA SOUTAR MRS H SOUTER MR J H SOUTH MISS JENNIFER LLA MS B SOUTHERDEN MR H SOUTHERN MRS K SOUTHERN MRS K SOUTHGATE MRS VALERIE SOUTHON V SOUTHORN MS C SOUTHWELL MRS SUSAN SOUTHWICK MRS G SOUTHWOOD MR WILLIAM SOUTTER MRS SHEILA SOWBY MRS J SOWDEN MS A SOWERBY MRS REBECCA SOWTER MRS EY MR H SPACK MR T SPACKMAN MRS J SPALDING MISS M SPARK MR R SPARKES MS J SPARKS MR P SPARLING MR D SPARROW E M SPARROW MR J SPARROW MR DAVID SPAUGHTON MR E SPEAKMAN MR C S SPEAR MRS J SPECK MRS BEATRICE SPECTOR MR M SPECTOR MR MARK NG MRS T SPEED MR GEORGE SPEIGHT DR H SPEIGHT MR R SPEIGHT MRS J SPEIRS MRS J SPELLER MR A SPENCE MR G SPENCE MRS G SPENCE MR IAN SPENCE MR M SPENCE MRS SYBIL SPENCE MR C SPENCER MS D SPENCER MR GRANT SPENCER MISS J SPENCER MR RICHARD ER MS V SPENCER MR WILLIAM SPENCER MRS M SPENCER-CLARKE MS PHILIPPA SPENS MRS A SPENSLEY MR S SPERL MISS MARJORIE SPERNICK MS M SPETCH MRS D SPICER MS G SPICER MR K SPICER MS M SPICER MRS PAULINE SPICER MR J SPICKETT MR L SPICKETT MR EGLER MRS S SPIER MR D SPIERS MRS M SPIERS MS P SPIERS DR E SPILLIUS MRS S SPINK MRS ANNETTE SPINKS MRS M SPINOULAS MR I SPIRO MR LUDWIG SPIRO DR M SPIRO MS M SPITERI MR IAN SPITTLES MR RICHARD SPITZ MS C SPITZER MS P SPIZEWSKI MR CHARLES Z MR D SPOONER MR PHILIP SPOONER MRS KARA SPORTELLI MS LYDIA SPOUDEAS SOURAS MR W SPOUGE MR G SPRING MR B SPRINGER MIKE SPRINZ MR D SPRUCE MRS JENNIFER SPRY MR J SPURGEON MR PETER SPURGEON MS C SPURLEY MRS F SPURLING MRS B SQUIERS MR RE MS C SQUIRE MISS ISOBEL SQUIRE MS JACQUELINE SQUIRE MRS SHEILA SQUIRE MRS T SQUIRE MR L SQUIRES MRS C SRIH MRS B SRINIVASAN MR H SROA MS L ST. LOUIS MR J STABLES MR P STABLES MS J STABRAWA MISS A STACEY MR K STACEY MR KENNETH STACEY MS EY MISS V STACHOWSKA MRS R STACKHOUSE MS K STAFFORD MR MICHAEL STAFFORD MR R C STAFFORD MR B STAGG MR R STAGG MR P STAINER MR DONALD STAINES MR D STAINTON MR T STALLARD MS J STALLIBRASS MS K STAMBROUSKIS MS P STAMP MRS O STAMPER MS E STAMPFER MR R STANBOROUGH MR E STANBROOK MRS A STANCIOFF MR DEREK STANCOMBE MRS JENNIFER STANDAGE MR E STANDEN MR J STANDEN MR J STANDING MISS M STANDING MRS A STANFORD MR JOHN STANFORD MR P STANFORD MR VAUGHAN STANGER MR V STANIC MS LEY MS CARYL STANLEY MR J STANLEY MISS JILL STANLEY MR M STANLEY MR NORMAN STANLEY MR P STANLEY MRS P STANLEY THE OLIVER STANLEY CHARITABLE TRUST MR D STANLEY-MARTIN AMY STANNARD MR M STANNARD MR P STANNARD MR R STANNARD MS OLGA LOVIC MS OLGA STANOLOVIC MISS H STANSFIELD MS A STANTON MR J STANTON MRS A STANWAY MR D STAPLEHURST MRS H STAPLES MISS MARY STAPLES MR DAVID STAPLETON MRS SUSAN STAPLEY MRS J STARK MISS C CLARK MR H START MR R STARTIN MR ALESSANDRO NO MR B STATER MR J STATHAM MRS S STATON MR J STATTON MRS JANE STAVES MR H STAVRI MR B STEAD MS H STEADMAN MISS L STEADMAN MRS LINDA STEADMAN MR PHILIP STEAR MR J STEBBINGS MR JOHN STEBBINGS MR M STE-CROIX MR PHILIP STEDMAN MISS M STEED AN STEEDMAN MR M STEEL MS P STEEL MR R STEEL DR ANNETTE STEELE MRS D STEELE DR H STEELE MISS M STEELE MR G STEELEY MRS CARYLE STEEN MR D STEER MRS D STEER MR D STEIN MRS F STEIN MRS JACK STEINBERG MRS LUCINDA STEINER MRS J OUSE MR M STELLMAN MR MARCEL STELLMAN MR P STEMP MRS G STENNING MRS ANNE STEPHENS MRS E STEPHENS MS G STEPHENS MR J STEPHENS DR AND MRS STEPHENS MR R STEPHENS MRS SYLVIA STEPHENS MRS A STEPHENSON MS G STEPHENSON J STEPHENSON MRS M ENSON THE HON LADY STEPHENSON MRS T STEPHENSON MR R STEPPE MS JULIA STERLING MR CHARLES STERMAN MR J STERN MRS JOAN STERN L STERN MS L STERN MR A STERNBERG DR A STERNDALE BENNETT MR H STERNER MR K STERROW MR PETER STERWIN PETER STERWIN TEVEN MR R STEVEN MR A STEVENS MRS A STEVENS MRS B STEVENS MR BRIAN STEVENS MRS C STEVENS MR CHRISTOPHER STEVENS MR DAVID STEVENS MISS E STEVENS MRS E STEVENS MRS F STEVENS MR GARY STEVENS MR I STEVENS MR J STEVENS MRS J STEVENS MRS JANE NS MR M STEVENS MR PAUL STEVENS MR R STEVENS MR A STEVENSON MS A STEVENSON DR B STEVENSON MR B STEVENSON MRS B M STEVENSON MR D STEVENSON MS E STEVENSON MISS G STEVENSON MR GAVIN STEVENSON MRS J STEVENSON MS M STEVENSON MR N STEVENSON TEVENSON MR RAY STEVENSON MISS C STEWARD MR MARTIN STEWARD MISS A STEWART MRS E STEWART MISS F STEWART MR J STEWART MS J STEWART MS JANET STEWART MISS JEAN STEWART MR JEFFREY STEWART MEG STEWART MRS S STEWART MRS V STEWART MR J STEWART-FITZROY MR EYHOR MR D STICHBURY MR C STICKLEY MRS JUNE STIFF MRS J STILES MR R STILES MRS MARION STILL MR STANLEY STILL MR F STILLWELL MRS L STIMAN MRS DIANE STIMSON MR R STINCHCOMBE MRS D STINTON MS J STIRLING MR TIMOTHY STIRLING MR A STIRRUP MR P LEY MRS B STOCK MISS M STOCK MR PETER STOCK MISS D STOCKEL MS J STOCKLAND MISS V STOCKLEY MISS J STOCKS MISS ANNE STODDART MS G STODDART A STOGDEN MS M STOJKOVIC MISS G STOKER MR ANDREW STOKES DR F STOKES MR HOWARD STOKES MR M STOKES DR S MR V STOKES MRS A STOKMAN DR L STOLL DR & MRS M STOLL MR H STOLLAR MS A STONE MR DEREK STONE DONALD STONE MRS J STONE MR J STONE MRS PATRICIA STONE MR RODNEY STONE MRS L STONE OF BLACKHEATH MR V STONE MRS Z STONE MS ZILLAH MS C STONEMAN DR JILL STONER MR B STONHOLD MRS WANDA STOPA MISS M STOPHER MR TOM STOPPARD MRS B STOPPS MRS B STORER MR E STOREY MRS FIONA STOREY MS I STOREY MR P STORM-LARSEN MISS FIONA STORRS MR B STOTHARD MR C STOTT MS RACHEL STOTT MRS T MISS ELIZABETH STOUT MRS C STOW MR D STOWE MS H STOWE MISS V STOWELL MRS A STRACH MR J STRACHAN MRS J STRACHAN MR R STRAKER MISS A STRANGE MRS L STRANGE MRS S STRANGE MRS L STRASSER MR J STRATFORD MR M STRATFORD LYNN STRATTON MR P STRATTON TRATTON MRS SUZETTE STRATTON MISS V STRAULI MRS I STRAUSS MRS L STRAUSS MR A STRAWSON MISS Y STREATFIELD MR B STREET MR G STREET MS E STREETER MS G STRIBLING-WRIGHT MR C STRIDE DR J STRIDE MRS N STRIDE MRS A STRINGER MR D STRINGER MS JANE FELLOW MS GERDA STRIPLING DR M STROM MR CHARLES STRONG MR JEREMY STRONG MRS K STRONG MR M STRONG MISS HELEN STRUDWICK MRS A STRUTHERS MRS A STUART MR C STUART MISS E STUART MS E STUART MR I STUART PROFESSOR JOHN STUART MR MORAY STUART TUART MS R STUART MRS R STUART-SMITH MRS DEBORAH STUART-STAFF MS A STUBBS MR KASTYTIS STUCINSKAS MR R STUCKEY REVEREND T STUCKEY MS C STUMPFL MR R STURGEON MR A STURGESS MR T STURGESS MR G STURROCK MRS S STURROCK MS B STYLES MR P STYLES- Y MR CEDRIC STYLIANOU MR CHRIS STYLIANOU MS PHILLIPA SUAREZ M SUATT MR M SUDDABY MR MATTHEW SUDDABY MR S SUDDLE MR J SUDWORTH MR J SUGAR MRS H SUGARMAN MR M SUGDEN MR PATRICK SUGRUE MR G SUHARAN MS O SULIMAN MR D SULLIVAN MRS DAPHNE AN MR E SULLIVAN MR K SULLIVAN MISS MARY SULLIVAN MRS V SULLIVAN H SULLY MR & MRS R SULTAN MRS S SULTAN MRS Y SUMITA MRS ANN SUMMERS MR G SUMMERS MISS KAY SUMMERS MR R SUMMERS MISS ANGELA SUMNER MR V SUMRAY MR S SUNDERJI MRS E RLAND MRS S SUNDERLAND MR KEN SUNSHINE MR F SUNTOOK MR H SURGUY MS S SURREY MR L SURRIDGE MRS R SURY MS B SUTCLIFFE MRS L M SUTCLIFFE MS C SUTHERLAND MRS E SUTHERLAND MR F SUTHERLAND MS J SUTHERLAND MR M SUTHERLAND MR OLIVER SUTTER MRS LING MR D SUTTON MRS E SUTTON MRS G SUTTON MR J SUTTON MRS J SUTTON MR SUTTON PROFESSOR R SUTTON DR TREVOR SUTTON MR V SUTTON MRS Y SUTTON MRS PAULINE SUVARNA MR P SVED MRS L SWABEY DR SHELLEY SWADE MISS S SWAFFIELD MR H SWAILES MRS J D MISS F SWAINE MS J SWAINE MR BILL SWAINSON MR J SWAINSON MR & MRS SWAINSON MRS J SWALES MRS C SWALLOW MISS SARAH SWALLOW MRS A SWAN MS F SWAN MR KENNETH SWAN MRS A SWANN MR P SWANN MRS S SWANN MS C SWANSON MR R SWANSTON MR M SWARBRICK SWARC MS D SWAYNE MRS M SWAYNE MRS M SWAYNE MR M SWEENEY STUART SWEENEY MRS M SWEET MRS R SWEET MRS D SWEETMAN MR G SWEETNAM MR RICHARD SWEETNAM MR T SWIATECKI MR AND MRS DAVID SWIFT MR GEORGE SWIFT MRS M SWIFT MS M SWIFT MRS S SWIFT MS L SWIMER IDLEHURST MRS J SWINGLER MR A SWIRLES MR C SWORD MR B SYDENHAM MRS CATHERINE SYDNEY MRS W SYED MR J SYERS MR C SYKES MRS C SYKES MR J SYKES MS M SYKES MRS J SYLVESTER MR R SYLVESTER MR R SYM MR J P SYME MS T SYMES DR D SYMINGTON MR AND SYMON MS P SYMON MISS GILLIAN SYMONS MS JEAN SYMONS MR PAUL SYMONS MRS J SYMS MS H SYNESSIO MRS H SZABO MRS A SZAREWSKI MRS P SZCZECH MR GRACJAN SZCZUKOWSKI MR K SZENDEFFY MRS A SZERVANSZKY MR Z SZKOPIAK MRS M SZKUTA MR M SZOSTAK MR SZPAKOWSKI MISS JANINA SZYNDLER MRS B TABATZNIK MR DAVID TABATZNIK MRS P TABNER MRS REBECCA TABOR MS M TABUTEAU MISS J TACKLEY MR RICHARD TAFFLER MR P TAGGART MS O TAHERI MS T TAIBO-SMITH MR DAVID TAINE MR B TAIT MS F TAIT MR W TAIT MRS D MRS H TAKAHASHI MR TAKAHASHI DR H TAKAMATSU MS MIKA TAKAMI MS Y TAKEDA MR H TAKEMOTO MR H TAKENOYA MR M TAKIN MS N TAKKIDES MRS A TAKLA MR K TAKYAR MISS S TALANTI MRS M TALATI MR J TALBOT MR R TALBOT MR L TALBOT KATHRYN TALINTYRE MRS G IS MS N TALLETT MR JOHN TALLON MR K TALSANIA MR ROBIN TAM MS KUNIKO TAMAI MS M TAMBOUKOU MR M TAMMARO MR RICHARD TAMPLIN MRS R TAMSETT B TAN MR B TAN MR L TAN MRS Y TAN MR S TANAKA MRS JANE TANDY MR L TANG MR M TANG MR R TANK MR DAVID TANN TANN MR CLIVE TANNER MRS D TANNER MR E TANNER MRS ELIZABETH TANNER MRS IRIS TANNER MR STEPHEN TANNER MRS V TANNER MR J TAPE MRS P TAPPIN MISS S TARAZI MS J TARBUTT MR S TARLTON MS S TARLTON MR C TARRANT MRS E TARRANT MR JOHN TARREL MRS A MRS HELEN TARSH MRS SALLY TARSHISH MS M TARVER MS IVANA TASKER MR J TASKES MR PHILIP TATA MR B TATE MR JONATHAN TATE MR D TATLOCK MR D TATLOW MRS E TATMAN MR I TATSUHARA MS M TATTERSALL MR P TATTERSALL MR C TATTERSFIELD MR G TAUNTON-COLLINS AVAKOL MISS A TAVAROZZI MRS R TAVENER MRS J TAVERNE MR R TAVERNER MR J TAVERNOR MRS I TAVKAR MISS A TAYLOR MR A TAYLOR MRS ANNE TAYLOR MR ANTHONY TAYLOR MR B TAYLOR PROFESSOR B TAYLOR MRS BETTY TAYLOR MR BRUCE TAYLOR MRS C TAYLOR MISS C DR CAROLE TAYLOR MR D TAYLOR MRS D TAYLOR MS D TAYLOR MR DAVID TAYLOR MR E TAYLOR MRS E TAYLOR MR F TAYLOR MRS F TAYLOR MS G TAYLOR MRS G TAYLOR MR G TAYLOR GERALDINE TAYLOR MR GILES TAYLOR MISS HILARY TAYLOR MISS TAYLOR MR I M TAYLOR Y TAYLOR MRS J F TAYLOR MR J TAYLOR DR J TAYLOR MRS J TAYLOR MS J TAYLOR MRS JEAN TAYLOR MS JEAN TAYLOR MRS JULIA TAYLOR MR K TAYLOR MRS L TAYLOR MR M TAYLOR MR M TAYLOR MS M TAYLOR MS M TAYLOR MRS MARGARET TAYLOR MR MATHEW C TAYLOR MR P R MRS P TAYLOR MS P TAYLOR MRS PAMELA TAYLOR MR PHILIP TAYLOR MR R TAYLOR MR RICHARD TAYLOR MRS R TAYLOR MRS S TAYLOR MR S TAYLOR MS S TAYLOR MR T TAYLOR TAYLOR JOYNSON GARRETT TAYLOR MADE JOINERY (BILDESTON) LTD MRS V TAYLOR MRS W TAYLOR TAYSOM MS A TCHEKEMAIN MR AND MRS TEAR MRS CATHERINE TEBB MISS M TEBB MR G TEDDER MR AMEDEO TEDESCHI MS T TEHRANCHIAN MS S TEHRANIE MR M TEICHMAN MRS SANDRA TEICHMAN MRS DIANETELGEN MRS L TELL MRS J TEMPERLEY MR A TEMPLETON MS E ETON MR JULIAN TEMPLETON MRS L TENN MR C TENNANT MISS P TENORIO MR GREGORY TERIAN MRS ROSEMARY TERIAN MS B TERLECKA-MUNNS MR R TERRELL MRS E TERRY MR L TERRY MRS M TERRY MRS P TERRY MR S TERRY MS SUSAN TESTAR MRS M TESTER MRS S TETERIS I TEWKESBURY MISS R THACKERAY MR S THACKERAY MRS D THACKRAY MRS DEIRDRE THACKRAY MRS J THADDEUS MR A THAKE MR DONALD THAKE MR H THAKRAR DR D THALLON MS PENELOPE THAM MISS CHRISTINE THATCHER MRS J THATCHER MR RICHARD THATCHER MR R E STON MRS J THEAKSTONE DR GINETTE THEANO MS C THEIL MISS SARAH THELWALL MRS G THELWELL MR B THEO MRS C THEODOLOU MRS G THERON MR I THIELE MR TORSTEN THIELE MR A THOMAS MRS AMANDA THOMAS MISS B THOMAS MR BARRY THOMAS MISS CHLOE THOMAS DR AS MR D THOMAS MR DEREK THOMAS MISS E THOMAS MISS ELAINE THOMAS MR G THOMAS MRS G THOMAS MS HANNAH THOMAS MISS HILARY THOMAS MR I THOMAS MRS J THOMAS MR J T THOMAS MISS J THOMAS MS J THOMAS DR & MRS THOMAS MR LLEWEYEN THOMAS MR L O P S MRS M THOMAS MRS M A THOMAS MISS M THOMAS MR M THOMAS MS M THOMAS MR N THOMAS MRS P THOMAS MS P THOMAS MISS R THOMAS MR R THOMAS MRS R THOMAS MRS S J THOMAS MRS S THOMAS REVEREND THOMAS MISS T THOMAS MR T THOMAS MS V THOMAS MR W THOMAS THOMAS MRS B THOMASON MR A THOMPSON MRS ANNE THOMPSON MR B THOMPSON MRS B THOMPSON MR BRUCE THOMPSON MR CHARLES THOMPSON MISS C THOMPSON MR D THOMPSON MR DENNIS THOMPSON MS DIANA THOMPSON MISS DOROTHY THOMPSON MR EDWARD THOMPSON

MRS H T THOMPSON MISS J THOMPSON MR J THOMPSON MRS J THOMPSON MS J THOMPSON MRS JOSEPHINE THOMPSON MRS K THOMPSON MRS M THOMPSON MS M THOMPSON MS MARIENNE THOMPSON MR & MRS P THOMPSON MR P THOMPSON MS P THOMPSON PATRICIA J THOMPSON
PENELOPE THOMPSON MR PETER THOMPSON MR R THOMPSON MR ROBERT THOMPSON MISS S THOMPSON MS YOLANDA THOMPSON MR N THOMPSTONE MR C THOMSON MR D THOMSON MR I THOMSON MR M THOMSON MS P THOMSON MR R THOMSON MR ROBIN THOMSON MRS T THOMSON
THOMSON MR H THOMSON MR J THORLEY MRS M THORLEY MISS J THORN MS J THORN MR N THORN MR J THORNBOROUGH MR IAN THORNBURN MS C THORNE MR GRAHAM THORNE MS K THORNE MR R THORNE MR ROBIN THORNE MR D THORNHAM MR A THORNHILL MRS G THORNLEY MISS N
THORNTON MS ELIZABETH THORNTON MRS HELEN THORNTON MS JOAHN THORNTON MR JONATHAN THORNTON MR KENNETH THORNTON MR P THORNTON DR R THORNTON MRS J A THOROGOOD MR JOHN THORP MR B THORPE MS L THORPE MS LESLEY THORPE MR H THORPE MRS E THORRIN
MS BECK'S THOSEEN MR S THOUGHTS-JOSEPH MRS B THRAVES MR M THUNDER MR DAVID THURGOOD MR J THURLEY MR P THURLEY MR R THURLOW MR D THWAITES MRS A THYNNE MR DEREK TIBBETTS MS A TICE MRS KATHERINE TICEHURST MRS
TICKNER MS P TICKNER MS STEPHANIE TICKNER MRS J TIDD MR DAVID TIDEY MR H TIDHAM MR WILFRED TIDSWELL MS A TIERNEY MS ANNE TIGER MRS B TIGER DR L TIGER MRS E TIKHOMIROV MRS T FILBURY MR W TILDEN MRS R TILDESLEY MR T HILLER MISS M TII
DR SAMANTHA TILLING PH D MBE MR JOHN TILLMAN MRS MARY TILLMAN MS A TILLYER MR C TILNEY MR JOHN TILZEY MRS G TIMBERS K TIMBERS MRS G TIMEWELL MS JOAN TIMMINS MR A TIMMS MR M TIMMS MRS R TIMOTHY MR ROBERT TIMS MRS J TIMSON MRS DOREEN TINDAL
ALBERT TING MS L TINGAH MR C TINGLE MS S TINHAM D TINLEY MR TINSLEY MR RICHARD TINSON MS S TIPLER MISS A TIPPER MS J JILL TIPPING MR & MRS O TISDALL MRS A TITLEY MR A TITMAS MS SALLY TITTERINGTON MRS S TOBI MRS T TOBIAS MRS JANE TOBIH MR LAURENCE T
MRS MARY TOBIH MR AND MRS P TOBIH SIR DAVID TODD I TODD MR M TODD MR N TODD MR TODD MISS SUZANNE TODD MRS T TODD MR CHRIS TODHUNTER MR M TODHUNTER MR ZORAH TODOROVIC MRS H TOFT MRS D TOFTS MR ANDREW TOLEY MRS S TOLIA MR R TOLLEY MS G TOLLI
MR B TOLLIS MS A TOM MR G TOM MRS I TOMACELLI MR NICHOLAS TOMALIN MR M TOMASSI MS A TOMASZEWSKA MR F TOMES MRS A TOMICH MS C TOMICZEK MRS M TOMKINS MR E TOMKINS MRS A TOMLIN MRS J TOMLIN MRS R TOMLIN MISS B TOMLINSON MISS H F TOMLINSON
I TOMLINSON MR S TOMPSETT MRS C TONER MRS ROSEMARY TONGE MS C TONGUE MRS I TONGUE MRS ANNE TONKINSON MR C TONKS MR J TONKS MR R TONKS MRS C TOOGOOD MR J TOOGOOD MS S TOOGOOD MR J TOOLE MISS C J TOOLEY W TOOMBS MI
TOOTOONCHIAH MS J TOPHAM MRS JAN TOPHAM MR D TOPLAS MRS C M TOPLEY MR T TOPPING H TORBLE MR R TORDAY MISS G TORNELLI MRS MAUREEN TORR MISS L TORRANCE MRS D U TORRY MR PAUL TORY MR STEPHEN TOSSWILL MR J TOTTMAN MR M TOULMIN-ROTHE MR ROB
TOURKOW MS AMANDA TOWER MR IAN TOWER MR G TOWILLS MR B TOWNLEY MRS A TOWNSEND DR C TOWNSEND MR L TOWNSEND MR S TOYAMA MRS E TOZER MRS A TRACE MRS F TRAFFORD LADY HELEN TRAFFORD MRS J TRAFFORD MRS D TRAMASEUR MS L
TRANFIELD MRS C TRANGMAR MR N TRANMER MR B TRAYNER MR B TREACHER MR H TREACY MRS S TREADWELL MR FRANCIS TREANOR MRS V TREBBLE MISS J TREBETI MISS D TREBING MRS U TREGARTHEN MISS L TREGEAR MR M TREGER MRS B TREGUER MR S TREHARNE MRS N TREH
MR MICHAEL TREICHL MR DAVID TRELIVING MS P TREMAYNE MRS P TREMBATH MRS H TREMLETT MRS P D TREMLETT MR M TREMNHEERE MR B TRENTON MR R TRESADERN MR U TRESISE MR H TRETHEWY MR CHARLES TREVELYAN MRS MARGARET TREVETT MR J TREW MR ROBERT TREW
TRIBE MRS A TRIBE MR J TRICKEY MR P TRIGG MRS H J B TRIGGER DE HURTIG MRS C TRILLO MRS K TRIM MR BARRY TRIMMER MR K TRIMMER MR SHASHANK TRIPATHI MS A TRISCOTT MRS S TRIST MR J TRITTON DR K TRIVEDI DR U TRIVEDI MRS L TRNOUSKI MRS A TROIANO MS P TR
MS J TROTMAN MS L TROTMAN MRS P TROTT MS H TROTTER MS J TROTTER MR J TROTTER MR R TROUT MRS M TROWBRIDGE MR C TROWER MRS S TROWAN MRS URSULA TRUE MR ROGER TRUELOVE MS MARIA TRUJILLO MR N TRUSSELL MS J TRUSSLER MR C TRUTER MBE MISS V TSAI K T
MISS H TSCHIERSCH MS SILVIA TSCUDIH MR I TSE MISS J TSENG MISS CHRISSY TSINHONTAS MR SAMUEL TSIPOTEY MR E TSITSOPOULOS MR C TSOUKIS MRS H TSUCHIDA MR T TSUKAMOTO MRS S TUK WEE TONG MR A TUCK MISS SARAH TUCK MR A TUCKER MR D TUCKER MRS D TU
MS ELIZABETH TUCKER MR G TUCKER MR H TUCKER MRS N TUCKER MRS NICHOLAS TUCKER MR S TUCKER MR THOMAS TUCKER MR W TUCKER MR WILLIAM TUCKER MRS A TUDOR DAWN TUDOR MRS F TUDOR MR FRANK TUDOR MRS J TUDOR MR QUI
TUDOR-EVANS MR G TUER MS MARY TUFFIN MRS S TUFFREY MRS CHRISTINE TUGWELL MR SIMON TUKE MS NORA TULETT MR B TULL MR E TULL MR CLIVE TULLOCH MR R TULLOCH DR KJELL TULLUS MR ROB TULLY DR IAN TUNBRIDGE MRS B TUNGATE MS K TUNKS MRS ELIZABETH TUN
MR M TUNHAH MRS C TUNNINGLEY MR A TUNSTALL MS M TUPMAN MISS HARRIET TUPPEN MR KEN TURBITT MR P TURK MRS J TURHAGE MR A TURNBULL MRS C TURNBULL MS M TURNBULL MR N TURNBULL MISS A TURNER MR A TURNER MRS A TURNER MS A TURNER
ANDREA TURNER MS B TURNER MR C TURNER MRS C TURNER MR D TURNER MRS EVA TURNER MR FRANK TURNER MS HELEN TURNER MR I TURNER MRS J TURNER MR JOHN TURNER MRS K TURNER MRS LOUISE TURNER MR M TURNER MR P TURNER MR R TURNER MR RIC
TURNER MRS S TURNER MS V TURNER MR W TURNER MS Z A TURNER MISS CLAIRE TURHEY MRS V TURNHAM DR A TURRALL MRS M TURRELL MS A TURTON MR A TURVEY MS A TURVEY MRS D TUTT MR F TUTT MRS J M TUTTON MR J TUTTON
TWAITES MR S TWANA MRS S TWEED MR J TWIGG MR W TWIGGER MRS C TWISS MS A TWITCHIN MR K TWYMAN MISS CAROLINE T¼E MISS M TYERMAN MRS PAMELA T½LE MS DORIS T½LEE MRS C T½LER MISS C T½LER MS C T½LER MRS H T½LER MS M T½LER MR R T½LER MRS R T
MISS S T½LER MS JENNIFER T½NDALE MR N T½NDALE MR M TYRELL MR I T½RIE MR CHRIS TYRRELL A T½SALL MS SOPHIA TZORTZI UBS GLOBAL ASSET MANAGEMENT UK LTD MRS A UDO-UDOMA MR A UDO-UMOREN MS O UDUKU MRS U UGLAND MRS A UKTU MS J H ULLRICH MR M UNNA
MISS A UMUNHA MR E UNCLES MS P UNDERHILL MS CAROLINE UNDERWOOD MS D UNDERWOOD MR SIMEON UNDERWOOD MR DAVID UNERMAN MISS H UNSWORTH MRS L UNSWORTH MRS C UNWIH MR O UNWIN MRS EILEEN UPHILL CAROLYN UPSON MS C UPTON MR M UPTON MS R UPTO
ROBERT UPWARD MS DAPHNE U'REN MR G URGA MS AHN URQUHART MR LOUIS URUOIS MR J USHER MR MATTHEW USHER MRS T USHER MR K USHERWOOD MR M USHERWOOD MR D USISKIH MRS S USISKIH MR C UTTING MRS M UTTING MR MICHAEL UVA MS M VAGO MR M VAID DR P VA
MS H VAILL MRS R VAIHER MS WENDY VAISEY THE LADY VAIZEY DR P VAKIL MR J VALE MRS P VALE MRS B VALENTINE MR J VALENTINE MR J VALENTINE MS H VALENTINE MR NEIL VALENTINE MR B VALIER-GROSSMAN MR H VALLANCE MRS L VALLANCE MS M VALLI MRS F
ALPHEN MR U VAN BLOMMESTEIN MR EDWIN VAN BOVEN DR JOHANNES VAN DE KOOT MR ISSA VAN DEN BROEK MS MARGARET VAN DEN DRIESSCHE MR W VAN DER LEE MS A VAN DER MEER MS H VAN DER POORTEN MR ERIC VAN DER R VAN DER POORTEN MR ERIC VAN DER R
ANNE VAN HAEUERBEKE MRS L VAN HOOF MS S VAN LANGENBERG MR A VAN LENHEP MS JANNY VAN MIHHEN MS S VAN OUDTSHOORN MRS J VAN POZHAK MISS J VAN R¼SSEN MRS J VAN SCHELLE MISS I VAN STAUEREN DR J VAN TILBORG MR P VAN UELSEN MRS S VAN BRUMMEN
VAHATA MRS G VANCOOTEN MISS SARAH VANDERLAAH MR L VANDOROS MRS E VANDRA MISS A VAM-OOSTEN MRS L VAHTOL MR J VANTRIGT MR G VAN-WAUEREN MR R VARD¼ MS A VARGAS MR P VARGA-WEICZ CATHERINE-ZOI VARDIS DR C VARLAAM MRS O VARLAKHOU PROFESSOR M VA
MRS S VARMA MISS A VARROW MR J VARTAN MRS SIAN VASEY MRS M VASS MR PAUL VATES MR A VAUGHAN MRS A VAUGHAN MR G VAUGHAN MRS S VAUGHAN MR T VAUGHAN MR W VAUGHAN-THOMAS MRS A VAUGHAN-WILLIAMS P VAUGHN DR M J S VAVRECKA MS M VAZQUEZ-FIGUEROA
CHRISTINE VEAR MR P VECCHIETII MRS I VEGRZ¼H MS B VEL MS S VELA MR PAUL VELLACOTT MR T VELUICK MR J VENABLES MISS U VENABLES MS A VENESS MR A VENHIG MS T VENN MRS N VENNING MS B VENUS MR O VERA MR INIGO VERASTEGUI MRS MADEL
VERCO MS G VERCOE MR M VERDEN MRS R VERE MR G VERHEUL MS P VERIT¼ MR PETER VERMAAT MR J VERME MS A VERNAU LADY VERHEY MS A VERNON MR GRAHAM VERNON MS J VERRELL MS PAMELA VERSCHUUR MS G VESE¼ MR H VESSELO MR M VETELE D VETTESE MISS D
MRS S VEYSEY MR R VIAZZANI MRS S VICARY MS ANDREA VICARY MS S VICARY MR D VICK MRS J VICKERS MS VERONICA VICKERS MR A VICKERY MR ALLAH VICKERY MS H VICKERY MRS L VICKERY MRS M VICKERY MR S VIGAR MRS E VIGE
MR A VIGGERS MRS M VIGGIAHI MR RATED VIJ MS KATHERINE VIK MR M VILACA MS LAURA VILLA MS L VILLASENOR MR MICHAEL VILLENEAU MR A VINCE MRS J VINCE MR N VINCE MS G VINCENT MS J VINCENT MRS JOYCE VINCENT MS SARAH VINCENT MR C VINCENZI MS H VINE
R VINE MR D VINE¼ MR P VIHHELS MRS F VIHHICOMBE MR B VINSON MRS S VINTER MR J VIRDEE MR MICHAEL VIRGO MR REZA VISHKAI MR D VISNIEWSKI MRS M VISSER MR A VITERBO DE SOUZA AZEVEDO MRS H VIUERSH MRS L VIUIAH MR P VIVIAN MRS A VOBES MISS J VOGE
S VOGEL MR H VOIGT MISS A VOLLER DR B VOLLMER MR DIRK VOM LEHH MR D VON ALLMEH MR M VON BREHTANO MR K VON BULOW MRS RIXA VON DEM BUSSCHE MRS J VON DER WEIDT CHRISTOPH VON DONHAHHI MR WOLF VON KUMBERG MR R VON MOTZ MR F VON OPPENHEIM MR G
SANDEH MR JONAS VON STEDIHGK MS B VON WANGENHEIM MR C VOORS MRS BARBARA VOSPER MR G VOSPER MR P VOULLAIRE ROBIN VOUSDEN MISS D VOWLES MR D VO¼CE MRS M VUJHOUIC MR S VYAS MR P VYFUHKEL MISS U VYAHHUKY MR PAUL VYSE MISS K V¼WAH
WACKERBARTH MR MASAHORI WADA MRS A WADDAMS MRS J WADDELL MISS C WADDLE MRS M WADE MR ROBIH WADE MS U WADGE MRS D WADHIA MRS M WADLE¼ MRS D I WAGNER MR E WAGNER MR ERIC WAGNER MRS IRENE WAGNER MRS L WAGNER MR O WAGNER MRS V WAGNER
WAGON MS ALEXANDRA WAGSTAFF MRS E WAGSTAFF MRS S WAGSTAFFE MR C WAIH MR D WAIH MR R WAINWRIGHT MR I WAIT MR C WAITE MS H WAITE MS MAR¼ WAITE MS MICHELLE WAITE MR T WAITE MR R WAITE MS H WAITZMAN MRS G WAJHTRAUB MRS MARG
WAKE MR A WAKEEM MR D WAKEFIELD MARK WAKEFIELD MRS S WAKEFIELD MR G WAKELIH MRS S WAKELING MRS J WAKEL¼ MR KEH WAKEMAN MRS C WALD MR RICHARD WALD MRS K WALDE MR C WALDECK MR D WALDEN MRS JENN¼ WALDEN DR A WALDMAN MR WA
MRS U WALDEN MR FLORIAH WALDGMANH MS G WALDRON MR ANDREW WALES MS DIANE WALES MR S WALE¼-COHEN MR B WALFORD MR A WALKER MS A WALKER MR ANTHONY WALKER MRS B WALKER MR B WALKER MR CHARLES WALKER MR D WALKER MS E WALKER MS F WA
MRS H WALKER MS HEATHER WALKER DR I WALKER MR J WALKER MR J WALKER MRS J WALKER MR J WALKER MS M WALKER MR M WALKER MRS M WALKER MARION WALKER MARTIN WALKER MRS N WALKER MISS NICOLA WALKER MS PHILIPPA WA
MRS P WALKER MS P WALKER MR PETER WALKER MR R WALKER MRS R WALKER MS V WALKE¼ MRS D WALKINGSHAW MR ALISTAIR WALL MS F WALL MR J WALL DR D WALLACE MR B WALLACE MRS M WALLACE MRS M WALLACE MRS MURIEL WALL
MS H WALLACE MS T WALLACE MRS U WALLACE MR R WALLACE-TARR¼ MS ALBINE WALLACH MR E WALLER MR Q WALLER MR J WALLE¼ MR B WALLHOUSE MRS URSULA WALLIMAH MR L WALLINGTON MS S WALLINGTON DEBORAH WALLIS F WALLIS MRS J WALLIS M
WALLIS MR HEIL WALLIS MR ROY WALLIS MR T WALLIS MRS JANET WALPOLE MR ANTON¼ WALSH MRS B WALSH MS E WALSH MS F WALSH MRS J WALSH MR J WALSH KATIE WALSH MRS M WALSH MR P WALSH MRS C WALSHE MS M WALTER DR MAGNUS WALTER MR A Q WAL
MRS B WALTERS J E WALTERS MRS J WALTERS MR ROBERT WALTERS MRS C WALTON DR A WALTON DR J WALTON MR PETER WALTON MRS S WALTON MISS U WALTON MRS P WAND MRS E WANG MISS JENN¼ WANG MRS L WANNELL MRS J WANSELL MR HEIL WANSTALL MR CHRIS WANT M
WANT MR JAMES WARBIS MR A MICHAEL WARBURG DR B WARBURTON MRS H WARBURTON MR RICHARD WARBURTON MRS A WARD MR D WARD MS DIANA WARD MS HELEN WARD MR I WARD MRS J WARD MR JEFFRE¼ WARD MR K WARD MR KEH WARD MR L WARD MR LESTER WARD
WARD DR PETER WARD MR P WARD MR PETER WARD MR PHIL WARD MR R WARD MRS U WARD MRS ¼ WARD MS ¼VONNE WARD MRS J WARD-CLARKE MR M WARDEH MR PETER WARDEH DR E WARDLE MR B WARDMAH MS J WARDMAN MR A WARDROP MR J WARE MR NICK WARE
WARE MRS S WARE MR TERENCE WARE MR D WARES MR J WARING MRS R WARING MR PETER WARLAND MRS ROSEMAR¼ WARNER WARNER CLASSICS MRS B WARREH MISS E WARREN MRS J WARREN MRS P WARREN MRS A WARRENDER MR C B WARRINER MRS S WARRINGTON MRS S WAR
MRS J WARTON MR K WART¼ MS E WARWICK MR S WARWICK MR P WASHINGTON MR P WASLE¼ MRS HANICE WASSEF MR D WASSELL MRS P WAT MR NEVILLE WATCHURST L¼NDA WATERHOUSE MR R WATERHOUSE MRS I WATERKE¼N MR ALAN WATERMAN MRS C WATERS MISS J WATERS
WATERS MRS H WATERS MS HANC¼ WATERS MR S WATERS MR J WATERSON MR W WATERTON MR B WATES MISS A WATKIH MS D WATKIHS MR WATKINS ¼ WATKINS MS JAN WATKINS MR MARK WATKINS MR SIMON WATKINS DR S WATKIHS M
WATKINS MRS A WATKINSON MS M WATKINSON MRS G WATKISS MRS U WATLING MRS C WATMORE MRS A WATSON MRS ALISON WATSON MR B WATSON MRS CATH¼ WATSON MR DAVID WATSON MRS H WATSON MISS FIONA WATSON MS G WATSON MR H WATSO
J WATSON MRS J WATSON MS J WATSON MRS JEAN WATSON MRS K WATSON MRS KELL¼ WATSON MR L WATSON MR M U WATSON MRS MARION WATSON MS PATRICIA WATSON MISS S WATSON MRS VALERIE WATSON DR PAUL WATT MS ROSEMAR¼ WATSON MR S WAT
CAROL WATTS DR B WATTS MISS E WATTS MRS J WATTS MRS M WATTS MRS R WATTS MS ROSEMAR¼ WATTS MS SANDRA WATTS MISS SUZANNE WATTS MS S WATTS-READ MRS L WAUGH MR HEHILLE WAUGH MR PETER WAUGH MR P WAHMARK MS J WEALE MRS K WEALSTEAD MR D WEARS
QUEENIE WEAVER MR P WEATHERALL MRS S WEATHERBURH MR A WEATHERHOGG MRS A WEAVER MRS P WEAVER MR S WEAVER MRS T WEAVER MRS A WEBB MR B WEBB MRS BARBARA WEBB MS C WEBB MISS CAROLINE WEBB MRS E WEBB MS H WEBB MS J WEBB MR J WEBB
WEBB MR J WEBB MR K WEBB MRS LAVINIA WEBB MR C WEBB MR M WEBB MRS M WEBB MR MICHAEL WEBB MRS N C WEBB MRS P WEBB MR R WEBB S WEBB MS GILL WEBBER MRS MARIA WEBBER MR W WEBBER MR A WEBER MRS ANNE WEBER MRS B WEBSTER MS C WEBSTER
WEBSTER DR G WEBSTER MISS J WEBSTER MR J WEBSTER MR N WEBSTER MR NORMAN WEBSTER MR P WEBSTER MISS XENIA WEBSTER MS JEAN WEDDELL MRS J WEDGWOOD MRS P WEDGWOOD MR R WEEDOH MS ALEXANDRA WEEKES MR N WEEKES MR JOHN WEEKES
WEEK'S MRS E WEEKS MRS PRISCA WEEMS MS S WEGE MS J WEGG MR E WEIGHMAH MS A WEIGHT MRS WEIL MRS T WEILER MS B WEILL MS JOAN WEINBERG MISS E WEINIHGER MR K WEINSTEIN MR M WEINSTOCK MRS A WEIR MS P WEIR MS SARAH WEIR MS D WEIS MISS D WEISER
MR WEISMAH MR G WEISS MR L WEISS PROFESSOR ROBERT WEISS MR J WEISSBART MR & MRS J WEISSMAN MRS J WEITZ MRS C WELCH MS E WELCH MS G L WELCH MS H WELCH MICHAEL WELCH MR PETER WELCH MRS S WELCH MR C WELCHMAN MS E WELD MR J WELD
MRS J WELDOH MS J WELFARE MR PETER WELFARE MRS S WELFARE MR C WELHAM MS S WELHAM MR C WELLER MISS D WELLER MR M WELLER MANFRED WELLING MRS S WELLING MISS D WELLINGS MR BRIAN WELLINGTON MR M WELLINGTON MR A WELLS MRS K WELLS MRS CHRISTINE WELLS
WELLS MR E WELLS MR I WELLS MISS J WELLS MS J WELLS MR L WELLS MRS NATALIE WELLS MR P WELLS MRS ROSEMAR¼ WELLS MR T WELLS MR B WELSH MS H WELSH MR S WELSH MS WELSH MR S WELSH MS TINA WELSH MR
WELTON MR R WELTON MRS W WEHBAN MRS G WEHBAH SMITH MRS C WENDELL MS H WENDT MR GEORGE WENHAM MR P WENHAM MRS G WENSLE¼ MS KAREN WENTWORTH MRS S WERB MR A WERNER MS M WERNER MRS ANN WEST MS C WEST MR R WEST MR E WEST MRS H WEST MRS J
MISS K WEST MRS K WEST MS KIM WEST MRS L WEST MR N WEST MR P WEST MS P WEST MR T WEST MR R WESTAWA¼ MR D WESTBROOK MR J WESTBROOK MR JOHN WESTCOMBE MRS BARBARA WESTERBERG MRS SUSAN WESTGARDT MRS P WESTGATE
WESTHEAD MRS MARIE WESTLE¼ MR S WESTMACOTT MR R WESTMAH MR A WESTMORE MISS C WESTMORE MR H WESTON MR J WESTON MR J WESTON MR A WESTRIP MR J WESTROPE MRS C WESTWELL MR H WESTWOOD MR ALAN WETHERALL MS U WETTEH MR T WE¼ MRS A
WHALE MISS D WHALE MRS L WHALE¼ MR E WHALLE¼ MRS SUSAN WHALLE¼ MS LORAINE WHARR¼ MR A WHARTON MRS C WHARTON MR R WHARTON MR S WHATELE¼ R WHATMOOR MRS P WHATMOUGH MISS S WHARTON MRS C WHEARDON MISS C WHEAL MS CATHERINE WHE
GILLIAH WHEATCROFT MR D WHEATLAND MR J WHEATLE¼ MRS M WHEATLE¼ MISS B WHEEL MR A WHEELER MR ANDREW WHEELER MR DAVID WHEELER MISS E WHEELER MR J WHEELER MRS J WHEELER MS M WHEELER MRS P WHEELER MISS P WHEELWRIGHT M
WHELAH MISS E WHELAH MR KEVIN WHELAH MRS A WHELLAMS MR C WHELLAMS MR J WHIFFIH MR J WHILLIS MR M WHILLOCK MR M WHIPPMAN MR T WHISKER MR U WHISTON MRS B WHITAKER MRS EMMA WHITAKER MRS MAR¼ WHITAKER MRS J WHITBURH MRS J WHITB¼ MR J WHIT
WITCHELO MRS E WHITCOMBE MR GU¼ WHITCOMBE MR A WHITE MS A WHITE DR ALAN WHITE MR B WHITE MR BRIAN WHITE MR C WHITE D WHITE DR DAVID WHITE MR E WHITE MRS F WHITE MRS G WHITE MR GEOFFRE¼ WHITE MRS IRENE WHITE MRS J WHITE MR J WHIT
J WHITE KERR¼ WHITE MS L J WHITE MS L WHITE MRS L WHITE MR M WHITE MRS H WHITE MR N WHITE MS N WHITE MR P WHITE MR PETER WHITE MR R WHITE MRS ROSEMAR¼ WHITE MR T WHITE MR U WHITE MISS MARGARET WHITE MR H WHITE MRS C WHITE MR C WHITE MR WHITEMAH MR WHITE MR MICHAEL WHITE MISS WHITE WHITE
MS I WHITEHEAD MR J WHITEHEAD MS JILL WHITEHEAD MISS L WHITEHEAD MS L WHITEHEAD MR P WHITEHEAD MR T WHITEHEAD MRS A WHITEHOUSE MR A WHITEHOUSE MS KAREN WHITEHOUSE MRS M WHITEHOUSE MR ANDREW WHITELE¼
WINIFRED WHITELE¼ MR W WHITELOCK MRS A WHITEMAH MR R WHITETHREAD MR L WHITEWA¼ MR MICHAEL WHITEWOOD DR Q WHITFIELD MR P WHITFIELD MR J WHITING MS J WHITING MR LAURENCE WHITING MRS A WHITLOCK MRS R ¼ A WHITMAH MR M WHITMARSH MRS A WHIT
MRS B WHITMORE MR J WHITMORE MISS ALEX WHITNE¼ MR B WHITNE¼ MRS EMA WHITTAKER MR P R WHITTAKER MR T WHITTAKER WHITTAKER MR & MRS A WHITTALL MISS M WHITTARD MISS T WHITTINGHAM MRS R WHITTINGHAM MRS B WHITTLE MR J WHITTL
S WHITTLE MS T WHITTLES MS C WHITWILL MR A WHITWORTH MS JULIET WHITWORTH MR MIKE WHMMAN MRS N WHMMARK MR DAVID WHMTE MS DENISE WIAND MRS M WICKENDEN DR G WICKENS MR S WICKER MR T WICKES MS E WICKHAM MISS H WICKHAM MS L
WICKHAM MISS B WICKINS MRS E WICKREMESINGHE MR A WICKS MR D WICKS MRS EILEEN WICKS MR H WIDDEN MR R WIDGER MISS H WIDHALL MRS P WIEDOU-FARLE¼ MR DAVID WIELD MRS S WIENER MISS I WIERSMA MR H WIESE MR S WIGART MR C WIGGIH MRS JENNIFER WIG
MS J WIGGLESWORTH MS SUSANHAH WIGHT MRS M WIGHT-BO¼COTT MR & MRS A WIGHTON MRS P WIGHTWICK MS H WIGZELL MRS H WILBRAHAM MRS J WILB¼ MR P WILCOCKS MR G WILCOX MRS C WILCOX MRS S WILCOX MISS T WILCOX MR W WILCOX MRS D WILD MR
WILD MR J WILD MRS K WILDBLOOD MR K WILDERODER MRS C WILDISH MS J WILEMAH MRS PAULA WILENIUS MR GARR¼ WILES MS S WILES MRS DOROTH¼ WILE¼ MRS HILAR¼ WILI MS E WILIAMS MR J R WILKES MR J WILKES MR KEVIN WILKES MR G WILKIHS MR M WIL
MR P WILKINS MR A WILKINSON MS C H WILKINSON MS C WILKINSON MR D WILKINSON MR DAVID WILKINSON MRS G WILKINSON MR HONOR WILKINSON MR HUGH WILKINSON MR J WILKINSON MRS JANE WILKINSON LAD¼ K WILKINSON
WILKINSON MRS P WILKINSON MR S WILKINSON MRS ROSAL¼H WILKINSON MR S WILKINSON MS SARAH WILKINSON MRS H WILKS DR MARK WILKS MR B WILLATTS MRS CARMEN WILLCOX MRS J WILLCOX MS T WILLETT MRS P T WILLE¼ MR S WILLEHS MR U WILL
MRS DOREEH WILLIAMS MR DOUG WILLIAMS MRS E WILLIAMS MR E WILLIAMS MS F WILLIAMS MR FRED WILLIAMS DR GRAHAM WILLIAMS MR GRAHAM WILLIAMS MR GREHUILLE WILLIAMS MR HEHR¼ WILLIAMS MRS H WILLIAMS MISS I WILLIAMS MR I WILL
J WILLIAMS MISS J WILLIAMS MRS J WILLIAMS MR J WILLIAMS MS JENNIFER D WILLIAMS MISS JULIA WILLIAMS MS JULIA WILLIAMS MRS JUNE WILLIAMS MRS KATE WILLIAMS MISS KATHARINE WILLIAMS MRS L WILLIAMS MS L WILLIAMS MR M WILLIAMS
WILLIAMS MS H WILLIAMS MISS MARGARET WILLIAMS MRS MARIE WILLIAMS MRS MAR¼ WILLIAMS MR H WILLIAMS MRS NORMA WILLIAMS MR P WILLIAMS MR PETER WILLIAMS MR R WILLIAMS MISS S WILLIAMS
WILLIAMS MR S WILLIAMS MISS S WILLIAMS MS S WILLIAMS MRS SARAH WILLIAMS MISS SIAH WILLIAMS MR T WILLIAMS MS U WILLIAMS MR U WILLIAMS MR U WILLIAMS MR V WILLIAMS MRS Z WILLIAMS-ASHMAH MRS U WILLIAMS-ELLIS MS A WILLIS
MR D WILLIAMSON MR J WILLIAMSON MRS J WILLIAMSON MS JO¼CE WILLIAMSON MR KEVIN WILLIAMSON MR P WILLIAMSON MRS U WILLIAMSON MR S WILLIAMSON MRS T WILLIAMSON MR C WILLIS MR IAN WILLIS MR KEITH WILLIS MR P WILLIS MR Q WILLIS THE W
PARTNERSHIP MR ROBERT WILLISHAM MRS S WILLISON MS DIANA WILLMENT MR J WILLMORE MS E WILLMOTT MS J WILLOUGHB¼ MR Z WILLOUGHB¼ MRS P WILLOW MR PATRICK WILLS MRS SUSAH WILLS MRS ¼UONHE WILLS MISS A WILLS-PACKER MR D
WILMINGTON MR Q WILMOT MR JAMES WILSON MRS M WILSHER MR A WILSON MRS ADRIENNE WILSON MS ANN WILSON MR ANDREW WILSON MRS B WILSON MRS B WILSON MS C WILSON MR D WILSON MS D WILSON MR DAMIAN WILSON MR DAVID WILSON THE HON G WILSON M
WILSON MS GWHHETH WILSON MRS HELEN WILSON MR I WILSON MR J WILSON MRS JANE WILSON DR JEREM¼ WILSON MR JOHN WILSON MISS K WILSON MR L WILSON MRS L WILSON MR M WILSON MS M WILSON MRS MARGARET WILSON MS MARGARET WILSON MRS M
WILSON MELANIE WILSON MR MICHAEL WILSON MRS H WILSON MR H WILSON MR NICHOLAS WILSON MR P WILSON MR R WILSON MR ROBIN WILSON MR R WILSON MS S WILSON LAD¼ STEPHANIE WILSON MS SUSAH WILSON MRS A WILSON-SMITH MISS M WILTON M
WILTSHIRE MRS P WIMMER MS K WIHMAR MRS B WINCH MRS C WINCH MR C WINCHESTER MR P WINCOTE MS C WINCOTT MS R WINDAL MS H WINDER MS M WINDISCH MS R WINDMILL MRS RIHA WINDSOR MS H WINE DR REHEE WINEGARTEN MRS SUELLEN WINER MRS J WINFIELD
WING MR HOWARD WINGFIELD MRS J WINH MR H WINH MR ADRIAH WIHHETT MRS A C WINNIHG MR H WINNING MR R WINNING MRS JACQUELINE WINNINGTON MR C WIHSLET MISS J WINSLOW MRS E WINSTON MRS B WINTER MR DAVID WINTER MR JOHN WINTER
K WINTER MS L WINTER MRS M WINTER MS MAXINE WINTER MR GORDON WINTERBOURNE MR GARETH WINTERS MS L WINTERS MISS C WINTERSDORFF MRS J WINTERTON MS ANNE WINTON MR A WINTON DR R WINWOOD MRS J WINYARD MISS ANGELA WISE MS C WISE MR F WISE
WISE MR JOHN WISE MR P WISE MRS MARIL¼N WISEMAN MR KEH WISHART MR DEAN WITHALL MRS JENN¼ WITHINGTON MR H WITHE¼ MS D WITTENBAKEP MR A WITZUM MRS R WOADWARD MR A WOLF PROFESSOR DAVID WOLFE DR K WOLFE MR C WOLFF MS D WOLFF
S WOLFF MS S¼LUIA WOLFF MISS J WOLFSOH MRS C WOLLAHD MISS A WOLOWICZ MS D WOLTON MR C WONG MRS J WONG MS K WONG MISS M WONG MRS RILBHE WONG-MOON ALICE WOOD MR B WOOD MR C WOOD MR CHRIS WOOD MRS D WOOD MR E WOOD MRS E
MS GILLIAH WOOD MR J WOOD REVEREND J WOOD MRS J WOOD MR JOHH WOOD MRS JUD¼ WOOD MRS K WOOD MR LANCE WOOD MRS M WOOD MRS MAR¼ WOOD MS M WOOD MRS N WOOD MRS P WOOD MS P WOOD MR R WOOD MRS S T WOOD DR PHIP WOOD MISS SUSAHHAH WOOD MR T WOOD
WOODALL A WOODALL MR A WOODCOCK MR AIDAN WOODCOCK MR P WOODFORD MR D WOODGER MR E WOODGER MRS SHIRLE¼ WOODHAM MR & MRS D WOODHEAD MR DAVID J WOODHEAD MR JOHN WOODHEAD MISS S WOODHEAD MISS ANNIE WOODHOUSE MR ROGER WOODHOUSE MRS
WOODHOUSE MR LEONARD WOODLE¼ QC MR A WOODMAN MS A T¼SALL MRS PAMELA WOODROFFE MS L WOODROOFE MS J WOODRUFF MS S WOODFUFF MRS CORIHHA WOODS D WOODS MR G WOODS MRS J WOODS MISS J WOODS MR L WOODS MR M WOODS
WOODS MS S WOODS MR STEPHEN WOODS MRS T WOODS MR E WOODWARD MR J WOODWARD MS P WOODWARD MR M WOODWARD MS ZOE WOODWARD MR WILLIAM WOODWARD MRS S WOODYARD MR R WOOLARD MR K WOOLASS MRS S WOOLCOTT MR D WOOLDRIDGE MR DUNCAN WOOLDRIDGE
ELEANOR WOOLDRIDGE MR GLENN WOOLDRIDGE MRS H WOOLDRIDGE MR S WOOLDRIDGE MR & MRS WOOLF MR H WOOLF MR C WOOLF MRS GILL WOOLFSOH MRS HAZEL WOOLGAR MRS ANGELA WOOLHOUSE MRS C WOOLLATT MR J R WOOLLER MISS B WOOLLETT MRS C WOOLLEHBECK
WOOLLE¼ MR A WOOLLE¼ MR JONATHAN WOOLLE¼ MR J WOOLLE¼ MRS KAREN WOOLLE¼ MR RO¼ WOOLLE¼ MR VICTOR WOOLLE¼ MRS C WOOLMER MR M J F WOOLMORE MARGARET WOOLMER MRS H WOOLNOUGH MR RICHARD WOOLRICH MRS P WOOLSE¼ MR C WOOH SUSIE WOOSLE¼
WOOSTER MISS H WOOTTEH MR W WORKMAN MR FRED WORMS OBE MRS JILL WORRALL MS R WORRALL MR S WORRALL MRS L WORRELL MRS H WORSFIELD MR P WORSLE¼ LAD¼ SARAH WORSLE¼ MR A WORTH MR I WORTH MRS MARGARET WORTH MR D WORTHING MR D WORTH MRS J WOR
MR M WORTLE¼ MR R WORTLE¼ MRS A WORTLE¼-MILLEK MR P WRAGG MR C WRAIGHT MR CHRIS WREHH MR D WREHTMORE MR A WRIGGLESWORTH MS A WRIGHT MR A WRIGHT MRS ALISON WRIGHT MS ANNE WRIGHT MR ANTHONY WRIGHT MR B WRIGHT MRS C WRIGHT MR D WRIGHT M
WRIGHT MRS E WRIGHT MRS ELIZABETH WRIGHT MR G WRIGHT MRS G WRIGHT MS GERALDINE WRIGHT MRS GILLIAH WRIGHT MRS I WRIGHT MR I WRIGHT MR J WRIGHT MRS J WRIGHT MS JENNIFER WRIGHT MRS JOANHA WRIGHT MR JONATHAN WRIGHT DR J WRIGHT MR H WRIGHT M
MRS M WRIGHT MISS M WRIGHT MR MAURICE WRIGHT MR N WRIGHT MS O WRIGHT MR P B WRIGHT DR P WRIGHT MR P WRIGHT MRS PATRICIA WRIGHT MRS R WRIGHT MR ROBERT WRIGHT DR S WRIGHT MR S WRIGHT SARAH WRIGHT MATTHEWS WRIGHTSON CHARIT¼ TRUST MRS J WRI
MR PHILIP WRIGLE¼ MR K WU MS MADELEINE WURZBURGER MR A W¼ATT MRS A W¼ATT MR L W¼ATT MR M W¼ATT MR J W¼BER MR R W¼LD MR A W¼LIE MR D W¼LIE MS H W¼LIE DR BARBARA W¼LLIE MR K W¼NNAH MISS C W¼N-JONES MRS J W¼NN MR M & MRS W¼NN
W¼NNE MR CHARLES W¼NN-EVANS MS ¼ YAMADA MRS T YAMAMOTO MR H ¼AMMOUNI MS M ¼ANAGISAWA MS D ¼ANHOULA MR G ¼APP MRS ZSUZSI ¼ARDLE¼ MR SERGE ¼ARED MRS J ¼ARNELL MR G ¼ARROW MISS CAROL¼N ¼ARWOOD MRS S ¼ARWOOD MS CATHERINE ¼ASS MS H
¼ASUTAKE MRS B ¼ATES MR DAVID ¼ATES MR & MRS ¼ATES MS EMMA ¼ATES MRS HELEN ¼ATES MR NICHOLAS ¼ATES MISS P ¼ATES MR STEPHEN ¼ATES MISS SUE ¼ATES MR W ¼ATES MR A ¼ATES-BELL FRCS MS A ¼AZICOGLU MR MD ¼EADON MR C ¼EAR MR V ¼EARGIN M
MR M ¼EATTS MISS C ¼EELES MR JAMES ¼EELES MS J ¼ELTON MISS G ¼ENDELL MR ALAN ¼EHTOB MISS C ¼EO MISS J ¼EO MRS M ¼EO MR G ¼EOMAN MR U ¼EOMAN MR P ¼EOWELL MR J ¼ERBURY MRS H ¼ERSSIAM MRS A ¼EULETT MISS JULIE ¼EUNG MR JOHN ¼IAHHAKIS MS
MISS KEIKO ¼OKOTA MISS K ¼ORK MRS L ¼ORK MRS K ¼ORK MRS K ¼ORK MRS H ¼ORK MRS M ¼ORK MRS C ¼ORKE MR E ¼OULE BARONESS ¼OUNG OF HORNSE¼ OBE MR A ¼OUNG MR B ¼OUNG MS B ¼OUNG MRS B ¼OUNG MRS C ¼OUNG MRS C ¼OUNG MR C ¼OUNG MR D ¼OUNG MRS G ¼OU
GWENDOLINE ¼OUNG MRS H ¼OUNG MR HUGH ¼OUNG MRS I ¼OUNG MR J ¼OUNG MRS J ¼OUNG MR J ¼OUNG MS JERUINE ¼OUNG MS JULIENNE ¼OUNG MS KATE ¼OUNG MISS M ¼OUNG MRS M ¼OUNG MR MALCOLM ¼OUNG MR H ¼OUNG MRS P ¼OUNG MRS PATRICIA ¼OUNG
PETER ¼OUNG MR R ¼OUNG MRS ROD ¼OUNG MRS S ¼OUNG MS S ¼OUNG MR STEVEN ¼OUNG MS JENNIE ¼OUNG MISS J ¼OUHGHUSBAND TED ¼OUNG-ING MR N ¼OUHGS MR S ¼OUNGS MS EVA ¼OUREN MR J ¼OURSTON MR H ¼OUSUF DR A ¼OXALL MRS I ¼U MRS HGET ¼UE
MURRAY ¼UGIH MS C ¼ULE MS U ¼ULE MS J ¼UNG MS E ZABORSZCZ¼ MS ZAGE MRS T ZAGORSKI MRS K ZAHARIEU MISS D ¼AHEDI MR C ZALEU MR S ZALIDIS MRS A ZAMBLERA MR H ZAMEL MISS ZANADANA MR R ZANELLI MR F ZANGRILLI MS C ZANOHI MR D ZARAKHOUITCH
U ZARB MRS K ZAREMBA MR S ZARGHAM MR P S ZATZ MR H ZAWADZKI MR RAFAL ZBIKOWSKI MISS C ZELKOWITZ MRS M ZELLI MR ROGER ZELUS MS X ZENTHER MS G ZIBARRAS MR H ZIEGELAAR MS CLARE ZIEGLER MRS K ZIEGLER SMITH DR ERNST ZILLEKENS MR Z
ZIMMERMAHN MS S ZMERT¼CH MS L ZOBENS MRS C ZOGOLOVITCH MRS A ZOLTOWSKI MR J ZOOB MRS R ZORNOZA MS M ZUCKERMAN MS JULIA ZUK MRS A ZURAWEL MRS M ZUSHI